Music
since the
First World War

Arnold Whittall

J. M. Dent & Sons Ltd
London

First published 1977
Reprinted 1983
First paperback edition 1988

Printed in Great Britain by
The Guernsey Press Co. Ltd,
Guernsey, Channel Islands, for
J. M. DENT & SONS LTD
91 Clapham High Street, London SW4 7TA

This book is set in Linotron Baskerville

British Library Cataloguing in Publication Data

Whittall, Arnold
    Music since the First World War
    1. Music, 1918-1976
    I. Title
    780′.904

ISBN 0–460–12567–2

Preface

Twentieth-century serious music has been dominated by two principal factors: the gradual loss of commitment to tonality, and the failure of twelve-note serialism to win more than limited acceptance. The more recent emergence of new, electronic sound sources and freer methods of notation and structural organization is obviously of major importance and they may eventually come to seem still more significant than features which are so intimately bound up with nineteenth-century developments, yet in the present work it is the implications of tonality's progressive decline and the exploration of strict and free varieties of serialism over the years since 1918 which receive the most detailed study. To begin a discussion of modern music in that year is clearly not to begin at the beginning, yet the date is as convenient as any as a starting point for a selective study of the most important techniques used by the most important composers of the last sixty years. Omissions are obvious and extensive, and the last composer to receive more than a mere mention was born in 1928: the most detailed attention is given to those whose work is complete and whose importance is incontestable.

It is hoped that the book will be particularly useful to advanced students, and the approach is, primarily, a technical one. It is still occasionally necessary to defend this kind of writing against the charge that verbal explorations of technical processes are irrelevant to the aural perception of meaning or, worse, deleterious to the emotional experience which is the stimulus to all artistic creation and the centre of all aesthetic response. It is true that it is probably impossible to make such writing aesthetically enjoyable in its own right, but I believe analysis can positively enhance the emotional enjoyment of a composition, provided that neither the analysis nor the experience is thought of as ending at a specific point in time. Analysis is as flexible as the analyst chooses to make it and, as a gradual, continuous process of exploration, can immeasurably deepen the aesthetic experience. What this book presents, therefore, is not a sequence of 'complete' analyses, but a basic introduction to the techniques which the major composers have used in their response to a situation in which the traditional foundations of music were being challenged, rejected, rethought and even, on occasion, reinforced.

I am greatly indebted to Neil Day for his work on the reduction and copying of the music examples. Former students of the University of Nottingham and University College, Cardiff may well recognize a good many of the ideas and idiosyncrasies which the book elaborates. But that it appears at all is due less to teaching experience than to the practical help and encouragement of my wife. She will understand why, in the end, I decided not to employ an enigmatic Wagnerian epigraph.

LONDON, DECEMBER 1975   ARNOLD WHITTALL

Note on the paperback edition

The publication of a paperback edition of this book, eleven years after the original, provides the opportunity to add brief postscripts to the three final chapters, to revise the Bibliography, and to make minor changes elsewhere. Comprehensive updating has not been attempted. The intention is simply to provide some perspective, eleven years on, for the ideas and arguments of the original text.

LONDON, OCTOBER 1987   A.W.

Acknowledgments

The author is grateful to the following publishers for permission to reproduce copyright material.

Anglo Soviet Music Press Ltd (U.K. agents, Boosey and Hawkes Ltd): Prokofiev, Symphonies Nos. 5 and 6; Shostakovich, Symphony No. 10. Associated Music Publishers, Inc., New York and reproduced by permission of G. Schirmer Ltd, London: Babbitt, Composition for 12 instruments © 1964; Carter, String Quartet No. 2 © 1961 and Cello Sonata © 1951, 1953. Boelke-Bomart, Inc., Hillsdale N. Y.: Schoenberg, String Trio. Boosey and Hawkes, Music Publishers, Ltd: Bartók, String Quartet No. 6; Britten, *Peter Grimes*; Strauss, *Capriccio*; Stravinsky, *Abraham and Isaac, Oedipus Rex, Pulcinella, The Rake's Progress, Requiem Canticles*, Symphonies of Wind Instruments; Xenakis, *ST/4*. Calder and Boyars Ltd and (in U.S.A.) Wesleyan University Press: Cage, *45' for a speaker* © 1954 by John Cage. Reprinted from *Silence: Lectures and Writings*. J. & W. Chester/Edition William Hansen, London, Ltd: Lutosławski, Preludes and Fugue; Nielsen, Symphony No. 5; Sibelius, Symphonies Nos. 6 and 7. Alphonse Leduc et Cie, Paris: Messiaen, *Technique de mon langage musicale, Méditations sur le mystère de la Sainte-Trinité*. Oxford University Press: Gerhard, Symphony No. 4; Vaughan Williams, Symphony No. 6. Colfranc Music Publishing Corporation: Varèse, *Déserts* © 1959, *Ecuatorial* © 1961, Intégrales © 1926. G. Schirmer, Inc.: Schoenberg, String Quartet No. 4 © 1939, reproduced by permission of G. Schirmer Ltd, London. Schott & Co., Ltd: Henze, *Elegy for Young Lovers*; Hindemith, String Quartet in F minor, String Quartet No. 3; Ligeti, *Lontano*; Schoenberg, *Von Heute auf Morgen*; Stravinsky, Symphony in C; Tippett, Concerto for Double String Orchestra, *King Priam, The Knot Garden*. Universal Edition (London) Ltd: Berio, *Circles*; Boulez, Piano Sonata No. 3; Stockhausen, *Prozession*. Universal Edition (Alfred A. Kalmus Ltd): Bartók, String Quartet No. 3 (© in U.S.A., Boosey and Hawkes, Inc., New York); Berg, Chamber Concerto, Lyric Suite, Violin Concerto; Janáček, *Káťa Kabanová*; Schoenberg, Suite, Op. 25, Variations, Op. 31; Webern, Songs, Op. 25, String Quartet, Op. 28; Weill, *Mahagonny*.

Contents

Introduction

Soon after the outbreak of the First World War, Ernest Newman wrote: 'How, we musicians may ask, can we contemplate without alarm and regret a possible set-back to the culture that, be its faults what they may, has given us Wagner and Brahms and Strauss and Hugo Wolf? . . . We might perhaps say that some such war was necessary for the rebirth of music. For there is no denying that, of late, music has lacked truly commanding personalities and really vitalizing forces. Now that Strauss has failed us, there is no one of whom we can think as having the seeds of the future in him . . . A few discontented spirits like Schoenberg have aspirations toward something new and more personal, but without the capacity to realize them . . . It is hard to believe that out of the new order of things there will not be born the figures and the ideas we long for. We can only hope that the result of the war will not be a perpetuation of the old racial hatreds and distrusts but a new sense of the emotional solidarity of mankind. From that sense alone can the real future of music be born.'[1]

Today pessimists will argue that modern art has remained unregenerate, failing to do more than reflect the most disturbing and negative aspects of the 'civilization' to which the First World War gave birth, and which the Second World War channelled still more decisively in the direction of ultimate catastrophe. A large majority even of educated musicians – performers, critics, teachers and academics – prefer the music of the past to any kind of modern composition. The assumption that the art of the past was better does not necessarily involve a parallel belief that the quality of life itself was better, though it may reflect the conviction that too high a price has been paid for most modern 'improvements.' Yet the common conclusion is that the modern age, with its unprecedented social and national conflicts and its remarkable technological and intellectual advances, is simply not an age in which worthwhile art can be expected to flourish: it is too unstable, too diffused, and art reflects this without being able to transcend it – hence, in music, the emphasis on discord, fragmentation and sheer diversity of style.[2]

Others will claim that those 'commanding personalities' and 'vitalizing forces' which Newman failed to discern have in fact appeared – some of them German, some not – and a new *musical* order of things has come about which, while certainly reflecting some of the unhappy aspects of modern civilization, has exorcised as much as it has imitated, and has laid firm foundations for future developments, some of which can already be foreseen. Much of the music written during the twentieth century may come to be seen as transitional, not merely between 'old' and 'new' styles, but also between very different concepts of what a musical composition can be and what a 'technique of composition', or even a 'language of music,' involves: but at the moment it is still widely felt to have an innate value independent of the 'rewards' to which it may one day be shown to have led.

In surveying such a recent and complex transitional process in the most abstract of the arts, it is peculiarly important to avoid emotive analogies with social or political events, but at the same time not to deny that associations exist between artistic and non-artistic phenomena. In 1914, Newman proclaimed a pervasive cultural decadence which gave rise both to the destructiveness of war and to the impotence of Strauss and Schoenberg. The hope was that, the festering boil having burst, all aspects of life would benefit from such a violent purgation: hence the optimistic anticipation of a new order. Much that is most inflexible in attitudes to modern art is rooted in such dangerous parallels, and principally, as far as music is concerned, in the assumption that the prevailing language and style of the period immediately before 1914 was 'decadent'. Music was in a state of change, or rather the constant process of transformation was broadening and accelerating in response to a feeling that the true decadence would be stagnation, the failure to appreciate that a static, self-repeating art ceases to be art at all. Composers who believed that tonality was no longer a living means of expression are therefore scarcely to be equated with ambitious military and political leaders who were prepared to accept the necessity for violence on a large scale to preserve what they believed to be the rights and relationships of existing societies.

The pace and character of stylistic change in the arts is inevitably affected by changes in society as a whole, whether those changes involve increasing repression or increasing liberalization. Inevitably, too, the stronger the ideological repression, the more the arts may come to reflect prevailing political beliefs: the case of the Soviet Union is paradigmatic, for in spite of the occasional relaxation of state interference, the character of Soviet music has been dictated since 1917 not by musical but by political considerations. Just as the great political revolution enforced a cultural conservatism rooted in a language which had grown up during centuries of 'decadent' political life, so the situation in Europe as a whole between 1918 and 1939 confirmed the general sense that true cultural revolution meant anarchy rather than progress. The need for self-renewal was greatest, naturally, in Germany and Austria, and important new developments could relate to this need; developments as different as the would-be popular, anti-romantic Epic Theatre of Brecht and Weill, with its palpable relevance to the extreme social tensions of the Weimar Republic, or the Schoenbergian serial method, reasserting the inevitability of rational linguistic evolution on the basis of the greatest German music of the past.

The prevailing conservatism in Britain reflected uncertainty in the face of postwar technical developments, and disillusionment with the soon-spent euphoria of the early 1920s, linked as this was with brief flirtations with those developments. Just as serialism was a new discipline, so 'neo-classicism' involved a 'purge' of all that was dangerously hysterical in pre-war late romantic music: it could encompass the lighthearted antics of *Pulcinella* and the austere tragedy of *Oedipus Rex*, and at its best it implied an intense concentration on the most direct kind of emotional expression: only the capacity for developing new forms was lacking. Some Americans became much involved with European neo-classicism; but in America itself, infinitely less disrupted by the war, experiment could proceed with the minimum amount of guilt. And it was here that the most extreme European reaction to the seriousness and complexity of late-romantic, expressionist art – Dadaism – eventually found its fullest exploration in music, when John Cage and his associates followed it through.

After the Second World War, all countries, with the exception of Soviet Russia, became involved in working out both the implications of the two great contrasted principles which had emerged during and after World War I: 'rational' serialism and 'irrational' Dadaism, and the possibilities of the new musical technology: tape recording, electronic synthesis, computer techniques. It was only as the best exponents of the more conservative modern techniques died that the initially radical new techniques, gaining perspective, came to be explored, extended, modified and even combined. Moment-form is the only major new structural concept to have arisen so far from this process, most important composers retaining some links, however tenuous, with older formal principles.

It is those composers who have sought new means of expression and may therefore well have more to offer the future than the present, who are more commonly accused of self-indulgence and self-defeating complexity; so it is not surprising that so many of them occasionally wish for the widest, simplest popularity. 'Music is only understood when one goes away singing it and is only loved when one falls asleep with it in one's head and finds it is still there on waking up the next morning . . . I always insisted that the new music was merely a logical development of [existing] musical resources. But of what use can theoretical explanations be in comparison with the effect the subject itself makes on the listener? What good can it do to *tell* a listener, "This music is beautiful," if he does not feel it? How could I win friends with this kind of music?'[3]

Schoenberg's *cri de coeur* may have been uttered in a rare moment of self-pitying disillusionment; on another occasion he could assert that 'the laws of art work in a way that contradicts the way the popular mind works'.[4] Yet it presents a crucial dilemma, to which Elliott Carter has also referred: 'serious music appeals to a longer span of attention and to a more highly developed auditory memory than do the more popular kinds of music. In making this appeal it uses many contrasts, coherences and contexts that give it a wide scope of expression, great emotional power and variety, direction, uniqueness, and a fascination of design with many shadings and qualities far beyond the range of popular or folk music.'[5]

Carter's standpoint is that of an unashamed intellectual, who approaches the deepest emotional issues not through intuitive improvisation but through elaborately rational processes. Many will argue that the explosion in popular music since 1960 – replacing the more sedate light and dance music prevalent in earlier decades – was in part provoked by the impotence of serious music, an impotence enshrined not merely in the attitudes of Carter, Schoenberg and others, but also in their commitment to technical processes which the listener must either ignore or analyse, since he cannot hear them as such, but only the music which results from their use. Suspicion of the role of intellectual formulations in modern music does much to account for the disenchantment with it among musicians themselves referred to earlier.[6] Yet the strongest case is not for discouraging complexity, or promoting foolish shotgun weddings with utterly incompatible pop techniques, but for encouraging both the more positive development of perceptible hierarchical qualities within complex music, and also the establishment of simpler kinds of serious music. As Part Three of this book will show, both possibilities are being pursued. As for the pop explosion, this was a decisive occupation of a ground which serious music has never sought to conquer, however interested both serious and popular musicians may occasionally be in building bridges between the two varieties. Where the two increasingly interact is in music, very different from that of Schoenberg or Elliott Carter, in which intellect is of less importance than instinct – intuitive music. In such music, the revolt is not so much against complexity as against its intellectual contrivance, involving high degrees of 'literacy' – of technical expertise. 'To deplore the [musical] illiteracy of the Beatles – or of any pop or jazz group – is nonsensical: for the essence of their achievement is that it is a return from literate and visual to aural and oral culture.'[7] This 'rediscovery of music as orgiastic magic'[8] is perhaps most tellingly enshrined in *Sergeant Pepper's Lonely Hearts Club Band,* the Beatles' LP, first issued in 1967, which Mellers defines as 'a ritual involving the young – through its electronic extension of musical sounds into the external world – in a ceremonial togetherness without the prop of church or state'.[9] Plenty of serious compositions may be felt to equate music with orgiastic magic – Stravinsky's *Rite of Spring,* Schoenberg's 'Dance round the Golden Calf' from *Moses und Aron,* Messiaen's *Turangalîla* Symphony, Stockhausen's *Stimmung*: but the relative sophistication of their musical means ensures an élitist aura. They 'contradict the way the popular mind works'. Even so, the relative popularity achieved by Stockhausen on mass cultural occasions like the Osaka World Fair may mark the first stages of a new relationship between the separate worlds of popular and serious music, and a relationship reflecting the increasing change in the nature of what is accepted as 'a composition'. Increasingly, even with serious music itself, the cultural conflict is not between 'radicalism' and 'conservatism', but between 'rationality' and 'irrationality' – reflecting a situation in which rationality itself is in a state of change.

'The cause of our current social crises . . . is a genetic defect within the nature of reason itself. And until this defect is cleared, the crises will continue. Our current modes of rationality are not moving society forward into a better world. They are taking it further and further from that better world. Since the Renaissance these modes have worked. As long as the need for food, clothing and shelter is dominant they will continue to work. But now that for huge masses of people these needs no longer overwhelm everything else, the whole structure of reason, handed down to us from ancient times, is no longer adequate. It begins to be seen for what it is – emotionally hollow, esthetically meaningless, and spiritually empty. That, today, is where it is at, and will continue to be for a long time to come.'[10] Pirsig's solution – to 'expand the nature of rationality so that it's capable of coming up with a solution'[11] – may itself seem little more than a rephrasing of his diagnosis, but his entire train of thought is highly relevant to anyone concerned with the present state and future development of modern culture – music included. There can be little doubt that society is changing in such a way as to make it more likely that the most radical and experimental aspects of present-day musical life will ultimately achieve wider acceptance than those aspects which seek to conserve the actual linguistic formulae of the past. Naturally, even our own radical processes will be superseded, but the expansion in the nature of rationality may also, if we are fortunate, be an expansion in the human capacity for understanding and enjoying the most ambitious and sophisticated products of the creative imagination.

Part One

The Survival of Tonality

Chapter 1

Symphonic Music 1

'The transition from composition which still emphasized key (while always containing many dissonances) to one where there is no longer any key, any tonic, any consonances, happened gradually, in accordance not with any wish or will, but with a *vision*, an *inspiration*; it happened perhaps instinctively.'[1]

This was Schoenberg's description of a process which, for him, was complete by 1909. Yet he was occasionally prepared in later years to employ the old system, and acknowledged that others would continue to do so. Evidently, the history of twentieth-century music would be radically different if all Schoenberg's contemporaries had immediately followed his example and if all subsequent composers had likewise accepted the transition from 'key' to 'non-key' as complete and irreversible. Instead, tonality of one kind or another has survived, usually preserving or adapting those freer relationships between chords and keys which had evolved by the early years of the century and which are often described as 'non-functional'.

This term is as suspect, and as useful, as 'atonality'. 'Atonality' is harmless enough once it is accepted that it means, not the absence of tones, but the absence of tonal harmony and key relationships; 'non-functional' may be understood to imply, not the total absence of logical harmonic procedures, but procedures which work in a different way from those of eighteenth and nineteenth-century music. This earlier tonal music is concerned with exploiting both the hierarchical properties of the circle or cycle of fifths – properties which establish degrees of relationship so that, for example, G major and F major are much more closely related to C major than are B major and F sharp major – and similar properties for the chords within any given key, tonic, dominant and subdominant triads being of greater structural importance than mediant or leading-note triads. Modern tonal music may well be more concerned with deliberate contradiction of these properties, or with playing off conflicts between a hierarchical interpretation of the tonal 'circle' and the anti-hierarchical situation established by a mode like the whole-tone scale – the kind of process pioneered by Debussy in his piano piece *L'isle joyeuse* (1905), with its structural exploitation of the tension between the whole-tone scale including A, and the diatonic scale, and key, of A major. Modern tonal composers may still employ conventional hierarchical relationships between keys, even if these are not established by means of traditional techniques of modulation, and key-feeling may be created by stressing single notes, or through various types of non-triadic chords. Key-feeling in this sense may even emerge in a serial or indeterminate piece: so may major and minor triads and other 'tonal' chords. What is less likely is that such references will be sufficient to create any aural sense of traditionally functioning tonality. In general, modern composers find it easier, and more desirable, to shun this than to attempt to avoid all hierarchical tendencies with regard to pitch emphasis or repetition.

Both tonal and 'non-tonal' composers may use traditional forms, and a relatively conservative tonalist like Sibelius may actually be more radical in his treatment of a traditional structural concept, such as sonata form, than contemporary serialists. Yet it is only to be expected that modern tonal music will provide by far the largest number of approachable, immediately appealing twentieth-century works in the concert repertoire. Listeners and analysts alike may often be tempted to exaggerate the traditional links of such works, but it is dangerous to assume that the symphonies of such composers as Carl Nielsen (1865–1931), Jean Sibelius (1865–1957) and Ralph Vaughan Williams (1872–1958) are likely to be structurally identical with the accepted designs of the past, simply because, by the radical standards of the 1920s, their styles were old-fashioned. Even the most senior tonal composers who were active after 1918 – Fauré, Janáček, Elgar – wrote instrumental or orchestral works which shun textbook stereotypes without ceasing to be 'symphonic' in the broadest sense.

The relationship of the two great Scandinavians to the German symphonic tradition has been well described by Robert Simpson: 'Nielsen, with his origins in Beethoven and Brahms, and Sibelius, with his in Beethoven and the Russian symphonists (with increasing awareness of Beethoven as he developed), together form an antithesis to the southern German-Bohemian, post-Schubertian-Wagnerian, completely romantic world of Mahler and Strauss. . . . What they shared was a common ideal, a desire for discipline and forceful economy achieved without sacrificing warmth of expression.'² In Sibelius this ideal finds its most remarkable outlet in the Symphony No. 4 (1911), which laid the foundation for the achievements of the last three symphonies and *Tapiola*, prefiguring the functional economy which is their most original quality. Nielsen's progress was less assured, his achievement more uneven in quality, but he produced at least one major symphonic masterpiece, the Symphony No. 5 (1922).

This symphony was the first since No. 1 to which the composer refrained from giving a general descriptive title, but the work had its origin in preoccupations which were far from abstract. Nielsen, whose Symphony No. 4 (1916), *The Inextinguishable*, ends in a mood of triumphant optimism, was dismayed by the more radical trends in postwar music: in the Fifth he sought to depict and resolve what he saw – and heard – as a conflict between false progressiveness, which he equated principally with the inhibition of genuine tonal motion as it might be sensed either in 'atonal' or anti-functional neo-classical music, and the true progressiveness of the naturally evolving tonal schemes which he himself favoured. The dangers of such musical autobiography are clear enough, but Nielsen's instinctive sense of how to temper personal involvement with intellectual control ensures that the work can be enjoyed purely as a battle between Good and Evil, even though the composer does not resort to the kind of parody of modernistic devices which he later attempted in the middle movements of the Sixth Symphony.

No evidence has so far come to light about the extent to which the unusual structural and tonal design was worked out in advance, or whether the composer simply allowed it to evolve during the process of composition. As with all the great modern tonal masters, ambiguity plays the crucial role on every level; from the large-scale structural exploitation of balance between fundamental changes of musical character and the continuous development of basic motives, to the small-scale but equally basic employment of chromaticism as a normative element, the appearance of pure diatonicism having a distinctly 'unreal' quality as a result. The structural basis of traditional thematic process – the return of initially stated ideas, not just their constant transformation – is most evident in the second movement: the basics of traditionally functional tonal harmony are pervasive, but Nielsen exploits the creation, frustration or fulfilment of expectations with undeniable genius. Since the main thematic elements are of the simplest kind, their changes of character tend to be easily perceptible, and even without that sense of perfect pitch which would enable a listener to identify the precise nature of the progressive tonal processes involved, it is impossible not to respond to the drama of the way in which such changes of tonal area are paralleled by strongly defined stages in the thematic process.

In the broadest terms, the 'programme' of the symphony involves a progression from uncertainty to security, from apprehensiveness to joyful exuberance, which is attempted, and frustrated, in the first movement; then asserted, challenged and ultimately reinforced in the finale. Every listener is likely to interpret the different stages of this process, and to identify the points at which changes begin or end, in different ways. In the context of the present discussion, it is less important to attempt to provide an accurate, detailed, emotional map

Ex. 1

of the work than to establish that its essential emotional progression is achieved by the consistent use of a particular musical language: indeed, the success of the work lies in the adaptability, as well as the coherence of that language. A comparison of the beginning and ending of the symphony is fruitful here. Initially, there seems to be total contrast, not merely of mood and tonality but of language itself. The tonality at the end is an unmistakable E flat major, affirmed not simply by the key signature and the final five-bar tonic chord, but also prepared by a thrilling dominant pedal. At the start of the work there is no key signature, and for several bars the key in use could be C major, A minor, D minor or F major. Only in bar 13, when the two bassoons begin to give greater emphasis to F and C than to any other notes, does F major emerge as the most likely key (Ex. 1).

Even though the F and C, in alliance with the A of the viola accompaniment, complete a tonic triad, the language is emphatically more chromatic than diatonic, more ambiguous than explicit, especially with reference to that all-important cadential definer of diatonicism, the leading note. Nielsen, like both Sibelius and Vaughan Williams, showed supreme skill in using the avoidance of the conventional leading note as a means of achieving the most productive tension between a chromatic foreground and a diatonic background. Only rarely does such a technique enable one to describe the music as modal, at least as far as the sole involvement of the old church modes like the Dorian or Phrygian are concerned; conventional hierarchical relationships may no longer obtain, either, but there is still an overall tonic or tonal centre to which all but the most uncompromisingly chromatic episodes refer. The specific point about the altered leading note is so important because, whereas at the very start of the symphony it leads to the most gripping kind of ambiguity – is the C in the violas the altered leading note of D minor? – at the end it contributes to the affirmation of E flat major. From Fig. 114 to within five bars of the end, the cadential harmony involves D flats not D naturals; the crucial chromatic feature of the entire symphony is therefore not eliminated but absorbed, a positive effect of colour rather than, as at the beginning, a force ensuring tonal ambiguity (Ex. 2).

This is Nielsen's most powerful technique: the harnessing and directing of forces which at first create ambiguity, until they become agents of resolution. It would be possible to undertake a rewarding but gigantic analysis of this symphony and consider the way in which every degree of ambiguity pertaining to every single note was incorporated

Ex. 2

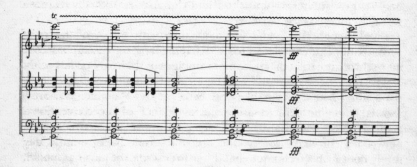

into a coherent overall scheme – how a note may be a tonic of one key or the dominant or subdominant of another, culminating in its potential chromatic function as an altered leading note or in some still more disruptive role. Yet of even greater structural importance is the way in which the more fundamental background shifts of tonality are organized. 'Shifts' is the crucial word, for there is very little stability in this work: chromaticism within keys and modulation between keys dominate the action and the intensity of the expression ensures an inexorably logical motion; for all the shifts of perspective, this background never totally disappears.

In the broadest sense, the two main parts of the first movement advance from F major to C major and on to G major, a process involving three similarly related areas:

F   C   G

subdominant→ tonic

             subdominant→ tonic

Such is the 'programme' of the movement, however, that not merely is G the most firmly established of the three, but the mood of its music casts it more as an *opponent* of F and C than as a relative. The comparative stability of G is no more a matter of the avoidance of all chromatic inflection than is that of E flat major at the end of the second movement, however. Stability is ensured principally by pedals in the bass, and the central conflict of forces is therefore appropriately launched when a dominant pedal in G major with a *stretto* above it (conventionally the means of preparing a final enhanced assertion of the tonic triad) is assailed by disruptive material from earlier in the movement, the very first statement of which (woodwind six bars after Fig. 31) has cancelled G major's F sharp leading note in favour of the more ambiguous F natural. A less subtle composer might have allowed his taste for naive symbolism to lead at this point not merely to the rapid erosion of all tonal stability, but to an even more desolate recapitulation of the opening material. Nielsen's purpose is very different, and reinforces the primacy of evolutionary factors in the work's form. After one of the most thrilling battles in all music, in which the dominant pedal is supported for much of the time by a subdominant one as well, a triumphant resolution on to the tonic triad of G major takes place (Fig. 37). As the climax subsides, however, the music begins to display all the signs of exhaustion, of losing the will to survive. It is not simply the continued presence of F naturals in the woodwind figure (five bars after Fig. 37), nor the expiring flutters of the aggressive side-drum figure which assist this rapid decline, but the way the final clarinet cadenza seductively transforms material which, in the violas six bars after Fig. 3, was one of the earliest signs of menace in the first part of the movement.

This coda, for all its gravity, indicates that the issue is unresolved: the serene music cannot itself eliminate all trace of the initial inertia, and it survives attack only to lose its own positive strength and drive. In this respect it may be significant that there has been no further progress along a purely tonal path. One might, for example, expect the second half of the first movement to have moved on from G major to D major, but, while D is indeed the last note of the final clarinet melody, it still functions as the dominant of G major. The chain has been broken, but a particular stage has been reached which is a whole tone above that from which the symphony began. The second movement is to end in the tonal area a whole tone *below* that in which the symphony began, and the change of direction is achieved with the elimination of inertia by energy. Yet anticipations of an even more basic tonal scheme than any hitherto discussed, involving such a symmetrical element –

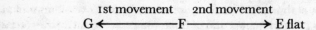

- are frustrated by the simple fact that the finale begins, not in F, but in the key as far away from F as possible: B major. There is some evidence of the working of a symmetrical element in the first movement, in the long passage between the two main parts (Figs. 24 to 25+15 bars), when 'negative' F is finally induced to yield to 'positive' G by the emphasis on A flat and D, the notes a minor third either side of F itself. This process of exorcism or neutralization cannot be considered purely in terms of symmetrical elements, however, for D obviously has an even more pressing function here as the dominant of G. Nor are the parallels between the two movements of the work symmetrically exact. The first movement begins indecisively in a grey key area, the second decisively in a bright area, its main internal contrasts involving darker keys and both faster and slower tempi (the first movement has only the basic tempo change from *Tempo giusto* to *Adagio non troppo*). The second movement undoubtedly presents the same basic conflict as the first, but the perspective is different, the outcome is different, and so – in a highly significant way – is the tonal scheme. Even though the early stages of the movement rapidly invert the ascending fifths scheme, to move down from B to E then down again to A, the sheer rapidity with which this occurs is a clear indication that a more elaborate process is now being prepared. If the conflict between inertia and energy is to be positively resolved, the fierce confidence of the finale's opening stages must be challenged and tested, and the diatonic clarity, with its almost mocking reversal of the first movement's hard-won progress, must be blurred by that more expressive and characteristic chromaticism which was Nielsen's most potent linguistic device (it will be noted that the A sharp leading note of B major yields to A natural when the movement is only eleven bars old). Nielsen dramatizes both the challenge and the conflict by undermining both the movement's dynamic momentum and its tonal confidence. After an exciting, unsuccessful attempt to recapture the initial B major (Fig. 6off.), the key feeling blurs and darkens, and the recall of the eerie alternations between D and A flat which had separated the two parts of the first movement similarly serve here (Fig. 67) not to press the claims of either key but to force a decisive change of mood as the only escape from the inertia of rhythmic stasis and tonal confusion.

In the first movement, the A flat and D neutralized the already negative F, and the D was carried over into the next stage as dominant of G major. But A flat and D also enclose B natural, and it is this crucial tonal plateau which is neutralized at Fig. 67 in the finale. Now it is the A flat (not the D) which achieves functional status with the establishment of F minor as the new key, and of a mood, as different as possible from the serene calm of the first movement's G major, which turns out to be energetic in the wrong way. The *Presto* fugue (Fig. 71), for all its hectic contrapuntal ingenuity, is too panic-stricken to achieve a genuine resolution: its climaxes lead only to disintegration, a new decline into exhaustion in which F minor is clouded but still not completely relinquished. It is now evident that a positive change of key – and, perhaps, insurance against the potential return of first-movement characteristics – can only be achieved with an extreme change, not of form but of mood. So a second fugue *(Andante un poco tranquillo,* Fig. 92), less self-confident than the G major counterpoint of the first movement but for that very reason more fully integrated into the entire expressive fabric of the work, begins what proves to be the final climb out of conflict. This fugue also shows that F is no longer merely a negative hindrance to the work's eventual fulfilment, but an element which must be transfigured rather than eliminated. Even when the B major-centred opening music of the finale returns (Fig. 99) to initiate a highly compressed recapitulation, it is soon diverted from its original path through the sharp keys, so that a final scheme of descending perfect fifths can function, starting with the F of the fugues, then moving to B flat as dominant of the concluding E flat. This is indeed the tritonal 'answer' to the finale's initial B-E-A, the resolution of the first movement's inconclusive F-C-G: the tonal scheme of the finale is a triumphant rethinking of the principles which governed the 'unsuccessful' first movement.

Nielsen's genius lies in shedding new light on, and extracting new dramatic purpose from, the simple idea of a difference between sub-dominant relatives and dominant relatives. The descending fifths of the finale – each tonic also a dominant of the next tonic – succeed where the ascending fifths – the subdominant relatives – of the first movement fail. In these admittedly basic terms, the supreme, strategic moment of unification and transformation comes at Fig. 110, where the woodwind and string alternations over the E flat major dominant pedal recall the similar moment of crisis in the first movement (Fig. 33). There a resolution was achieved only to turn to ashes: now there can be no question of frustrating the victorious assertions of E flat: it is not merely the last lap of a long journey, but a totally convincing conclusion to the arguments which that journey has created. It has been claimed that the Fifth Symphony is merely a transitional work, a preparation for the 'new spiritual equilibrium' of the single-movement Clarinet Concerto (1928), with its avoidance of 'progressive' tonality.[3] Yet the sweep of the argument and the breadth of design in the symphony make it an altogether more memorable experience than the concerto: it is not only Nielsen's masterpiece, but also one of the greatest and most original of all modern symphonic works.

The achievements of the three symphonies which Sibelius completed after 1918 cannot be easily summarized, but they stem from a determi-nation to pursue the implications of the masterly Fourth, rather than to retreat from its austere perfection into a safer world of the better known and the well tried. The Fifth Symphony was first completed as a four-movement work during 1914–15, but in 1918 it was revised and the first two movements fused. 'Integrating extremes of movement may have been the troublesome problem; in the first movement the difficulty is once and for all solved. This astonishing piece moves gradually, almost imperceptibly, from a great Wagnerian-Sibelian drifting into a pace that recalls the Beethoven *scherzo*.' Having 'achieved a virtually complete sonata movement in a very short time, and over a basic pulse of vast slowness,' Sibelius expands the structure to include a fast movement which is, in essence, 'another immense recapitulation'.[4] It is scarcely surprising (though profoundly depressing) that such a radical yet organic transformation of the traditional sonata design should have passed uncomprehended. The rest of the work is structurally simpler, though the process of thematic transformation in the finale has the kind of inexorable cumulative effect which only the greatest masters can achieve. The crux is in the almost imperceptible establishment of a broad tempo (Letter N), and in the consequent accumulation of extreme harmonic tension against the firmly established bedrock of the tonic key. Sudden shifts of tonality to keys a minor third either side of E flat – C between Letters E and F, G flat at Letter I – contrast with the balancing *major* thirds of the first movement and are the more effective for being clearly perceptible contrasts to a main key; indeed, Sibelius never wavered in his control of this most traditional of symphonic principles: not for him the progressive tonality of Mahler, or Nielsen.

The epic concerns of Sibelius's Fifth Symphony are by no means absent from his last orchestral works, but they are presented with even greater concentration of form and through material the more eloquent for its extreme economy. After the prolonged struggles with the Fifth there came a five-year period of virtual silence, and the Sixth Symphony (1923) is still sometimes characterized as a gentle, unassuming piece, a reaction against the grandeur and drama of its mighty predecessor. Regression of a kind might be inferred from the reversion to a four-movement pattern, and the use in the first three movements of flexibly adapted sonata-form schemes. Yet the dramatic tensions which justify the use of such schemes arise from a supremely skilful deployment of a harmonic language of the greatest refinement and sophistication, in which chromaticism functions with even greater dramatic force than in the broader paragraphs of the Nielsen Fifth. The texture is a marvellously fluent blend of contrapuntal and harmonic events, but the nature of those events, and of the way they evolve, is governed by Sibelius's sovereign feeling for purposeful ambiguity.

The most fertile tension in the Symphony No. 6 is between the diatonic tonality of D minor and the Dorian mode on D. Yet this is merely the first stage in a whole network of relationships which expands to embrace F major, C major, G minor and B flat minor, with their capacity for degrees of diatonic or modal interdependence. This is, in fact, the symphony *par excellence* about tonality, but it never becomes merely an intellectual exercise; indeed, the third movement is one of the wittiest in the entire symphonic repertoire, with canons which seem to mock the contrapuntal earnestness of other parts of the work. Expressive impulse and technical process go hand in hand. For example, the first movement begins with gently interacting polyphonic lines using only 'white-note' material: these gradually achieve greater homophonic solidity and chromatic ambiguity, culminating in a chord which might be expected to resolve into D or G, but which is startlingly underpinned by a C natural, and so is directed towards C major: when first heard in bars 17 and 18 of the movement, this chord had resolved smoothly on to a triad of D minor, and so this new event is both structurally significant and expressively potent. Another striking effect occurs at the climax of the finale (p. 80), where a treble *forte* assertion of B minor is diverted with superfine dexterity on to the tonic second inversion of D minor (Ex. 3).

Ex. 3

Such instances could be multiplied, especially those involving a rapid return to the principal tonal area from some remote point, but should not detract from the fact that the entire work is organic and deeply eloquent, in spite of its relatively small orchestra and the almost miniature dimensions of the individual movements.

Sibelius's last symphony, completed in 1924, is in C major and in one movement. 'The most remarkable aspect of Sibelius's Seventh Symphony is that it is an *organic* symphony in one movement; not merely a long movement in which various sections correspond to slow movement, scherzo, and so on, but a single, indivisible organism.'[5] Great works have indeed been written on the four-movements-in-one principle, but Sibelius's Seventh is not one of them. Without wishing to follow those who argue the superiority of Sibelius's scheme to a four-in-one – it is different but not *ipso facto* better – the sheer originality of his achievement must be reiterated, since it outdoes that of many younger composers of the time, whose *styles* were much more adventurous than their musical structures. The Seventh Symphony was at one stage called 'Fantasia sinfonica', and one certainly cannot demonstrate the symphonism of the piece solely by reference to an 'average' structural concept of the symphony. For most listeners, however, the coherence of the design and the majestic logic of the material and its treatment provide sufficient justification for the title: it is not just a symphony, but a new stage in the evolution of symphonic form. 'As a musical structure the Seventh is at once the grandest and most subtly organized that Sibelius ever achieved, and its form shows no trace of compromise with any vestigial symphony in separable movements.'[6]

Although the Seventh is not a four movements-in-one design, this does not invalidate the terminology of traditional structural analysis. The presence of thematic statements and restatements, along with strong contrasts of mood and tempo, provide a basis for defining the structure as the diversification of a unity. The most important thematic statement of the opening *Adagio* and its continuation (p. 9, bar 2 to p. 10, bar 3) reappears reorchestrated in the final section of the work (p. 68, bar 2 to p. 74, bar 7), and the coda (p. 74, bar 8 to the end) balances the first part of the first section, tonally and thematically. To this extent, the terms 'exposition' and 'recapitulation' are appropriate, but qualifications are needed. The exposition is in the tonic key throughout, with only incidental deviations, and the main thematic statement (the awesome trombone theme, Ex. 4a) is prepared for (after the introduction) by a solemn procession mainly for divided strings (pp. 5–9) which is never recapitulated. Since its purpose is to provide a suitable climax for the entrance of the most majestic theme in the work, the same effect cannot be repeated: the two later recurrences of the theme are differently prepared.

The importance of the trombone theme as an embodiment both of a mood and of a tonality is reinforced by its appearance at the centre of the symphony (pp. 30–6), still in the trombone but in the tonic minor and in a significantly varied shape (Ex. 4b).

Ex. 4

a.

21

b.

If this is felt to constitute *development* of the theme, then the central segment of the overall sonata scheme can be added, and we can view the work as comprising a single sonata-form design with other elements separating and linking the three basic sections. Sibelius may very well have had some such intention at one stage, but his 'exposition'. 'development' and 'recapitulation' are not sufficiently conventional to suggest that they have done more than provide a background principle to be greatly modified in practice. On grounds of tonality alone, the very strong emphasis on a single key suggests rondo rather than sonata, and may indeed be a relic of Sibelius's intention to compose a 'Hellenic' rondo as the finale of his original three-movement scheme. So rather than over-categorize, it is surely sufficient to note the unifying function of the first and third statements of the trombone theme, while recognizing that the second statement confirms the thematic unity and also reflects an important stage in the emotional progress of the symphony.

Development can most obviously be found after the first statement of the trombone theme has run its course (pp. 12–20), and discussion of the ascending scale and other motives from the introduction gradually evolves towards a less explicit reliance on C and a much faster tempo. No sooner is this scherzo-like liberation achieved, however (*Vivacissimo.* p. 23), than Sibelius begins to prepare the return both of C (though minor) and of the trombone theme (p. 30). This passage is a particularly subtle example of Sibelius's mixing of formal functions. The *Vivacissimo* has the potential to become an independent scherzo section, its material derived from that of the earlier exposition but its tonality distinct (G sharp minor perhaps). Yet no sooner is it launched than its more urgent function is revealed: not to reinforce a new mood, but to mark, as it begins, the most distant remove so far reached from basic mood, key and material, and to prepare for the early return of more fundamental elements. The return will not be 'complete' – of course: it is too soon for that – and at the very end of the C minor statement of the trombone theme, the music throws out an emphatic reminiscence of the *Vivacissimo* idea, bending the key briefly towards a surprising E major (p. 36).

So far the work has revealed two basic levels, the 'slow' (introduction and trombone theme; central recurrence of trombone theme; recapitulation of trombone theme and coda) and the 'fast' (the abortive 'scherzo', which is paralleled by the *Vivace* section from pp. 59–64 immediately before the build-up to the final return of the trombone theme, p. 68). With transitions mediating between these extremes we seem to have a near-symmetrical arch form. Yet one section of the work remains unaccounted for: the extended *Allegro molto moderato* (pp. 40–59), which is itself ternary with an introduction! Gerald Abraham and others have shown how the material of this section derives from previously stated motives. But what is its structural and tonal function? An obvious effect is to prevent the form from falling into 'predictable' symmetry. Yet at the same time the music here seems to mediate between the extremes of tempo and mood which the 'arch-form' elements propose. If mediation is one factor, postponement is another, for the interpolation performs a function not dissimilar to that of the non-recurring central part of the 'exposition' in ensuring that a statement (the last in this case) of the main theme of the whole work is placed in the most telling and satisfying position.

Tonally, the function of the *Allegro molto moderato* is equally essential to the dramatic yet organic unpredictability of the structure. It restores a pristine C major to counter the *Sturm und Drang* of the central, minor-mode trombone statement and its hectic but transitional aftermath. Yet its own middle section recalls that aftermath, and the tonality darkens, so that the main material returns in a diatonic E flat major (p. 54). Thus the 'episode' does not merely postpone the clinching return of the main theme, but prepares the ground for the most dramatic tonal event of the entire symphony: the recovery of C after its displacement by E flat, a situation prefigured but not fully realized by the first 'scherzo' and central trombone statement. This new function ensures that the second scherzo is no carbon copy of the first, but a still more urgent search for the stability necessary to end the symphony.

Tapiola (1925), a tone poem inspired by the landscape and legends of the far north, was Sibelius's last important work. We have no evidence that Sibelius intended it as a disguised Eighth Symphony, yet it is difficult not to see it as the final stage in a process of symphonic compression. In the Seventh Symphony, strong contrast had a positive role to play: in *Tapiola* it is more a matter of concentration on different aspects of a single idea. Hence the feeling that there is no genuine symphonic progress through argument to resolution but, instead, the exploration of a landscape seen in a single frozen moment: a painting. *Tapiola* raises the paradox of time and timelessness far more acutely than many more radical works which contrast measured and unmeasured material. But whether or not the differences between it and the Seventh Symphony are definable as the differences between non-symphony and symphony, the sheer severity of its design makes it easy to accept as a last word.

It now seems that it will never be known whether Sibelius began or even completed another symphony after *Tapiola*. Maybe a work was written and then destroyed in an excess of self-criticism. Maybe Sibelius's failure to write an Eighth had little or nothing to do with musical problems. Nothing can minimize the fact that the long silence was a tragedy, both for Sibelius himself and for modern tonal music. Yet the originality and perfection of the last three symphonies is such that it is difficult to imagine how their creator could have continued along a path of further refinement and exploration. Perhaps if the late works had been less successful he would have written more: in which case, it was not self-criticism but self-awareness which led to thirty years of silence.

Ralph Vaughan Williams made a much slower start than Sibelius: if he had stopped composing at the age of sixty his very finest works would not exist. So it was only after 1915 that he began the series of seven symphonies (Nos. 3–9) which, while less innovatory in purely structural terms than the later Nielsen and Sibelius, have strong roots in a language in which a modality and thematic character closely related to folk music were brought into fruitful confrontation with the much more dramatic resources of modern tonal chromaticism. Vaughan Williams's four finest symphonies – Nos. 3–6 – seem to invite discussion as two pairs, Nos. 3 and 5 being essentially pastoral and reflective, Nos. 4 and 6 tougher and more active. Yet this parallel soon breaks down when matters of technique are considered. For example, No. 3 ends by moving away from the principal tonal centre of the work, while No. 5 – in many ways just as subtle an example of the propulsive ambiguity of diatonic and modal interactions – affirms the purest tonic harmony in its final bars. No. 4 ends vehemently with a chromatically spiced but uncompromising cadence in the principal key of F minor: the conclusion of No. 6 could not be more different – unless it were demonstrably atonal – since the passive, eerie alternations of E flat major and E minor triads, both in second inversion, serve less to establish the ultimate primacy of E minor as tonic for the whole work than to confirm that the symphony has been fundamentally and persistently concerned with the undermining of keys by those a semitone or a tritone distant. Since all four symphonies are in four movements it is certainly instructive to compare them purely at the structural level; but useful though it may be to discover what, for example, the relative proportions allotted to development sections or second subject groups may be, there is still greater value in attempting to identify the workings of the musical language which brings the forms to life.

As far as the Symphony No. 3 (the *Pastoral*, completed in 1921) is concerned, the relationship between reflectiveness of mood and ambiguity of language is strikingly close. What might have been a symphony in G major – or in G minor – or even in the Mixolydian or transposed Dorian modes – becomes a symphony about what happens to G as a tonic when a wide variety of pressures – diatonic, chromatic, modal – are applied to it. The use of flowing rhythms, lyric thematic ideas, and the major or minor triad as principal harmonic unit, ensures that the tensions which this language generates rarely become overt. Indeed, a better sense of focus is found in later symphonies, where there is a more effective balance between drama and lyricism, and a genuine opposition is suggested between cycle-of-fifths hierarchies and other forces.

The Symphony No. 4 (1934) is a fine example of economically organized form, vividly unified thematic process and tautly controlled chromatic harmony. The Symphony No. 5 (1943) is again more lyrical, but this does not invalidate a truly dramatic tonal scheme in which the modally oriented ambiguities of the first movement are recalled and diatonically dissolved in the serene coda of the finale. Yet it is the Symphony No. 6 (1947) which, of all the nine, deserves the closest study: it is the nearest Vaughan Williams came to a truly Sibelian concentration, for although only the most basic sustained notes link the four movements – *Allegro, Moderato,* Scherzo *(Allegro vivace)* and Epilogue *(Moderato)* – there is an undeniable sense of continued consideration of the same essential issue throughout. Since that issue, in its simplest form, is the clashing semitone, the Sixth Symphony might even be regarded as a further essay on the subject matter of the Fourth: after all, such a subject is of inexhaustible interest to a modern composer committed to tonality but acutely conscious of the factors which most insidiously call it into question.

The purely thematic unity of the work is prominent, and an important contributory factor to the general sense of highly concentrated processes at work. Even when contrast of mood is almost total, as with the *cantabile* second subject of the first movement, there are clear motivic connections with first-subject material. Yet the greater the underlying thematic connections, the more important a purely tonal conflict between opposites and alternatives becomes. In the first movement this involves not only E major and E minor, but F minor and E minor, C minor and B minor, B flat minor and B minor. What might potentially be a straightforward, traditional scheme of E minor-B minor-E major is complicated by the tendency of tonic and dominant to be shadowed by keys a semitone away. Moreover, when the mediant achieves prominence at an early stage (Fig. 4), it is not as G major but minor, whose own mediant, B flat, is to play a crucial role later in the work.

No sooner has the first movement countered its brief, confident assertion of E major with E minor, than the triad as such vanishes and a single E is left to die away against the B flats with which trumpets launch the second movement (Ex. 5).

Ex. 5

The tritonal opposition is expressed through a theme which constantly pits major and minor seconds against the B flat, and although the F minor-E minor argument is referred to during the course of the movement, the B flat, reiterated relentlessly in the later stages, provokes despairing assent from the rest of the orchestra in one of Vaughan Williams's most powerful climaxes. The price of assent seems to be the avoidance of a root position triad of B flat minor, however; instead, first inversions of G minor and G flat major bring the semitonal oppositon into the foreground of the argument again. At the end of the movement this has shifted to the even more basic level of B flat/C flat [B], and it is one of the roles of the Scherzo to carry the harmonic/tonal argument into an entirely new area. Its contrapuntal texture involves entries of the tritone-generated theme a perfect fifth apart, thus increasing the structural significance of the conflict between semitones at a crucial stage. The underlying tonal argument is thereby sustained and intensified, especially when C minor, a potential bridge to the 'real' dominant, B, achieves prominence in the 'trio' (Fig. 16). With the return of the Scherzo, however, any progress towards a final resolution is halted by the welter of imitative entries of a theme which contains so much contradiction within itself, that even triadic harmony is scarcely possible in such a context. The return of the trio theme as a barbaric march (Fig. 39) halts the atonal drift by focusing on a persistent if unstable A flat, but in a chilly transition the tritonal material returns again, to be finally summarized by a bass-clarinet line descending over two octaves from F to E.

The knowledge that Vaughan Williams connected the finale of the Sixth Symphony with the speech from *The Tempest* ending 'We are such stuff as dreams are made on; and our little life is rounded with a sleep,' is still no preparation for the extreme, anti-romantic bleakness of this Epilogue. It is not so much an image of death as of life laid waste. The analogies with post-nuclear landscapes are as apt here as with Varèse's slightly later *Déserts*. Yet if the music is a suppressed *cri de coeur*, its organization is highly disciplined. The threads are gathered together, as the semitones and tritones of the opening idea demonstrate. When the tonic E is at all firmly emphasized, however, it is in a stifled Phrygian cadence and on an icy minor ninth chord. Only at the very end does the return of pure triads crystallize around the G natural of the first violins. Clashes have become oscillations, and although there is still enough 'function' left in the D sharp of the penultimate chord for us to sense a resolution from something subordinate on to something basic, the absence of root position and more decisive rhythmic treatment ensures little sense of true finality. We are at the opposite pole from where we began: the cataclysm which launched the argument has been exhausted. The argument itself is unresolved (Ex. 6).

The Sixth Symphony marked the end of an important phase in Vaughan Williams's creative life, a phase which produced his finest and most appealing music. To some extent, it was a phase of unresolved

Ex. 6

alternatives, so that it is possible to argue that the Fifth and Sixth Symphonies belong to quite different, even mutually exclusive worlds of feeling, which were only integrated in the last three symphonies.[7] These are an old man's music and are likely to grip the listener less forcefully than their predecessors. They are by no means negligible, but they seem at times to be repeating well-tried effects. Even without a high regard for these works, however, there can be no doubt that Vaughan Williams was a symphonist of exceptional individuality and skill, whom none of his British contemporaries could match. The most prolific symphonists among them, Arnold Bax (1883–1953) and Havergal Brian (1876–1972), both have their passionate partisans, but even when they have received their due from posterity it seems unlikely that Vaughan Williams will suffer in comparison.

His greatest near-contemporary was Gustav Holst (1874–1934), who would probably be ranked much higher if he had found accepted forms more attractive and relatively radical harmonic devices less appealing. Even so, the fine tone poem *Egdon Heath* (1928) is by no means unsymphonic in form and method, and it is tragic that Holst did not live to finish the symphony for which a Scherzo was completed in 1933. Vaughan Williams's debt to Holst was deep. Even the Ninth Symphony originally had a programmatic idea centring to some extent on the Thomas Hardy country which *Egdon Heath* so memorably portrays. In his old age, one of the finest of all twentieth-century symphonists was still finding inspiration in the landscape of the country whose most personal and primitive forms of musical expression he had done more than anyone to integrate into the mainstream of modern musical development.

In France there was no symphonist of the stature of Nielsen, Sibelius or Vaughan Williams, and the concern of Albert Roussel (1869–1937) for continuing the symphonic tradition can be used as evidence that even his best work displays 'more sense than sensibility, more integrity than imagination'.[8] Roussel's best works are the songs and ballets (notably *Bacchus et Ariane*, Op. 43, 1930) and the short descriptive pieces and choral compositions, like Psalm 80, Op. 37 (1928). The three symphonies which he composed between 1919 and 1934 are still worth close attention, however, if only to demonstrate the kind of problems facing a composer who was no structural innovator, and who did not want to compose wholeheartedly neo-classical (or anti-romantic) symphonic works. In the Symphony No. 2 in B flat (1919–21), the last of the three movements is the least conventional in form, but at the same time it unifies the work as a whole by developing first-movement material. The Third Symphony in G minor followed in 1929–30, but structural problems here are if anything more pronounced than in the earlier work. In particular, the design of the opening *Allegro vivo* is flawed by a second subject which does not balance the main tonality clearly enough and at the same time seems too detached from the mainstream of the movement as a whole. Such dangerous diversity of material also weakens the finale.

One diagnosis of Roussel's difficulties sees him as attempting to extricate himself from the influence of Prokofiev's style – especially his ballets *Chout* and *Le Pas d'Acier* – and David Drew, whose convincing thesis this is, examines the Fourth Symphony in A major, Op. 59 (1934), as the crucial work in which 'Roussel attempted to come to terms with his problems'.[9] The first movement *(Allegro)* has similar flaws to that of No. 3, yet the rondo-like finale is far better than its predecessor and the central movements – a *Lento molto* and a Scherzo – have impressive moments, notably the climax of the *Lento*.

Of Roussel's French contemporaries, only Maurice Ravel (1875–1937) belongs to the present chapter, by virtue of his two piano concertos. Even if we agree that 'with regard to overall form, Ravel's music has nothing very valuable to offer',[10] these concertos, composed so close to one another, yet so strikingly different in certain basic respects, deserve some discussion.

The Concerto for Left Hand in one movement and the Concerto in G in three movements were both completed in 1931, and while the former is an imaginative reconstitution of the world of Lisztian romanticism, the latter unites – and transmutes – a wide variety of less grandiose sources: Scarlatti, Mozart, Saint-Saëns and Gershwin among them. Both works also have an admixture of that Spanish flavouring which Ravel found so difficult to resist, and indeed the G major was initially planned as a Basque Rhapsody for piano and orchestra. The fashion-conscious aspect of the two-hand work is obvious, but inoffensive when the result is so light and elegant. Gershwin's *Rhapsody in Blue*, which enjoyed a great vogue in Europe during the late 'twenties, has left distinct echoes behind, but there is more parody than imitation in Ravel's work and more good humour than a composer seriously jealous of popular trendsetters would be likely to display. Sonata and rondo-type movements frame the elegant *Adagio* whose main melody, apparently inspired by Mozart's Clarinet Quintet, captures for some the spirit of a Fauré song. The dissonant climax before the return of the melody (piano accompanying cor anglais) is evidence that Ravel could still contrive a dramatic effect of appropriate proportions. This charming work is never merely superficial.

Greater concentration is to be expected from the single-movement Left-Hand Concerto, which relates to the sombre grandeur of *Gaspard de la Nuit*, as the G major does to the delicate fantasy of *Le Tombeau de Couperin*. The dark, doom-laden orchestral opening and the rhetorical piano entry certainly conjure up visions of heroic confrontations, of impossible odds challenged, with the obvious technical limitations of a single hand appealing to Ravel's delight in ingenuity. The form may not be ideally balanced, since the slow Sarabande which precedes the main fast music does not unfold with totally convincing momentum, and the *cadenza* which its return provokes near the end seems over-long, but the sardonic dance elements of the main *Allegro* have ample verve and bite. In spite of increasing illness, Ravel in his later years was far from effete and self-indulgent, or able only to convince in languid moments like the *Adagio* of the G major concerto. It can indeed be argued that 'in certain respects, the most consistent and the most innovatory of Ravel's late works is that much maligned piece, *Bolero*',[11] but the 'calculated mating of the sophisticated and the barbaric', which determines the quality and character of *Bolero* (1928), is more attractively harnessed to rather more symphonic aims in the Left-Hand Concerto. Both *Bolero* and the concerto are easily vulgarized in performance, but, like the *Don Quichotte* songs, Ravel's last composition, the concerto has an aura of romantic bitterness which is disturbing and hauntingly memorable.

Chapter 2

Béla Bartók

Béla Bartók (1881–1945) completed his Second String Quartet in October 1917, and Halsey Stevens rightly says that 'the whole direction of Bartók's later writing might be deduced from this one work'.[1] Then in his thirty-seventh year, Bartók had gradually developed a personal style from two principal sources: other composers, most notably Liszt, Strauss and Debussy; and folk music, which played a vital part in his life from 1905 onwards. Of all his earlier works it was probably the one-act opera, *Bluebeard's Castle* (1911), which marked the most decisive stage in the establishment of this style, which, for all its various impressionistic, expressionistic and nationalistic components, clearly involved a reinforcement of tonality at precisely the time when Schoenberg was confirming his abandonment of it, and even Stravinsky (in *The King of the Stars*) seemed to be bracing himself to follow suit.

When he completed the opera, Bartók had still not written a wholly satisfactory instrumental work: the String Quartet No. 1 (1909) has many remarkable qualities, but it is not a completely coherent conception. It may therefore have been fortunate, as far as his long-term development as a composer was concerned, that *Bluebeard's Castle* was rejected by a Budapest competition jury. Discouraged, Bartók devoted himself to the collection and arrangement of folk music, only returning to serious composition when war broke out and travelling became difficult. Now at last he was ready to profit from the stylistic synthesis of the opera and to create a convincing 'abstract' design. The Second String Quartet (1915–17), like its contemporary, the ballet *The Wooden Prince* (1914–16), took a significantly long time to complete, but it laid the foundations for the next twenty-five years of creative achievement.

The principal tonal centre of the quartet is an A which, although it only emerges gradually and is not established or exploited through traditional triadic progressions, functions as a tonic for the first and third movements of the work. (Its close relative, D, is the centre for the

31

Scherzo.) The avoidance of such triads involves a parallel avoidance of emphasis on the interval of the perfect fifth, and it is clear that the tritone and minor third, with their function of dividing the octave symmetrically and thereby of contradicting and conflicting with traditional hierarchical relationships within the octave, are already suggesting not merely particular types of thematic material but a new kind of tonal organization. The work uses forms which are clearly derived from traditional models, though the slow third movement is freer in this respect than most of Bartók's later finales. There are also motivic interrelationships between the movements, thematic unity serving to reinforce tonal unity. The character of the music clearly involves the transformation (rather than the direct quotation) of national rhythmic and melodic features, and the second movement is one of the most directly folk-inspired pieces which Bartók ever composed. These, then, are the main characteristics of the work, and they were to be continued, developed and reshaped – but never abandoned – in all Bartók's later compositions. He remained a tonal composer, however much he may at times have shunned the triad or manipulated short motives in so concentrated a manner as to suggest an interest in serialism; and he remained committed to the sonata and ternary structures in which tonality functions most fundamentally. There is often a powerful tension between a wholly traditional harmonic and structural background and what Bartók has actually written, but such tension enhances both the appeal and the approachability of the music, and nowhere more profoundly than where his use of intervallic and structural symmetry displaces traditional hierarchies.

The Second Quartet was first performed in March 1918, but it was *The Wooden Prince* which at last brought Bartók a degree of public success – and with it the long-delayed first performance of *Bluebeard's Castle* in May of the same year. The completion of the quartet did not provoke an immediate outburst of creative activity, however. The publication of folk music still occupied much of Bartók's time, and although he composed another ballet, *The Miraculous Mandarin*, in 1919, its controversial, erotic subject matter deterred any theatre from accepting it, and the music remained unperformed until 1926. There is a vehement intensity in the two violin sonatas (1921–2), and the commitment to tonality itself seems in danger of being lost; but they confirm that the medium of chamber music would be of continuing significance for Bartók as he sought to follow up the achievements of the Second Quartet.

The commitment to traditional structures in the sonatas is also far from whole-hearted, and the apparent reluctance with which the rhapsodic, large-scale first movement of No. 1 discloses a basic adherence to sonata form may be the main reason for the general opinion that it is not a complete success. Bartók himself evidently accepted this verdict, since he was willing to let the work be played without it. The harmonic direction of the second and third movements is certainly more clearly focused, and with the appearance of more specifically Hungarian material the virtually atonal impressionism which Bartók seems to have learned most directly from his Polish contemporary Szymanowski is less apparent. The two-movement Second Sonata is the finer, with clearer form and surer harmonic control. There are nevertheless signs that Bartók's desire to demand a high degree of virtuosity from both players helped to dictate a somewhat disjointed, episodic form in the second movement; and the overall scheme, presenting problems which are not all solved with equal success, may have prompted a further attempt at a single-movement scheme with two basic parts, in the String Quartet No. 3 (1927).

A less aggressive, experimental tone is struck by the Dance Suite (composed in August 1923), which exists in orchestral and solo piano versions. It was the work which, in Bartók's own view, closed the first phase of his career. After three years (1923–6) in which his only works were a handful of folksong transcriptions, a flood of new compositions established him unmistakably as one of the greatest modern masters. In them his reactions to the two innovatory giants of the postwar musical world – the neo-classical Stravinsky and the serial Schoenberg – can be clearly observed; in particular, Bartók seemed to share their concern to keep lyricism, and with it any overtly romantic qualities, in a subordinate position. Nevertheless, there was no likelihood of Bartók's becoming a whole-hearted disciple of either: his own ideas were now too clear-cut, and his own genius too strong, to permit any decline into stylistic subservience.

Of all Bartók's mature compositions, the Third String Quartet is perhaps the most imaginative in form and the most intense in expression. Both the imagination and the intensity are rooted in compression: the work is in one movement and lasts little more than fifteen minutes. Yet the compression serves to sharpen the contrasts between dramatic and lyric types of material, between contrapuntal and harmonic textures, and it also presents one of Bartók's most rigorously organized arguments between tonal centres; the argument is at once about degrees of relationship (old and new) and about the need to affirm a single supreme centre, which may ultimately be diatonically, if not triadically, asserted. The single movement of the quartet is divided into four sections: Part One, Part Two, the Recapitulation of Part One, and Coda. Within such a compressed scheme, one would expect a high degree of unity in every dimension, but it is the most fundamental technical feature – the type of conflict between tonal centres – which is the most basic unifying factor. Thematic interrelationships are less important, less immediately perceptible, pertaining principally to the first and third, and second and fourth sections respectively. The main thematic contrast is *between* rather than *within* sections, however, and this reinforces a crucial duality which is one way in which the funda-mental tonal argument is carried through.

The forms of the individual sections are not as easily absorbed into pre-determined ternary or sonata schemes as are most of Bartók's later designs. In Parts One and Two the structures serve to prepare and present a particular tonal conflict (C sharp versus C natural) – a conflict which takes very different forms in both but is resolved in neither. To this extent the same essential issue is approached by way of two radically different types of material, and two forms which have an ancestry in ternary and sonata design, but which are adapted to the unique purposes of this particular work.

Part One is slow, Part Two is fast; Part One is lyrical and builds to a melodic statement of gravely simple beauty; Part Two is hectic, dramatic (and distinctly more folk-like); its climax is an essentially harmonic, virtually athematic confrontation of the most aggressive kind, in which the tonal, and therefore the structural issue is for once completely on the surface. There is still no resolution, however, and the third and fourth sections of the work, with their remarkably free rethinking of the issues presented in the first two parts, ultimately resolve the problem by sheer vital force, though in a way which proves that, as in all hierarchical tonal schemes, rivals are also to a degree associates.

Any brief analysis of so subtle a score needs above all to demonstrate the way in which the thematic process is itself a function of the tonal process. In Part One, the main motive – a rising fourth and falling third – has a 'white-note' form which can press the claims of both C and D as tonal centres, and a 'black-note' form associated with C sharp. The tensions of this first Part are mainly the result of combining various manifestations of these two forms at strategic points, a process which begins in the sixth and seventh bars, and is also of considerable importance between Figs. 3 and 5 (plus two bars), and between Fig. 11 and the end of the Part. Although the central segment of this ternary scheme evolves away from the original form of the basic motive, it provides clear indications that C sharp is truly central (cf. four bars before Fig. 9), and that the issue at stake is more its survival than its supremacy. With the return of the basic shape in the final stages of Part One, however, it is evident that in the simplest sense the white-note melodic version is dominant, while C sharp and G sharp are given greatest prominence in the bass (Ex. 7).

Ex. 7

This stasis is expressed in its most basic form four bars from the end of Part One, with a 'chord' (C sharp, G sharp, G natural) which confirms that an important element in the conflict involves the orthodox dominants of the tonal centres, and their ambiguous position in Bartók's scheme of things. G natural, as a dominant, may be a powerful agent of C natural in conventional terms, but as the tritone relative of C sharp and with a position precisely midway between one C sharp and another, it may in the end be given an even stronger function in that connection.

The analytical work of Ernö Lendvai becomes especially relevant at this point.[2] Lendvai has argued that Bartók made systematic use of a tonal system involving relationships between 'axis' tones (a tonic axis might be C/F sharp; E flat/A; its dominant G/C sharp; B flat/E; and subdominant F/B; A flat/D) and of Golden Section proportions and Fibonacci series to determine both the structure of a particular work, and even the character of particular types of material.[3] As ways of reinterpreting and reinforcing tonality and traditional formal designs, these theories have much to recommend them, even if the evidence that Bartók made conscious and consistent use of them is far from conclusive. As far as the Third String Quartet is concerned, the 'axis' theory can help to clarify the sense in which pitches a tritone apart are in *association*, rather than in conflict, as members of the same axis group, whereas pitch centres a semitone or whole tone apart conflict rather than associate. Put another way, the principal 'background' conflict in the Third Quartet is between the tonic C sharp and the subdominant F sharp: but the subdominant is represented most frequently by its tritonal associate, C natural. The other important conflict is between the tonic C sharp and the dominant G sharp, but here, too, G sharp is represented by its tritonal associate, D. In this way the graphic 'hemming in' of the central C sharp by pitches a semitone on either side provides a concentrated representation of the equally symmetrical situation in which C sharp is 'attacked' by pitches a perfect fourth away on either side (G sharp and F sharp).

In Part Two of the quartet, the mood changes and the tonal argument modulates with it. Immediately, in the D natural-E flat trill of the second violin, the shift can be perceived, and the new, scalic, thematic material confirms the location of this new stage in the conflict of semitones. Just as, in Part One, the argument was pursued principally through the conflict between 'white' and 'black' note forms of the main motive, which in development tend to interact, so in Part Two the same essential principle is established in the early stages.

Attempts to define the overall form of Part Two in terms of a single archetype are unsatisfactory, and it may well be that Bartók here achieved a blend of variation and sonata form of the kind attempted later by Webern in the first movement of the String Quartet Op. 28 and the Variations for Orchestra Op. 30. Yet the presence of modulatory features in Bartók's case naturally creates a much greater closeness to the traditional sonata model, and his 'variations' are equally perceptible as stages of development.

The exposition of the second Part is certainly over at Fig. 5. Before that Bartók has established his two thematic elements: first, the modal-triadic 'white-note' cello idea, which immediately provokes a brief 'black-note' retort, but is allowed some canonic development before a fully worked-out 'black-note' theme is stated. At Fig. 3, this is heard in the first violin (it is not, of course, exclusively 'black-note': the most important thing about it is that it is centred on E flat, D natural's dominant-axis opponent), and is unfolded in immediate combination with the cello triads, pointing up at once their similar motivic constitution and a tonal conflict which the sharing of F natural and C natural does nothing to alleviate (Ex. 8).

Ex. 8

The first stage of variation/development (Figs. 5–7) inverts the 'black-note' idea, and suggests a transitional function in its double departure: from the confrontation between two versions of a similar basic shape, and from the conflict between D and E flat. This section actually restores the C sharp/C conflict for much of its length, and also includes a subsidiary clash between F and E.

The fierce and concentrated logic of the developmental processes between Figs. 7 and 36 are best studied directly in the score, but some general points concerning texture and the direction of the tonal argument can be made verbally. Once the fundamental terms of the harmonic issue have been restated, between Figs. 7 and 8, in the reiterated D/E flat/A unit, the composer gradually shifts the emphasis away from tonal conflict as such into a polyphonic development of the basic motives, which enables the purely tonal argument to operate on a larger scale. At one bar before Fig. 12 a long series of canons begins, initially involving only the two violins (tonal centre C, moving to E), then, at Fig. 14, shifting to the viola and cello (centre A), back to the violins at Fig. 15 (centre D) and viola and second violin four bars later (centre G). All this, using the cello version of the basic motive as thematic material, is merely a preliminary flexing of muscles, however: the canons so far having involved assent rather than conflict. At Fig. 16, all four instruments are involved for the first time in a double canon by inversion, principally at the tritone with C and F sharp as the most basic 'poles'. Once again, the more fundamental tonal oppositions of Part One are recalled, though in a context where the absence of C sharp itself confirms that the conflict as such has not been renewed: in so pervasively contrapuntal a texture, no clear feeling of tonal centre can emerge at all.

An important new stage begins at Fig. 19 with the restoration of D (supported by both F natural and A natural) as tonal centre for a passage of concentrated canonic development of the 'black-note' motive. As the music descends sequentially, so the area of C sharp/C is touched on: as if to prevent this gaining in importance, the texture solidifies, canon disappears temporarily, and both D and E flat are added to form a four-note cluster (four bars before Fig. 23).

The rest of the development section can be divided into two main parts. Between Figs. 23 and 31 the 'black-note' version, restored initially to its original E flat basis, sweeps aside a renewed attempt at canons on the 'white-note' version. Clashes between D/E flat yield again, as they did at Fig. 5, to C sharp/C: there is an unmistakably recapitulatory quality here, but at the climax the prime associate of D/E flat – A – is fully in control (Fig. 31).

The final variation, or stage of development, then achieves the greatest contrapuntal concentration yet. It begins as a 'double fugato' centred on A, the axis relative of C and the most powerful opponent of C sharp. After 'orthodox' answers on E, the subject (deriving from the 'black-note' motive) gradually builds up a sequence of *stretti* which inhibit the emergence of any clear tonal direction. A stasis similar to that at Fig. 23 seems the only possible outcome. But this time the cluster is a whole tone higher: instead of C/C sharp/D/E flat we have D/E flat/E/F. It is the F which, as E sharp in enharmonic disguise, runs on into the recapitulation at Fig. 36 and helps to confirm C sharp rather than D as the principal tonal centre (Ex. 9).

It is this substitution, engineered by Bartók with sovereign inevitability, which provokes the virtual collapse of the thematic process in the closing stages of Part Two, and the naked clashes, not between C sharp and D, but between C sharp and C natural, the original *alter ego* for which D has in effect been acting as a substitute throughout Part Two. Of course this has to remain unresolved. At four bars before Fig. 49, C sharp in the cello underpins a full C major triad in the upper instruments. In the rapid collapse which ensues, the two notes parry

Ex. 9

each other like duelling fencers, and when the cello 'resolves' its last
C sharp on to a D, this is the very reverse of a triumphant compromise
but an admission that the whole issue remains in doubt (Ex. 10).

Ex. 10

sempre ff

After the brutal *dénouement* of Part Two, when the attention has been focused on tonal issues to the exclusion of thematic issues, the third section (Recapitulation of Part One) reasserts the thematic process but suspends the tonal argument almost completely. Bartók's title for the section is only approximate: it is an allusive re-studying of the thematic material of Part One, with virtually nothing in the way of exact repetition. Yet its function is not only to reassert the thematic process, but to prepare the ground for the final thematic *and* tonal argument of the Coda. It has an oddly hesitant foreboding which creates no sense of anticlimax or of marking time. In fact its psychological necessity and appropriateness are more remarkable than its technical function within the scheme of the work as a whole. The C sharp/C natural conflict is still to be heard (e.g. five bars after Fig. 3), however, and the final bars seem to be moving decisively in favour of C sharp, when the Coda suddenly takes over in a mood of barely suppressed hysteria and firmly rooted on a cello C (Ex. 11).

The Coda is at once a thrilling reworking of material from Part Two and a final establishment of the fact that C natural is subordinate to C sharp. The last cadence, with its long 'dominant' preparation in which the bass note G sharp has C and D naturals strongly in evidence above it, indicates that, if this were a simple diatonic ending, then C natural would *really* be the leading note B sharp, and would therefore need to resolve on to its tonic (Ex. 12).

Such functions are scarcely relevant here, but the final chords serve both to summarize the conflict which has provoked the entire work and also to project a satisfying outcome to that conflict. The constitution of the chords also reinforces the structural importance of major and minor seconds, and perfect fifths and tritones, to the fabric of the work as a whole. Ultimately, the greatness of Bartók's Third Quartet lies in the

lucidity and coherence with which music of such passion and power is planned and presented. It was a triumph which the composer never surpassed.

During the remaining sixteen years of his life, Bartók produced a series of instrumental compositions which refine and reflect the explorations of the period between the third and fourth quartets. It was not a period of major innovations and many of the works display similar methods. Nevertheless, there is nothing in the least monotonous about Bartók's exploitation of his hard-won stylistic maturity, and even in those works where structural symmetry is all-pervading, the material is treated with unfailing inventiveness. The predictability of large amounts of exact repetition is always avoided, even though the conflict between rival tonal centres is normally less intense and triadic har-

Ex. 12

monies more frequent than in the Third Quartet. Bartók continued to produce folksong transcriptions, and in 1939 completed the large *Mikrokosmos* sequence of 153 progressive piano pieces, his most important educational legacy. His personal life was severely disrupted by the outbreak of the Second World War. Like many, he sought refuge in America: unlike many, he found absence from his native land almost unbearable, and ill-health and public indifference made his last years miserable and less crowningly productive than might have been hoped. In view of Bartók's long struggle for creative stability and public acceptance in Hungary – which he attained without facile compromise and by intensifying rather than diluting his commitment to what he believed to be the most fundamental cultural features of his own nationality – his early death in exile remains one of the tragedies of twentieth-century culture. More than any other great European composer, he was a victim of political forces: the man who had sought to integrate progressive artistic ideas into the fabric of a nation's life was in large part himself destroyed by the Hitlerian perversion of nationalism.

A study of the major compositions of the period from 1928 to 1945 reveals the establishment of a new equilibrium, wherein the 'poise' of structures in which many basic features are predetermined is projected through material of great appeal and compelling plasticity. There are three five-movement works: the String Quartets No. 4 (1928) and No. 5 (1934) and the Concerto for Orchestra (1943). Parallels between the quartets are easily demonstrated: the themes and forms of the first and fifth, and the second and fourth movements are related in each case, with the central movement acting as the pivot of the 'bridge' or 'arch'. The greater forcefulness of the Fourth String Quartet is accounted for largely by the fact that it has only one slow movement (the third), whereas in the Fifth the second and fourth movements are both slow. The other significant difference is that the later work starts with unmistakable tonal emphasis, on B flat, whereas the main centre of the Fourth Quartet – C – emerges far less obviously or immediately. The greater radicalism of the Fourth is also inferable from its tendency to be 'all-thematic', whereas the Fifth, though with no shortage of contrapuntal writing, is not so easily analysed in virtually serial terms. Since there is always the temptation to proceed with the discussion of these two powerful works in mutually exclusive terms, it is important to emphasize the long, finely shaped melodic writing of the Fourth Quartet's central movement and the discordant expressionism of the Fifth's outer movements. The Fifth probably has the wider expressive range, encompassing the enchanting delicacy of the third movement's trio and the blatantly bitter naivety of the last-minute classical parody

(Finale, bar 699), while the Fourth has the more concentrated dramatic impact, its tonal argument reflecting the fierce subtleties of its near-contemporary, No. 3.

In the much later Concerto for Orchestra, a less intense work, the intellectual implications of symmetry are not pursued further, or even as far. As with the Fourth Quartet, there is a central slow movement of considerable expressive power – and the material is linked with that of the introduction to the whole work – but the atmosphere of the flanking pairs of fast movements is a good deal more relaxed than is the case with the quartets. Bartók's own note on the work speaks not of symmetrical equivalences but of 'a gradual transition from the sternness of the first movement . . . to the life-assertion of the last one'.[4] Technically, apart from its dazzling exploitation of the orchestra, the texture ranges from intricate polyphony to sumptuously harmonized, folk-derived melody, including another brief parody recalling that in the Fifth Quartet, though this time there is a specific victim: the 'Fascist' march theme from Shostakovich's Seventh *(Leningrad)* Symphony. The concerto has disappointed those who prefer Bartók's more adventurous earlier style, and the forms of the individual movements, particularly the second and fourth, are indeed uncomplicated to the point of obviousness. Yet the play with tonality, at times triadically enforced, at times less simply presented, is as vigorous as ever, and as convincing. For a work which is sometimes described as a 'dilution' of Bartók at his best, its style is still unmistakably that of its creator, and him alone.

The three four-movement works from this period are notably diverse: the Music for Strings, Percussion and Celesta (1936), the String Quartet No. 6 (1939) and the Sonata for Solo Violin (1944). These are in fact the only major mature works in which Bartók ever employed a four-movement scheme, unless it is argued that the Third String Quartet itself belongs under that heading. It is certainly not inappropriate to consider the structure of the Music for Strings, Percussion and Celesta alongside that of the Third Quartet, for although the former is in four distinct movements rather than four linked sections, the sequence of moods (neither beginning with a 'symphonic' *allegro*) can be equated and there are thematic links between all four movements of the 'Music', extending the alternating links of the Third Quartet and prefiguring the 'motto' theme of the Sixth. Most importantly, however, the two works provide perhaps the most impressive examples (apart from the Second Quartet) of that 'transition' of mood to which Bartók referred in his note on the Concerto for Orchestra; true, the Coda of the

Third Quartet is perhaps too hectic and concentrated to be described simply as 'life-asserting', but it brings the work to a triumphant as well as intellectually convincing end. The Music for Strings, Percussion and Celesta, by contrast, fits Bartók's terminology precisely. It would be oversimplifying to say that the chromatic searchings of the start are dissipated in diatonic radiance at the end: there is never any real doubt about the central function of A, the first note of the work, but there is a world of difference between the lugubrious counterpoint to which it gives rise in the first movement and the exciting thrummed major triads which launch the finale.

The 'Music' is also notable for its use of that opposition between tritone and perfect fifth which was so basic to the Third Quartet, and it is the more explicit here in view of Bartók's willingness to employ simple triadic harmony (in the sonata-form second movement, C, F sharp and G are cunningly deployed, and this element is inverted – F, F sharp and C – in the arch-form third movement). The essential tritone is, however, A-E flat, unchallenged in the initial fugue, but in effect forced, or encouraged, to resolve on to A-E (though not to disappear) in the rondo-like finale.

This 'tonic axis' also has an important function in the Sixth String Quartet, a work very different from the Music for Strings, Percussion and Celesta in its overall character and shape. In a sense, the shape is the reverse of that of 'Music', with the fastest movement coming first and the slowest last – Bartók's first slow finale since the Second Quartet, and one of his simplest yet most deeply expressive inspirations. As the Second Quartet showed, ending in slow desolation does not necessarily mean ending in tonal ambiguity, but in the Sixth Quartet, for the only time in his mature output, Bartók does not conclude with an absolutely explicit tonal emphasis. Instead, two of the members of the tonic axis, D and F, coexist with their respective fifths. In view of the fact that the cadential progression of bars 84 and 85 involves a very clear movement on to D and A from their tritones, and the further fact that the D and A remain sounding after the cello's F major triad has died away, those who wish to allot a single centre to the work will associate this ending with the conclusion of the first movement and choose D. If it is D, however, it is with a crucial and unusual degree of ambiguity which is only acceptable because it is implicit in the material and manner of the work's generating idea (Ex. 13). This idea is a 'motto' theme (Ex. 14), which prefaces each of the first three movements and forms the principal subject of the fourth. It

Ex. 13

will be noted how clearly the first phrase of the motto outlines the tonic axis, with its span of G sharp to D. But the motto as a whole presents a move away from such decisiveness, with a positive assertion of ambiguous intent in the prolonged 'D', which acts as a C double sharp resolving on to D sharp (bar 8).

Ex. 14

Tonal explicitness does not seem required of such a melancholy theme, so that although the tonal framework of the piece as a whole remains faithful to the axis principle – B is central to the March, A flat to the March's 'trio', F (ironic major triads) to the Burletta, D to its central *Andantino* – the finale itself starts from an A minor triad, which could be a 'real' dominant but which is powerless to establish any permanent effect because of the highly chromatic nature of the motto theme, whose harmonization it initiates. Even the return of first-movement material in the central section of the movement does nothing to press any relevant tonal claim. In fact the suspense becomes truly agonizing, the issues so delicately balanced that no decisive outcome is rationally conceivable. For that the motto theme itself would have to change its nature.

At the end of the score Bartók wrote 'Saanen Budapest, 1939, VIII-XI'. A few months later he was in America, and although he returned briefly to Hungary to settle his affairs, the Sixth Quartet was a true farewell, an ending the sadness of which is all the deeper for being so economically expressed. It may in a technical sense be 'inconclusive', but when the end is reached the listener knows instinctively that there is no more to be said.

Bartók's last four-movement composition was the Sonata for Solo Violin which he wrote for Yehudi Menuhin. Completed in March 1944, it is in many respects the best of all the American works. The toughness and intensity of the music recall the finest pieces of the 1920s, and the four movements do add up to a sonata rather than a dance suite, so there is no exact, neo-classical parallel with Bach. True, the first movement is marked 'Tempo di ciaccona', but this refers more to the character of the first theme than to the structure of the whole, a sonata form in which the second subject, centred on E flat after the G of the first, is much more lyrical in character. Development deals only with the first theme, and after a recapitulation which itself involves further development, the relatively restrained coda changes the tonal emphasis from G minor to G major.

Bartók's skill at fugal writing can often be observed, but the second movement of this sonata is the only example of a complete fugue in the late works, apart from the first movement of the Music for Strings, Percussion and Celesta. A four-voice fugue for a violin naturally requires the greatest skill if the result is not to seem severely strained or even ugly. Bartók's fugue is a severe affair, with a terse, aggressive subject and the use of many contrapuntal and violinistic devices, as when a statement of the subject (bowed) is combined with its own inversion (plucked), but it is written from a profound understanding of the potentialities of the instrument. It is demanding, for both player and listener, but never ungrateful or unrewarding.

After such concentration a degree of relaxation is essential, and the third movement, a slow 'Melodia' is expansively lyrical without ever losing itself in sentimentality, even in its more florid later stages. The *Presto* finale is a rondo with two episodes, in which G is re-established as tonal centre after the C of the fugue and the B flat of the Melodia: no axis structure here.

All Bartók's concertos (excepting the first for violin of 1907–8) are in three movements; so, from the later period, are the Sonata for Two Pianos and Percussion (1937), which the composer also transcribed as

47

a concerto for two pianos and orchestra, and two slighter pieces, *Contrasts* for violin, clarinet and piano (1938) and the *Divertimento* for string orchestra (1939).

The whole of Bartók's final period – a period in which the tonic triad, not just the tonic note, is restored to a degree of prominence – is framed by the Second and Third Piano Concertos (1931 and 1945 respectively), for the Viola Concerto was left in too incomplete a state to qualify as true Bartók. The two piano concertos present two distinct types of form, both of great importance for Bartók. The first type, found in the Second Concerto, relates to arch form, with sharing of material and character (though not, in this case, form) between the outer movements. The second type, that of the Third Concerto, is more traditional, lacking symmetrical parallels and involving outer movements quite distinct in character, the finale lightening rather than reflecting the mood of the first movement. For purposes of analytical comparison, it is worth concentrating on what are probably the two finest representatives of these structural types from the late period, the Sonata for Two Pianos and Percussion and the Second Violin Concerto (1938). The fundamentally asymmetrical form of the Sonata is compensated for by a more obvious exploitation of internal pitch symmetry involving the tritone (note, for example, the progression of the slow introduction from F sharp to C and the replacement of F sharp by G in the third bar of the main *Allegro*). There is in any case an obvious difference of character between the works, since one would hardly expect the same kind of emphasis on lyrical melody in a work for two pianos and percussion: here there is a more epic tone, at least in the first movement, with much contrapuntal interplay to set off the massive harmonic climaxes, yielding to an expansive *bonhomie* in the finale which can at times seem too self-consciously jolly. Much of the material of the sonata reflects the limitations of percussion instruments in its concentration on simple reiterated motives, but there are more haunting moments: for instance, the second subject of the first movement (bars 84ff.), and the central episode of the second movement in which the two pianos generate a dramatic dialogue of riveting tension.

The sonata is not the most spontaneous of Bartók's works, and the exactness with which the first movement conforms to 'Golden Section' proportions might have something to do with that; the Second Violin Concerto is, however, that rare phenomenon, a modern masterpiece wholly characteristic of its creator which uses traditional textures and structures in a fresh and valid way. The danger with symmetrical interrelationships is always that they may produce mechanically predictable results: here, however, the finale, for all its clear derivation of theme and form from the first movement, has that extra degree of informality which is precisely right for the work.

The concerto's character is immediately established by the way in which the lyric first subject, triadically introduced, though its progressions soon cease to be conventionally diatonic, moves into more energetic transitional material. This might sound perilously close to the reverse of what an effective sonata-form movement should propose, but it works superbly well, since Bartók's melodic ideas have exactly the right air of controlled freedom to warrant the more business-like passage work of the transitions. 'Formality' is well integrated into this first movement by such effects as the inversion of the first theme in the development (bar 194) and of the transitional material in the recapitulation, the 'twelve-note' second subject (stated over a pedal) and the hints of axis relationships (the development begins on F major triads). But it is precisely the capacity of aristocratic poise and peasant vigour not merely to co-exist but to interact which makes this movement such a fine one.

'Aristocratic poise' may likewise describe the theme of the central movement's set of variations, centred on G with prominent C sharps. Violinistic conventions (e.g. the double stopping at bars 43ff.) are functionally integrated as in few other modern concertos, and the variety of mood achieved against the background of the charmingly contemplative theme makes one regret that Bartók did not write more sets of variations.

The finale, its sonata structure and material paralleling those of the first movement at every point, is itself a large-scale variation, much faster than the original and in triple time. No work of Bartók's better demonstrates the satisfaction which can accrue from such a tonally-centred, thematically unified technique, in which evolution and repetition are held in such delicately purposeful balance. The concerto is just as 'progressive' a work as one from which thematic unity is completely absent, even though it may rely more on conventional details of figuration and form than the Third or Sixth Quartets.

The high level of achievement in three such different works as the Third and Sixth String Quartets and the Second Violin Concerto shows the remarkable range of which Bartók was capable. Yet these works have a still wider significance. Of all twentieth-century composers who have accepted and preserved the fundamental principle of tonality, Bartók was perhaps the most successful at justifying that preservation through his parallel adaptation of traditional formal elements: yet he never wrote a mature work called 'symphony'.

Chapter 3

Igor Stravinsky

'In borrowing a form already established and consecrated, the creative artist is not in the least restricting the manifestations of his personality. On the contrary, it is more detached, and stands out better, when it moves within the limits of a convention.'[1]

In 1918, Igor Stravinsky (1882–1971) was cut off from his native Russia by war and revolution: it was an appropriate moment for new stylistic explorations. *Les Noces* (completed in short score in April 1917), employs a language which, in its concentration and vigour, is already remote from the expansive, romantic exoticism of Stravinsky's earliest compositions, but the work retains strong links with the thematic characteristics of *Le Sacre du Printemps*. It is these links which *Pulcinella*, begun in 1919, most conspicuously severs. The new ballet was 'my discovery of the past, the epiphany through which the whole of my later work became possible. It was a backward look of course – the first of many love affairs in that direction – but it was a look in the mirror too'.[2] *Les Noces* was the high point of Stravinsky's creative response to Russian rituals: *Pulcinella* was Stravinsky's first essay in a new style, commonly called neo-classical.

The reliance in *Pulcinella* on pre-existent material – principally attributed to Pergolesi – is of a relatively extreme kind, with some movements being closer to arrangements than parodies or recompositions. It is far from being utterly un-Russian: 'the D minor tenor aria . . . is a Russian dance, and the horn counter-melody at no. 65 is far closer to Tchaikovsky than to Pergolesi';[3] what is involved is not a complete break with an exhausted early idiom, but a radical reorientation, not merely with regard to that idiom, but in relation to the entire history of music.

Other elements were involved in that reorientation. Stravinsky was later to state that 'the musicians of my generation and I myself owe the most to Debussy',[4] and apart from the specific debt of *Pulcinella* to the *commedia dell 'arte* elements of Debussy's late sonatas, all the works of the succeeding period up to the early 1950s demonstrate a commitment to a concept of tonality which, in its avoidance of the kind of 'rules' – the generally accepted hierarchic principles – of preceding generations, owes much to Debussy. As Chapters 1 and 2 have shown, there may well be a significant tension between the traditional background and modern foreground in such a style, and this tension is likely to involve rhythm as well as harmony, with regular accentuation and harmonic functionality alike displaced. The most memorable moments in Stravinsky's neo-classical music nevertheless often occur when triads fulfil a final, cadential function, and there is still a sense of discord resolving on to concord, or of a distinction between chromatic and diatonic entities. This is the practical application of that concept of 'polarity' which Stravinsky described in his lectures, *The Poetics of Music*,[5] as 'poles of attraction' which 'are no longer within the closed system which was the diatonic system' and which can be brought together 'without being compelled to conform to the exigencies of tonality'. Of its nature, however, such a view relates significantly to the 'closed system' of tonality: its entire justification is the way it modifies rather than rejects traditional precepts. And nowhere is Stravinsky's modification of those precepts more striking than in what has been shown (by Pieter van den Toorn in particular: see Bibliography) to be a consistent use of the 'octatonic' scale (alternate half/whole or whole/half steps) as a substitute for the major or minor scales. This makes possible a much richer range of modal harmonic relationships (as with Messiaen's octatonic Mode II: see p.217).

Stravinsky's friend Pierre Suvchinsky, acting as devil's advocate, has argued that Stravinsky's 'descent' after *Les Noces* proved his failure to understand the general ideas of his time, and that his failure to follow up the 'wild music' of his early years was due to the malign influence of the writer Arthur Lourié, who was responsible for ensuring that 'the savage of genius, the man who was all "creative instinct" and "natural talent", came to be thought of as a mere arbiter of taste, pontificating about the glories of Gounod'.[6] If Stravinsky ever suffers a severe decline in esteem, it may well be this kind of argument which gains support. It will be the object of the ensuing discussion of the music to suggest why such a view is unjustified. As late as 1960, however, Robert Craft quotes Stravinsky himself as commenting: 'Let's say that I was a kind of bird, and that the eighteenth century was a kind of bird's nest in which I felt cozy laying my eggs.'[7] He proved that, even if the new classicism demanded the absence of 'savagery', it could still serve the demands of a wide range of expression, from the frothiest wit (the Octet) to a stark tragedy *(Oedipus Rex)*, which would surely have satisfied even Debussy in its utterly anti-Wagnerian atmosphere. In truth, Stravinsky seems to have been much less ambivalent in his loathing of Wagner than Debussy was: apart from the famous account in the autobiography of his visit to Bayreuth, and the strictures in the lectures about music which is 'more improvised than constructed' and 'the perpetual becoming of a music that never had any reason for starting, any more than it has any reason for ending', the knife could still flash in 1963 when, after a performance of *Don Carlos*, he claimed Verdi, not Wagner, as 'the true progressive'.[8] Such are the prejudices of creative necessity, and they show that Stravinsky's music was always based on a deep response to a past which was a lively storehouse, full of stimulating images and ideas which he could make his own or use to give his own their fullest expression. So no single label will do for Stravinsky, and least of all one which implies that his music lacks 'expression' or romantic feeling. Stravinsky was not ultimately an 'intellectual', and he himself claimed, again in *The Poetics*, that music is betrayed by being turned into 'an object of philosophical speculation': discussion of his style is therefore most useful when it deals with matters of function and relationship.

Stravinsky's use of traditional titles– Sonata, Concerto, Symphony – is not evidence of any naive desire to produce carbon copies of classical structural models, but demonstrates his belief in the extent to which such models could be reshaped without losing their essential identities. The resulting tension between old and new can also be found in the individual harmonic units which range, as previously noted, from simple triads to complex and, in themselves, atonal aggregates. To study the relationship between borrowed stylistic elements and Stravinskian transformations is a fascinating but difficult process, and the difficulty lies in description and definition.

Pulcinella has already been described as an extreme example, in its use of relatively untransformed material. Certainly the Larghetto and Gavotte are examples of movements which, from the purely harmonic viewpoint, are virtually arrangements. Stravinsky-isms appear more in matters of spacing and instrumentation. Given the simple nature of the borrowed material, moreover, it is not surprising to find that harmonic modifications principally take the form of introducing a freer use of diatonic dissonance, rather than 'chromaticizing' simple diatonic elements. The Coda is a good example. Here the key of C major is implied both by the short tag which provides the main thematic element and by the C major triads which are the strongest harmonic features of the first seven bars. The other chords in those bars show a thickening-out of the harmonies (unacceptable in the eighteenth century) implied by the top and bottom parts. We could still provide conventional labels for them, but the speed at which they move ensures that they are heard as relatively discordant subordinates to the tonic chord, into which they all resolve. To this extent, we can still sense progression, and this sense is equally strong in the final bars of the work, where 'perfect' cadences articulate the flourishes on the triad of C major. As long as the bass continues to move clearly from dominant to tonic, we can experience the cadential effect, even if the 'dominant' chord is not a simple triad but an eleventh with the third omitted. We can relate what Stravinsky actually writes to a functional cadential progression, and hear one against the background of, or as a replacement for, the other (Ex. 15).

Ex. 15

A major problem with Stravinsky, as with other modern composers who retain links with the processes of the tonal past, is the extent to which we can define the 'actual' in terms of the 'model', and the only adequate answer lies in the individual ear, the individual sensibility. Analysis may show on paper that this progression is traditionally functional while that one is merely an assertion, but with Stravinsky of all composers, context is everything. He had rejected traditionally functional harmony, but in doing so he enhanced the distinction between tension and resolution which those functions articulated.

The most notable characteristic of the short Symphonies of Wind Instruments (1920) is its avoidance of pure triads, even in cadential contexts. At once, the tension-relaxation element becomes less rigidly defined, and chords, which in a particular rhythmic context may seem more discordant, can lose such connotations under different conditions.

The final section of the work (Fig. 65 onwards) can be regarded as an expansion from one basic progression, and again the term progression is appropriate in spite of the absence of pure triads, for some of those elements, which in a C major perfect cadence need resolution, do resolve. One B rises to C, though another remains stationary. The lower D and A flat resolve by step, the upper D does not. The F falls a step to E. Such a progression can be expressed even more simply as two ninth chords, one minor and one major, but it is a crucial aspect of Stravinsky's reappraisal of individual chords that the traditionally fixed root-third-fifth-seventh hierarchy is broken down.

The final section, summarized in Ex: 16, is in two parts. The first is dominated by its initial chord and reflects its internal tension, the clash between A flat and G which prevents the G major triad at the top of the chord from functioning diatonically. So this first section, for all its repetitiveness, has no clear tonal direction, and we experience less a process of tension and relaxation than a state of suspense. There is still a thematic process: the music is not static, but it does not yet contain the means to resolve its own tension. The crucial stage in this process occurs between Figures 70 and 71. Here, for the first time, the initial chord resolves outwards on to another chord with strong C major qualities and when that chord in turn is abandoned the A flat has shifted to the upper area of the harmony and can be resolved on to a G.

The second part of the section begins with a chord, the upper segment of which is identical with that of the initial chord of the first section, but the lower segment is more euphonious, and the whole is diatonic to C major. All that remains is to show that even this chord is inconclusive – too tense – and to resolve it on to a harmony which combines triads of G major and C major (and therefore includes E minor). For the third time the bass moves down from D to C, and this time the ambiguous A-B flat clash is avoided: a resolution indeed (Ex. 16).

The Symphonies of Wind Instruments is a 'radical' work both in its freely coherent form and in the absence of any traditionally triadic harmonic progressions. Similarly, while it ends in C (or on C), it is

certainly not in the sense that the Symphony in C (1940) employs that key. There is perhaps a greater sense of resolution in the Symphonies of Wind Instruments than there is of clarification, yet its concentrated intensity indicates why a pure triadic end could not have been employed. Such endings often work best when the mood is exuberant and witty: cf. the end of the Octet (1923) or of the Piano Concerto (1924); at times the intention seems almost ironically naive, as in the bald E major harmony (no fifth) at the end of the Piano Sonata (1924). The most epic, heroic work of this period, *Oedipus Rex* (1927), ends with dissolving stresses on pitches which are associated with traditionally close relatives yet are not stated with such explicit cadential finality. The ballet *Apollo* (1928) accepts the perfect fifth above the bass in the final stages, but a degree of harmonic ambiguity is ensured by the use of sharpened fourth and naturalled seventh.

The Symphony of Psalms (1930) has a systematically progressive scheme of basic tonal and harmonic relationships.[9] Since the first movement begins with an E minor triad and ends with a G major triad, this establishes not merely a precedent for structural motion between tonal areas a minor third apart, but also for defining those areas principally in terms of triads – root, third and fifth. What makes the rest of the work particularly satisfying is that while the structural motion is continued – the E flat of the second movement, the C of the third – neither is finally expressed in simple triadic form. The second movement adds supertonic and submediant notes to the major triad, while the finale subtracts the dominant, leaving only the tonic and mediant, the tonic doubled several times over.

Such nice distinctions may seem too nice, and therefore unnecessary. A tonic can still be felt as a tonic, whether we have a single note emphasized or a chordal 'aggregate' of six or seven. Yet it is precisely in his exploitation of the relationships within a tonic chord – and of the listener's responses and expectations in respect of those relationships – that Stravinsky shows such unsurpassed imagination. The hostility of Schoenberg and others to such neo-classicism seems likely to have contained a strong element of unwillingness to recognize the exciting vitality which Stravinsky could display in spite of his 'failure' to follow the 'inevitable' move into totally chromatic serialism.

Just as Stravinsky's tonal harmony is flexible enough to include traditional chord progressions as well as his own personal inventions, so too it is possible to find 'modulation' as well as 'juxtaposition' of different keys or tonal areas. The issue of tonal relationships cannot be considered independently of form, however, and so it is best approached in respect of two very different types of work, represented here by the opera-oratorio *Oedipus Rex* and the Symphony in C.

It might seem heavy-handedly unfunny, in view of its subject matter, to begin a discussion of *Oedipus Rex* with the remark that it is about the discovery of relationships: but in purely musical terms this is apt. Most commentators have sought parallels between the events of the plot and the sequence of tonal centres, Eric Walter White describing the work as 'an inspired example of the use of mode and key to achieve psychological insight in musical terms'.[10] Certainly, whether or not the sequence of centres which the work presents was contrived as a precompositional scheme, or whether each new centre was chosen simply as the most appropriate at any given point, the final result is a musical organism with specific and definable properties.

The whole work begins on B flat (minor key in tendency) and ends on G (also minor key in tendency): so there is an overall progression between relatives a minor third apart. This progression also functions as the basis for the first of the two acts, though here the final G is major mode and asserted triadically with added notes in a context stressing its closeness to C. Of the other principal tonal centres in Act I, C and E flat stand out, both with major key associations. The only unrelated note to be stressed with any persistence is B. We may therefore summarize the situation in Act I as involving specially strong associations between two pairs of keys each a minor third apart: G and B flat, C and E flat. If B were to be present on equal terms, its associate would be D, the dominant of G.

In the early stages of Act II, D appears as a centre for the first time, approached initially from G but associated (more 'orthodoxly' in the context of the work) with both its upper and lower minor thirds, F and B. The two pairs of relationships from Act I continue to receive prominence, but at the climax of the drama – Oedipus's moment of truth, when he realizes that he has murdered his father and married his mother – the F/D pair are stressed until, with the appearance of

F *sharps*, the other association, that between D and B, is logically suggested (Ex. 17).

Ex. 17

The final stages of the work give G the supremacy (with some use of its lower minor third, E), and C and E flat appear as subsidiaries. B flat does not reappear in its own right, having been as it were cancelled out by the implied Bs already mentioned.

Like any interpretation of facts, this summary is clearly a 'slanted' one. It does not account for every possibility in the harmonic organization of *Oedipus Rex*, but it does isolate what I believe to be a factor of special importance: Stravinsky's exploitation of the dominant note.

If G minor is the main key of the work, then D, its dominant, has an important role. Indeed, Wilfrid Mellers chose to regard the key of D major as central, saying that the opera is dominated by the search for it, and defining it as 'the key of the inner light'.[11] To accept this view we must also accept that the music to which Oedipus sings the words 'Lux facta est' is in D major (Ex.17). The *chord* of D major has appeared earlier in the work, as has the key of D minor, yet this, it is urged, is the only time that the *key* of D major appears. The obvious counter-argument is to claim that the music is not in D at all, but in B minor. By this time mediators will be suggesting that it could be either, depending on how one hears it, and that, surely, ambiguity is of the essence here. A particular situation has arisen in which the composer is seeking an idea of clarificatory simplicity: all is light – but all will become dark. So he uses his most expressive device: the major third without fifth (or root?). In doing so, he highlights a situation in which the strongest tension is between major and minor thirds (one way in which *Oedipus Rex* is a precursor of the Symphony of Psalms is now clear). But that is only the beginning: other tensions exist, between triadic harmonies and non-triadic harmonies; between asserted key-associations and traditional modulatory means of moving from one to another. Stravinsky relies very much on our expectation that the 'dominant' will confirm the 'tonic': by contrast, the minor or major third is ambiguous: it tends to suggest, not affirm. Hence the way in which D as a centre is held in reserve, while G is established rather by way of B flat and C. And the moment of ultimate truth, when the 'inner light' receives outward expression, sees the clarity of the 'true' dominant being clouded by the stark reality of its minor third associate. The positive serenity of the end of the Symphony of Psalms can be interpreted as C major confirming the original dominant G, even though the dominant note itself is absent from the final chord. The tragedy of Oedipus, by contrast, ends with the complete collapse of 'dominant' certainties. The minor third *ostinato* summarizes the main structural feature of the work, and the entire final passage (Fig. 201ff.) contains only one D natural. This is still 'tonal' music. But in its bleak austerity it seems the only possible outcome of a drama in which the technical processes have paralleled the events of the plot with perfect precision. The strongest association after that of the minor third is the perfect fourth – the C and G of the central chorus. Here the music seems on the verge of the expansion that would focus on tonic and dominant as mutually dependent entities. Psychologically, their failure to articulate this function is profoundly right: it gives *Oedipus Rex*, not a negative excellence, but a coherence deriving from a positive integration of subject and style which is disturbing and intensely dramatic.

Oedipus Rex was composed against the structural and stylistic background of the 'number opera' from Handel to Verdi, and tradition had established no set of absolute precedents for the handling of tonal relationships within the form, nor whether there should in fact be any overall scheme, relating to one principal key, or not. With the Symphony in C, however, the precedents were more precise, and the tensions between foreground and background are altogether more absorbing. In *Oedipus*, for all its separate 'numbers' – arias, ensembles, choruses –, Stravinsky was involved with what was in dramatic terms virtually a new form. The Symphony in C is the closest he ever came to the most common structural scheme of a classical symphony, and the work is one of his most impressive assertions of the artistic need for order: not all-pervading symmetry, but coherent process, in which the mutual interdependence of tonality, harmony and theme is fully and imaginatively worked out. People sometimes express surprise that this often genial and refined symphony could have been written in what Stravinsky himself described as 'the most tragic year of my life' – it was the year in which his first wife died. Yet that is precisely the time when a work like *Oedipus Rex* could not have been written, for without detachment Stravinsky's classic objectivity would surely have crumbled into formlessness. The Symphony in C is an affirmation, though it ends with unassertive restraint. It is not so much the work of a composer triumphing over tragedy as it is of one whose art transforms rather than imitates life.

The title provokes two questions: 'symphony in what sense?' and 'in C in what sense?' As to the first, there are four separate movements – the outer ones thematically related – which preserve much of the essential nature of traditional symphonic structure. The parallels between it and any symphony by Haydn, Beethoven or Tchaikovsky (Stravinsky admits having had symphonies by those composers to hand) are naturally not exact, but the differences are meaningful to no small degree precisely because they are deviations from something approximating to a norm. Critics of the work will point to what they define as its 'static' or 'balletic' character, so any defender of its symphonism must demonstrate the presence of dynamic processes, and those processes are often most apparent in the motivation for structural 'deviations' from a generally accepted symphonic norm, which modify the concept but do not contradict it.

As for the second question – 'in C in what sense?' – the same kind of answer might suffice: not a classically functioning C major, but an unmistakable emphasis on a tonal and harmonic area associated with C as tonic. Here, too, there are 'deviations', however: and just as Stravinsky will reshape sonata form, so he will modify the relationships within the traditional C major scale to produce elements which are then consistently employed. Not surprisingly, these elements involve the establishment of ambiguities: what is involved, as Peter Evans observes, is the 'simultaneous acknowledgement and denial of classical precedent'.[12]

In *Oedipus Rex*, the whole issue of the relationship between a tonic and its mediant, subdominant and dominant, is fundamental with regard both to chords and key areas. The Symphony in C, too, is concerned with this matter, as the opening illustrates (Ex. 18).

Ex. 18

The main motive of the movement is stated at once, but with greatest emphasis given to its first note, B. In a work which began with clear C major harmonies, its true function as leading note would probably be perceived at once. Here the context is ambiguous. With the rapid movement away from C to G in bar 2, and the presence of F sharp in the harmony of bar 4, the B might rather be the mediant of G – or the dominant of E minor. And what Stravinsky is doing, as the whole of the first movement illustrates, is regarding chords of C major, G major and E minor as possessing particularly strong resemblances, especially C major and E minor, with their common pitches, E and G. The presentation of the first theme of the sonata exposition (Fig. 5ff.) shows what is in essence another version of the situation at 'Lux facta est' in *Oedipus*. There we had a major third which could either be one triad without a root or another without a fifth. Here we have an accompani-

mental minor third, and although the melodic line supplies the missing
root, suggesting first-inversion harmony, the essential quality of the
passage lies in the absence of the root from the bass, and therefore of a
full triad (it is hard to feel, here, that the Bs in the oboe are completing
E minor triads).

This is tonal music in which the tonic note is subordinate: and its
authority is not so obvious as to render its presence unnecessary. The
entire harmonic character of Stravinsky's style rests on this ambiguous
treatment of single notes, the real presence of which is vital if a tonal
scheme is to achieve adequate solidity and coherence. The issue has
become, yet again, one of thirds. In the first movement we have an
exposition which ends in E, and a development which ends in E flat (in
neither case is the dominant note excluded). And a root-position
C major triad is only firmly established in the coda (Figs. 71 and 72),
before the final chords of the movement resolve on to a combination of
E minor and C major – with E in the bass! (Ex. 19).

Ex. 19

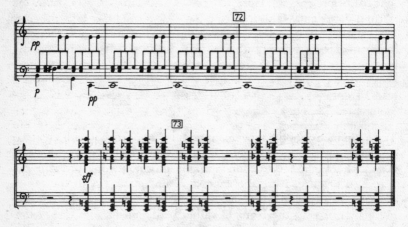

The use of sonata form in this movement is such as to give maximum
dramatic focus to the tonal harmonic issues involved. The first subject
tends to move 'flatwards' from C to D minor and F, raising the question
whether the second subject will be in the (orthodox) dominant. The
balance between diatonic and, however briefly, 'atonal' passages (e.g.
the first subject restatement and the short transition, pp. 6–8) serves to
keep the whole issue of the relationship between tonal clarity and

structural process alive, and in the second part of the transition passage the harmony clears and settles on to a long dominant preparation, using the dominant seventh of G major.[13] At its climax this provokes contradiction, and the second subject section, which begins at Fig. 19, is in a mainly diatonic F major. (This means that the characteristic minor third oscillation in the bass is between A and C.) The section ends with more tonal and thematic drama; a darkening into B flat minor provokes a move into the true dominant which is impermanent from the start, so that the exposition can only reach a point of adequate finality by moving up to E major.

As Cone has emphasized, the recapitulation is notable for the way in which the main second subject restatement (now 'on' C) is moved between the two parts of the transition passage: this means that the long dominant preparation (now on G) comes at a later, more dramatic point, for its function is no longer to prepare a surprise deviation of tonal area late in the movement, but to balance a coda which gives new developmental emphasis to the movement's main motive (see horns, one bar before Fig. 62). Here, as dramatic tension increases, comes the second dominant build-up of the movement, and this time the final clarification can take place, even to the extent of allowing C major its moment of root-position stability. The reshaping of the recapitulation, and the 'redundant development' or first part of the coda, have perfectly fitted the need to dramatize the problems of a tonal centre which cannot, literally, root itself until all the tensions of a chromatically-dominated harmonic language have been – if not resolved – then adequately rehearsed. The movement is in modified sonata form, but the modification is organic, not arbitrary: it arises from the nature of the material, not from theories about how sonata form may best be revised for modern purposes. It is not intended to survive this one movement, but here, and possibly only here, it is perfect.

A similar sensitivity informs the three remaining movements. The slow movement adopts the subdominant F as principal tonal centre, the Scherzo the dominant G. Not unexpectedly, the finale returns to C, yet it is not a C purified of the ambiguities so vital to the first movement, and by no means absent in slow movement and Scherzo. The actual presence of first-movement material ensures that the same issues are reviewed, and the calm processional ending, as different in character as possible from the terse cadences which concluded the *Moderato alla breve*, achieves the uneasy finality of a portmanteau C major/E minor/G major chord rooted on E (Ex. 20). At this late stage, the tonality as such cannot be questioned, yet the essential ambiguities cannot be wholly eradicated, and the ending is the more satisfying for their presence.

Ex. 20

The two major works of Stravinsky's last decade as a tonal composer are the Symphony in Three Movements (1945) and the opera, *The Rake's Progress* (1948–51), which are respectively his most ambitious 'abstract' and theatrical projects. Discussion of the symphony must begin with the nature of its symphonism, which is structurally less clear-cut than in the Symphony in C. Even if we regard 'Three Symphonic Movements' or 'Concerto for Orchestra (with concertante piano and harp)' as more appropriate titles, and give due emphasis to the composer's own remarks about the specific stimuli which the work reflects – 'a documentary film of scorched earth tactics in China' for the first movement; a scene called 'Apparition of the Virgin' intended for the film *Song of Bernadette* for the second; and 'reaction to the newsreels and documentaries . . . of goose-stepping soldiers' and other wartime connotations for the third[14] – the work must stand or fall on the effectiveness of its overall design. In sonata-form terms, the opening fast movement is finely organized to ensure that considerable internal contrasts do not result in any loss of the tremendous momentum generated by the opening paragraph, with its extreme tension between simple motivic shapes and the chromatic clashes of the harmony. The considerable extent of the central development (Figs 34–88) prepares a compressed and reshaped recapitulation, whose main function is not simply to re-establish the inexorable dynamic temper of the exposition, but to resolve this out into the uneasy stability of the final bars, where the war between A flat and G is temporarily settled in favour of the latter as the fifth of a seventh chord on C. That this is not another Symphony in C will only be decided in the finale, where the initial clash between G and A flat grows into an overall tonal clash between C and D flat, the latter ultimately triumphing.

The languid *Andante* (centred on D) does not contribute directly to this titanic conflict, though it serves to keep the clash of semitones in focus, and in its own recapitulation (linked by an Interlude to the finale) the dramatic return of C as a tonal centre is effectively foreshadowed (from one bar before Fig. 138 onwards).

The March-Finale has such an irresistible forward thrust that it can afford to be fairly loosely organized around recurrences of the main material and the first movement's 'motto'. The underlying agent of propulsion is the 'war' between C and D flat (with its dominant, A flat), but this is less immediately perceptible than the array of orchestral effects, ranging from dazzling tuttis to eccentric moments of chamber music, like the 'fugal' duet for trombone and piano at Figs 170-2.

Other less ambitious instrumental works of the 1940s – the Sonata for Two Pianos (1943-4), the Ebony Concerto (1945) and the Concerto for Strings (1946) – display Stravinsky's continuing willingness to adapt the traditional tonal forms: a willingness which persists into the 'transitional' Septet (1952-3) with its ternary first movement: exposition-fugue-recapitulation. This period is nevertheless dominated by a group of stage works, with the relatively lightweight *Danses Concertantes* (1941-2) and *Scènes de Ballet* (1944) preceding the much more substantial ballet *Orpheus* (1947), after the completion of which only the strikingly austere Mass (1948) precedes *The Rake's Progress* itself.

The climax of *Orpheus* (two bars before Fig. 137) shows a clear link with the Symphony in Three Movements. Yet the ballet as a whole is dominated not by such energetic outbursts as by the elegiac restraint of the First and Third Scenes. The music for the Furies takes second place to that for Orpheus and Eurydice, and there are no simpler nor more memorable bars in Stravinsky's whole output than the F major *pas-de-deux*, which starts with such tenderness and breaks off near the end in anguish as 'Orpheus tears the bandage from his eyes. Eurydice falls dead.'

This humanizing eloquence is much less evident in the Mass, where personal religious feeling rarely breaks through the veil of liturgical objectivity. There is joy in the Sanctus, earnestness in the Credo, and a kind of self-denying abasement in the Agnus Dei. Stravinsky has surely succeeded here in his oft-quoted aim of writing 'very cold music'. Yet there is undoubted majesty in the very economy, and in the use of the ten wind instruments. The Mass is the most important anticipation of the mood of the later, serial 'Requiems' – and this in spite of its frequent reliance on harmonic rather than contrapuntal textures and the capacity of its tense progressions to resolve out *quasi* – tonally.

65

The juxtaposition of 'mass' and 'opera' inevitably evokes the names of Mozart and Verdi, and it is Mozart's influence which pervades the subject and style of *The Rake's Progress* more profoundly than any other. It might have been predicted that Stravinsky would remain as remote as ever from that musico-dramatic through-composition which he vilified so entertainingly in his various writings. It was less inevitable that the result should be no artificial parody of pre-Wagnerian operatic conventions but a work which is entertaining and moving in its own right, while the Auden-Kallman libretto has no recourse to social and psychological analysis of the kind so brilliantly exploited by many modern opera composers. The secret lies in the utter rightness of the subject; the 'fable' is a morality: the object is not to create sympathy for the destroyed protagonist but to learn from his destruction and avoid one's own: hence the overriding parallel with *Don Giovanni*. Unlike the typical modern operatic 'victim', Tom Rakewell deserves his fate: but his very weakness of character has given Stravinsky the chance to provide him with appealing and attractive music, direct yet idiosyncratic, and these qualities extend into the work as a whole.

Though his largest work, *The Rake's Progress* is not an encyclopedia of Stravinsky's neo-classicism. The more powerful expressive tensions of *Oedipus Rex*, the Symphony of Psalms, *Apollo* and *Orpheus* are missing; but within the narrower focus of comic conventions the opera does offer the most substantial display of Stravinsky's rhythmic resource and tonal-harmonic richness, showing, too, his superb skill as a writer of vocal lines in which 'old' conventions are given new expressive life. Ex. 21 is from Act One Scene Three.

The Rake's Progress was first performed in Venice on 11th September 1951, a few week's after the composer's sixty-ninth birthday, and less than two months after the death of Arnold Schoenberg. In spite of all that has been written about the opera itself, we have no real idea of how Stravinsky saw his own future at this time. Having composed his most ambitious neo-classical work, did he feel a need not merely for renewal but for change? Was he conscious that the death of Schoenberg gave serialism a 'historical' perspective which made adoption of it just another kind of neo-classicism? Whatever Stravinsky's thoughts may have been, his music shows that the testing and adaptation of serial processes was a gradual affair, beginning in 1951–2 with the composition of the Cantata on Old English Texts and ending on 21st March 1958 with the completion of *Threni*, his first completely twelve-note work: Stravinsky then remained committed to twelve-note techniques

Ex. 21

for the rest of his life. The works from the Cantata to the ballet *Agon* (1957; the immediate predecessor of *Threni*) are 'transitional', both in the sense that tonal and serial elements may be juxtaposed or combined in them, and in the sense that the serial elements are not necessarily twelve-note. Stravinsky's first twelve-note movement (and the order is not strict even then) is the tenor aria 'Surge, aquilo' from the Canticum Sacrum (1955). Ultimately, the significance of *Threni* is not just that it shows Stravinsky accepting the particular virtues of an all-inclusive twelve-note technique, but that such a technique has led to the loss of all *tonal* feeling. In *Threni* Stravinsky became not merely a twelve-note composer, but an atonal composer, and although the later twelve-note works may emphasize certain pitches from time to time, and attach structural significance to such emphasis, the possibility of tonally-centred serial music, which the transitional works contemplated, had clearly been rejected.

Chapter 4

Symphonic Music II

The first chapter on tonal symphonic music dealt principally with composers who, in respect of date of birth, were the seniors of Bartók and Stravinsky. This chapter gives its main emphasis to Hindemith, Prokofiev and Shostakovich, who were born between 1890 and 1910 and thus came to creative maturity after the principal issue of early twentieth-century music – to retain or abandon tonality – had already been raised.

There can be few composers whose first decade of mature creative work is as remarkable as that of Paul Hindemith (1895–1963). As early as the String Quartet in F minor, Op. 10 (1918), essentially traditional elements of form, tonality and texture are projected with a vigour and purposefulness going well beyond mere youthful exuberance and indicating a formidable combination of intellect and sensibility. This quartet was completed before Stravinsky's first neo-classical work, *Pulcinella*: there can be no question of any influence. Yet Hindemith's opening shows an equal facility for translating baroque gestures into modern terms (Ex. 22).

The harmonic sweep of the music is boldly shaped, with bitonal conflicts emerging clearly at a fairly early stage. The forceful energy could indicate a knowledge of Bartók, though it is probable that Hindemith only discovered both Bartók and Stravinsky after the end of the war. A particularly impressive feature of the first movement of this quartet is the presence of strongly contrasted lyric material. There is none of the aridity or monotony which was to afflict so many of Hindemith's later, more ambitious projects.

Hindemith was extremely fortunate in the short term, for the cultural atmosphere in postwar Germany strongly favoured brittle, sardonic, parodistic yet far from superficial creative work. A remarkably large proportion of the flood of compositions which he produced between 1918 and 1930 is of high quality, with abundant vitality, delicacy, wit and variety of expression. The Sonata for Cello and Piano Op. 11, No. 3 (1919) is one exception, for the neo-classic/post-romantic stylistic range seems less well motivated than in the First String Quartet, Ex. 22

weakened as it is by an over-extended structure (an ill omen). At the other extreme, all but one of the seven works called Kammermusik are unfailingly attractive and interesting, the occasional brashness tolerable simply because there is an unmistakable sense of fun in the treatment of baroque and classical devices: for example, the throwaway cadences which are particularly evident in Nos. 3 and 4. The Kammermusik No. 4, Op. 36 No. 3 (1925), for violin and chamber orchestra, is probably the best of the set: one only needs to compare it with the later, more orthodoxly planned Violin Concerto (1939) to sense the lowering of temperature and loss of vigour which had taken place in little more than a decade. The main fault to be found with individual movements of the Kammermusik set is the same as that of the 1919 Cello Sonata: unduly protracted formal schemes, where the material is simply not interesting or imaginative enough to warrant such thoroughgoing exposure of its properties. In particular, the slow movement of the Organ Concerto (Kammermusik No. 7, Op. 46 No. 2, of 1927) is as dull as anything from later decades.

Apart from the Kammermusik series, to which we might append the unambiguously neo-classical Concerto for Orchestra Op. 38 (1925), Hindemith wrote three more string quartets during the 1920s, of which No. 3, Op. 22 (1922) is the most highly regarded. It is a work which merits close study both for the way it shows the composer's confidence and flexibility in the treatment of traditional forms and tonal relationships, and also for its clear anticipations of weaknesses which were to increase in later years.

The Third String Quartet is in five movements and has a main tonal centre of F sharp, which is firmly established only in the finale. Clearly defined 'progressive' tonal schemes can work very well (Nielsen's Fifth Symphony was also completed in 1922) but Hindemith seems to be attempting an ambitious dual scheme here: first, a conflict between a gradual progression towards F sharp via both relatives and opposites (e.g. C sharp and C); and also a more general process of clarifying tonality out of atonality and bitonality. The work begins with a *fugato*

Ex. 23

which can, in retrospect, be seen to hint at F sharp at cadence points, but which, in its own terms (the terms imposed by the contradictory directions of the two phrases of the fugato theme itself), has no clear tonal centre at all (Ex. 23).

The second movement provides strong contrast in every respect, being fast, vigorous and firmly anchored on C sharp. Ironically, the weakest moment is the only contrapuntal passage, a *quasi-stretto* (from four bars before Letter M) which marks the transition at the end of the middle section of the ternary scheme. If this is a structural miscalculation, expanding what would be better compressed, the final C sharp major triad sounds an inconceivably tame outcome of the toughly discordant idiom which the movement employs for most of its length (hints of Bartókian influence, specifically the oscillating minor-third motive of the second movement of his String Quartet No. 2, are strong here).

It is, however, the central movement of the work which is the weakest, a leisurely, meandering and repetitive affair, which seems to be aiming at a kind of nonchalant serenity, but which alternates an oddly toothless bitonality – 'bite' being easy to achieve by combining clashing keys – with an equally uningratiating modality. The very restraint is evidence of Hindemith's over-confidence, the rhythmic monotony robbing the ultimate arrival on the bi-modally coloured F sharp triad of all conviction (Ex 24).

After this, the brief, improvisatory fourth movement comes as a relief, with its distinct suggestion of the Kammermusik style. Though centred firmly on C, the music creates a strong sense of progressive conflict which carries over into the blander rondo-finale with its much

Ex. 24

more explicitly neo-classical material. This is a well-balanced movement with ample internal contrasts, but the conclusion again seems
tame, perhaps because a full, pure (if *pizzicato*) F sharp major triad two
bars from the end actually precedes the final thematic statement (in
octaves).

As a whole this quartet displays a disturbing tendency to lose focus,
both in its diversity of thematic character (the lyric material so much
less convincing than the energetic, neo-classical shapes) and in its
range of harmonic language, with resolutions seeming forced and
unearned. With hindsight it is all too easy to diagnose the symptoms of
later disease: but even in the immediate context of the early 1920s this
quartet shows that Hindemith could not invariably sustain the ideal
balance between a desire to exploit traditional forms and the employment of a flexible tonal musical language involving a high degree of
chromaticism. The more serious the intention, the less successful the
result.

The best of all Hindemith's neo-classical works is probably the opera
Cardillac (1926). Though unambiguously a number opera, its forcefulness and vitality relate directly to the fact that the composer's 'last link
with Expressionism' can be found in it, a link which was removed in the
unfortunate revision which he undertook in 1952.[1] His second major
opera, *Mathis der Maler* (1934–5), while not totally dissimilar in subject
matter to *Cardillac*, is less obviously divided into separate numbers, and
gains, inevitably, in fluency and continuity. At a much later date,
Hindemith attempted another large-scale study of the relationship
between the artist and society in *Die Harmonie der Welt* (1956–7), in
which the principal character is the Renaissance philosopher Johann
Kepler. From the purely dramatic point of view the work is weighed

73

down by the absence of a conventionally unfolding plot, and while it is firmly structured musically as a gradual, systematic progress towards the ultimate E major, there is little of the compelling vitality of *Cardillac* or the unaffected expressiveness of *Mathis der Maler*. Hindemith's very different final opera, *The Long Christmas Dinner* (1960), based on the play by Thornton Wilder, has much more direct dramatic appeal.

It might seem naive to relate Hindemith's retreat from the vitality and abrasiveness of the early style to a response to the political disaster which afflicted Germany at the end of the 1920s. Yet there can be no doubting the affiliation between the social and political instability of the postwar, pre-Hitler period and the at times aggressive, at times morbidly languid music of Hindemith, Weill and others. Culture and society were very much of a piece in the Weimar Republic, and Hindemith's later music exhibits all the symptoms of an attempt to exalt Apollo and debase Dionysos: to provide, whether intentionally or not, a spiritual antidote to the poison of fascism. In these terms Hindemith's later music fails when it seems too negative: when it avoids issues, goes through the motions. It is certainly no mere matter of a 'retreat' into tonality and explicitly traditional forms, for other composers – Prokofiev, Shostakovich and Britten the most prominent – were able to find ample vitality and purpose in such elements long after the end of the Second World War, thereby demonstrating that tonality could survive the demise of neo-classicism itself. What is lacking in so many of Hindemith's later works is fundamental dramatic tension. In exile, after 1937, he aged too gracefully, the 'triumphs' too easily achieved, without anger, much less despair.

Naturally, with such a prolific composer, there are moments when so general a view fails to apply. Calm resignation is appropriate and deeply moving at the end of *Mathis der Maler* and, on a smaller scale, at the end of the Second Piano Sonata (1936). Geniality can also play a positive part, as in the finale of the Cello Concerto (1940) or the deservedly popular Symphonic Metamorphoses on themes of Carl Maria von Weber (1943). Even in works like the Violin Concerto (1939) and Clarinet Concerto (1947), where dull, leisurely, lyric flow is the predominant quality and one longs for a touch of the old eccentricity or vulgarity, the climaxes are powerful and cunningly placed. The Sonata for Cello and Piano (1948) has a first movement, marked Pastorale, in which a highly effective, if gentle, tension is generated by flexible harmonic direction and changes of accent and by a fugato texture which is, for once, more fanciful than ponderous. Even in as prosaic and soporific a work as the *Harmonie der Welt* symphony (1951), the music may suddenly, briefly, spring to life with a wierdly orchestrated episode (cf. the finale, bars 150–167), which recalls the old – young – Hindemith. Yet his last chamber work, the Octet (1958), is a sad ending to a career which had begun with the F minor Quartet. Here, there is ample geniality, and the occasional flicker of true creative imagination (the ghostly march ending the second movement, with its scurrying string figuration). Yet as the melody at Letter C of the third movement shows, a composer stands or falls by the appropriateness of his material, and the pedestrian protraction of this unimaginative idea is ultimately what counters the effectiveness of other parts of the work.

A simple way of summarizing Hindemith's career is to say that he progressed from Kokoschka to Kepler. It is a far cry from the modish, garish expressionism of Kokoschka's *Mörder, Hoffnung der Frauen*, which Hindemith set as a one-act opera in 1919, to the grand philosophical issues of the much later dramatic work, *Die Harmonie der Welt* (completed 1957). Hindemith was nothing if not a practical musician, as his prowess as violist, teacher and conductor proved. But his delight in theoretical speculation, allied to a conviction that tonality was a universal, indestructible law of nature, never inspired a practical compositional breakthrough which would have excused all the theoretical inconsistencies and inaccuracies. So he remains the most striking example of a modern composer, whose early career was consonant with a particular atmosphere, the intensity of which was a measure of its impermanence. It is immeasurably sad that Hindemith's later music gives no more than an occasional flicker of a positive conservatism which could have balanced the youthful excesses of the 1920s: the cultural cure for political insanity proved to be sadly dull and colourless. But to someone so closely involved it may have seemed that caution was the only sanity.

Apart from Hindemith, the only other major composer born in the 1890s was the Russian Sergei Prokofiev (1891–1953). At first he seems a conveniently similar instance of a brilliant prodigy whose creative growth was redirected at midpoint by inescapable political and social factors. In Prokofiev's case, however, it is far less justifiable to praise his early, more radical works at the expense of his later, more conservative ones: the operas and symphonies which form the most important part of his output in the 1920s are all surpassed by those he wrote after his return to Soviet Russia in 1933 (he had left his native land in 1918 and lived mainly in Paris). Perhaps the only genre in which his earlier achievement is superior is the concerto – No. 3 for piano (1917–21) being commonly regarded as his best.

If Hindemith's problem was increasingly how to invent material suitable for the substantial instrumental forms he favoured, Prokofiev's was to assess the extent to which traditional forms were suited to the individual cast of his thematic thinking. The contrast between hectic drama and more restrained lyricism which he could encompass was very marked in the 1920s: the opera *The Fiery Angel* (1927) and the associated Symphony No. 3 (1928), together with the ballet *Le Pas d'Acier* (1927), represent the extreme limit of Prokofiev's aggressive anti-romanticism, reflecting similar preoccupations in Stravinsky, Bartók and Hindemith while never sounding like mere imitations. Yet the ballet *The Prodigal Son* (1929) and the related Fourth Symphony (1930) operate at a much cooler temperature. These works opened the way for a more positive blend of lyrical and dramatic qualities which Prokofiev was to explore in several of his finest compositions: the ballet *Romeo and Juliet* (1936), the Fifth and Sixth Symphonies (1944 and 1947) and the opera *War and Peace* (first version 1942). It was not until 1944, eleven years after his return to Russia and fourteen years after his last essay in the form, that Prokofiev returned to the symphony as such; but there is a remarkable sense of confidence in the fact that the Symphony No. 5 was composed in only one month. The principal virtue is precisely that which was lacking in Nos 2, 3 and 4: a disciplined control of tonal and thematic relationships which owes nothing to programmatic schemes. Yet the most impressive thing of all about the work is the extent to which its debt to the traditional four-movement plan serves to enhance the originality of the result. In many respects this is a truly 'classical' symphony, but there is no pastiche or parody of classical style. The music is wholly personal to Prokofiev in its characteristic moods of wistfulness and wit, and its certainty of purpose, however instinctive, gives it the stamp of genius.

The least 'classical' feature is that the first, sonata-form, movement is an Andante rather than an Allegro, and the only possible structural miscalculation lies in the use of a faster tempo for the second subject (*poco più mosso*, Fig. 6), which is difficult to gauge effectively in performance, and can undermine the inexorable growth of the movement rather than acting as a truly dynamic contrast. Since the first subject is basically lyrical, Prokofiev creates tension by harmonic means, with the simplest and most orthodox of background tonal relationships (the exposition ending in the dominant), coloured by chromaticisms which are always just prominent enough to disturb the main tonality without obscuring it unduly. The richness of the orchestration is a further factor making for purposeful monumentality, but the use of E naturals in the spare harmonic support for the opening B flat major melodic phrase is the clearest statement of intent: even if the traditional hierarchy of the cycle of fifths is preserved, the disruptive tritone has a part to play (Ex. 25).

Ex. 25

The first-subject paragraph unfolds organically, with varied statements of the main theme, and the second subject, itself far more chromatic *melodically* than the first, leads to the main climax of the exposition at Fig. 8, with the firm establishment of the dominant F in the bass for the first time. Only at the end of the exposition, in the codetta between Figs 9 and 10, is there a strong contrast of thematic character, an 'afterthought' which is to grow in significance as the work proceeds.

There is a fine development section in which increasing dramatic excitement is achieved by a thorough exploration of all the thematic ideas, and a widening of tonal perspective culminates in an emphasis on E major which is the most impressive fulfilment of tritonal opposition (five bars before Fig. 17). The tonic key of B flat remains the essential foundation throughout the recapitulation, but the more agitated mood, which the return of the codetta theme six bars after Fig. 22

revives, inspired one of Prokofiev's finest passages, the thirty-six-bar coda, in which the lyric-epic character of the main material is transfigured and reinforced with a powerful logic as the phrases climb up from their B flat pedal bass. The final cadence might seem slightly selfconscious in its avoidance of conventional plagal or perfect harmonies, but it concentrates chromatic tensions – with an E natural in a suitably prominent position – and diatonic resolution into the smallest possible space (Ex. 26).

Ex. 26

The scherzo (*Allegro marcato*), which comes second, provides the first truly fast music in the symphony. Yet the first two bars indicate that this is not going to be a wholly lighthearted affair. It is a *danse macabre*, whose obsessive ticking accompaniment achieves symphonic rather than balletic status by virtue of its flexible support for a cumulative construction with much variety of harmony and phrase-length. The 'trio' is more conventionally dance-like, and the bright-eyed innocence of its opening and closing statements (*Meno mosso*, Figs 36 and 47) makes the more heavily orchestrated return of the scherzo at Fig. 48 the more sinister. The diabolical intensification of this recapitulation never becomes over-elaborate, however, and the driving direction of the harmony issues ultimately in a discordant, chromatic but undoubtedly final cadence in D minor.

The *Adagio* in F major begins with what is surely Prokofiev's most hauntingly beautiful melody. The three-bar *ostinato* introduction proposes a strong tritonal element (F–B–C in the bass), which the melody itself incorporates along with other chromatic features. As the Adagio proceeds, however, it is clear that a more fundamental alternation between E major and F major is involved, which, in terms of the basic tonic of the whole work, is highly dramatic. The middle section of the movement has a rather formal rhetoric which does not attain to the same very high level as the outer parts, but the *ostinato*-dominated transition from its climax at Fig. 71 to the return of the main idea at Fig. 72 is powerful in its very simplicity. With the main theme there also returns the F/E alternation. The conflict is resolved in a closing paragraph of the greatest lyrical beauty, the most crucial harmonic moment being at Fig. 76, where the E as root of E major becomes the bass of a first-inversion C major triad. This effect shows that triadic harmony can still function with validity and originality when apparently 'non-functional' tonal relationships are involved.

The finale is marked *Allegro giocoso*, and begins with an introduction whose uncomplicated smile is barely clouded by quotation of the earnest first subject of the first movement (Fig. 79). Even when the main *Allegro* theme is launched, tritonal and other chromatic clashes at first impinge little on its diatonic good humour. The danger, then, is that the movement may seem to have too little to do with what has gone before, and that, in seeking to be naively life-enhancing in orthodox Soviet fashion, it may sever its connections with the truly symphonic essence of the work as a whole. Prokofiev avoids that pitfall triumphantly by allowing the material to generate its own inexorable momentum – a technique which is the most positive relic of his early manner and which has already worked well in the second movement. Simple exuberance becomes fierce energy, with any potential monotony resulting from motoric rhythmic assertions kept at bay by the tonal argument between diatonic and chromatic elements around the fundamental B flat. The ending is at once exhilarating and disturbing. Since this was a wartime symphony, associations between vigour and violence need not be suppressed, but the finale has no need of programmatic props to justify it: it succeeds because it concludes the whole work in an appropriate way, continuing its arguments and resolving its tensions.

Prokofiev's Sixth Symphony was first performed in Leningrad on 11th October 1947. Its main musical ideas were to some extent 'inspired by the war years,' but the titanic conflicts which are expressed so uncompromisingly may owe at least as much to an intention of Prokofiev's to dedicate the symphony – his Op. 111 – to the memory of Beethoven: although Prokofiev makes no attempt to match the Olympian serenity of the Arietta of Beethoven's Op. 111, the C minor Piano Sonata, the terse forcefulness of the sonata's opening *Allegro con brio ed appassionato* can be sensed behind the more expansive but no less tragic character of the symphony's *Allegro moderato*.

The achievement of the Sixth Symphony is the more remarkable in view of an approach to both structure and key relationships which is considerably more original than that of No. 5. It is in only three movements, with an apparently extreme contrast between the first and third dramatically undermined with the reappearance of the first movement's second subject near the end of the finale – a very different effect from the incidental reminiscence of the first movement's first theme in the introduction to the finale of the Fifth Symphony. On one level, the Sixth Symphony is more diffuse than the Fifth: contrasts within movements tend to be greater. Such is the composer's skill, however, that the result is never episodic, and the cumulative build-ups to perorations which avoid the conventional diatonic affirmations so beloved by Soviet 'aestheticians' are structured with a master hand.

The first movement (*Allegro moderato*) is a large-scale sonata design, in which the modifications are the result of perceptions about the character and potential of the artless yet eloquent main theme. On its first appearance it is framed by an introduction and a continuation both of which are more decisive in character: the 'questions' raised by the theme itself concern its tonality or modality (A flat? E flat? B flat?) and also its capacity, as a melodic rather than motivic entity, for symphonic development (Ex. 27).

Ex. 27

Prokofiev's answer is to develop the theme at once in an extended, tonally fluctuating context, which finally comes to rest on the region of B minor (the enharmonic submediant of E flat minor) for a second subject (*moderato*) of even more tragically lyrical cast than the first (Fig. 10). With only the briefest exceptions, this paragraph is in a pure Dorian mode on B, creating the atmosphere of a kind of epic pastoral. So the first really dramatic surprise – and the act which generates the central conflict of the movement – is that which ensues at Fig. 13. A further related idea, though more assertive, fails to launch the development, but prepares the return of the first theme, rooted on G sharp (Fig. 15). After a further statement on D sharp (i.e. the tonic) at Fig. 16, the exposition ends on to the original dominant: B flat.

The home key is regained, but with a new tempo (*Andante molto*) and a new theme (Fig. 17), more expansively lyrical than anything heard so far, for which the typically ticking accompaniment is a perfect background. With a shock of surprise, this is countered (Fig. 20) with an *Allegro* faster than the original, and the main theme centred on G. The 'true' development – some consider it a developmental recapitulation – is now under way, and there is no longer any question of the capacity of the main theme to bear developmental processes. In perspective, the delaying role of the Andante (could it not be the 'real' second subject?) is seen to be dramatically essential, the goad stirring the main material from reflection into action. At Fig. 29 a mighty dominant pedal is heard, and the most hectic assertions of main-theme motives surround it. This is the crux. The first subject has the capacity for development of the kind that reveals its latent intensity, but it cannot be transformed into a convincingly triumphant assertion. With superb control, as the dominant pedal persists and harmonic tension crystallizes around it, Prokofiev slows and quietens the music. What is prepared is the recapitulation of the 'second subject' in the tonic key (Fig. 33), which then links up at Fig. 36 with the *Andante molto* theme, whose greater chromatic density had earlier provoked the main development. For the second time, the first theme follows on from it, but now at the *original* tempo and, of course, in E flat minor (Fig. 37). The first bar is again 'developed' to achieve an overwhelming *harmonic* climax on the submediant major chord (C flat). A coda then ends the movement, with dark timbres undermining the otherwise positive presence of the major third in the final tonic chord.

The extent to which Prokofiev has risked incoherence in the interests of ambiguity in this movement may be apparent from the above analysis. It is far less 'safe' a structure than that of the first movement of the Fifth Symphony, but it succeeds because it shows that the *Andante molto* theme has a positive function of contrast, which in the recapitulation leads to its enclosure by the two main ideas of the exposition. Of course, in the most concentrated sonata-form movements such additional perspectives are not needed, but, given the lyric nature of Prokofiev's initial material, his skill in the creation of such a profoundly dramatic design cannot be overpraised.

Even more daring was his decision not to insert a lightweight Scherzo at this point, but to deepen the tragic atmosphere still further with a large-scale Largo. The taut chromaticism of the A flat-centred opening is as uncompromising harmonically as anything in Prokofiev's works of the 1920s, yet the singing theme for trumpet and violin (one bar after Fig. 1[42]) has a selfconfidence which anticipates an ultimately serene ending. It is therefore possible to feel that the violent eruption at the end of the first part of the movement is less organic and inevitable than the climax of the first movement; yet it still acts as an effective foil to the more relaxed central episode. This in turn is grafted on to a compressed recapitulation in which the main theme now precedes its original introduction. The music calms down, but the harmonic issue remains ambiguous until the last two bars restore the tonic chord of A flat major.

The opening theme of the finale (*Vivace*) seems much more straightforwardly playful than that in the Fifth Symphony, not least because of the virtually exclusive diatonic use of E flat major. After only ten bars, however, the insertion of a more earnest and aggressive dotted rhythm outlines a conflict which is to have extraordinary repercussions (Ex. 28).

At this early stage we might expect a simple battle between 'good' and 'evil', ending in the triumphant enthronement of the playful main theme, well equipped as it is with the potential for triadic fanfares. Most of the movement proceeds in a way which makes this probability a real one: nor would it be very difficult to compose an ending comparable to that of the Fifth Symphony, with a less bland but still essentially affirmative fantasia on the opening theme. It is only when the recapitulation is launched that it becomes clear that Prokofiev is composing a disintegration of the main theme rather than an apotheosis. Under the guise of development, the direction becomes hesitant and the main key is lost. All seems well again when the chief contrasting theme returns in the dominant key (at Fig. 34 [94]) but increasingly hectic development of the initiating motive of the first subject destroys that security, and what might once have been the clinching tonic-key return of the main theme has undeniably ominous overtones. When, at Fig. 49 [109], the accompanying rhythm for the contrasting theme comes round again, there is at first no theme at all, just the sustained clash of A natural against B flat. When thematic statement does return, it coincides with the gradual loss of rhythmic impetus, and a descent towards minor tonality. At Fig. 53 [113] the second subject of the first movement returns, marked *Andante tenero*, and it sounds almost consolatory in spite of its E flat minor modality. It

Ex. 28

yields to a harmonic outburst of unparalleled intensity but unclear direction, with thematic roots back in the main body of the finale. After a pause the menacing dotted rhythms return, merging not into 2/4 joviality but into remorseless 6/8 reiterations of harmonies which, in a final cadence, resolve on to a major triad as conclusive but as untriumphant as any major triad can be.

The Sixth Symphony was Prokofiev's last great orchestral work and it was a worthy climax to a career which, whatever it may have initially tried to reject, ultimately succeeded in confirming the continued relevance of the most fundamental traditional techniques. In 1918 Prokofiev referred to sonata form as 'the most flexible musical form,' and it was its adaptability which formed the basis for the triumph of the Sixth Symphony's first movement. Tonality, too, was a flexible resource which he came to use as skilfully as any other modern master. In affirming the roots of his language, and of his own profound romanticism, Prokofiev, at the cost of baffling his Soviet colleagues, transcended the limitations of his own earlier experiments and fulfilled himself through reinterpretation rather than rejection.

Dmitri Shostakovich (1906–75) came to creative maturity at precisely the time when tonal sonata form might justifiably have been felt to have no future save as a vehicle for affectionate or sardonic parodies like Prokofiev's Classical Symphony (1916–17). Yet he first achieved fame with a four-movement symphony (No. 1 Op. 10), written in 1926 when he was still a student, and when he died his huge list of works was dominated by fifteen symphonies and fifteen string quartets, with several concertos and substantial chamber works (notably a piano quintet and two piano trios). Coupled with the pressures of his situation as a Soviet composer, this contribution can easily be interpreted as evidence of arch-conservatism, suggesting that, even within his own stylistic terms of reference, Shostakovich failed to explore alternatives, or to adapt to changing circumstances. Yet one of the most remarkable things about his output is the absence of carbon copies, the sheer variety of forms employed. Not all are equally successful, but it is precisely because Shostakovich achieved a distinctly personal manner and continued to explore its structural implications that he can be regarded as one of the great modern symphonists in the romantic tradition.

Shostakovich's acceptance of that tradition was clear from the first, even if it took him a decade to work out how to continue it in a positive, coherent way. The broad dimensions of the First Symphony enabled a large number of obvious influences – the early Stravinsky, Prokofiev, Hindemith and the late Mahler among them – to survive without eliminating all traces of emerging originality. It was probably the conscious effort to achieve greater concentration in combination with political 'relevance', which led to the less than totally coherent single-movement plans of the Second and Third Symphonies (1927 and 1931). In the same year as the First Symphony, Shostakovich had composed the single-movement First Piano Sonata, which provides plentiful evidence of his openness to the more radical composers of the West – Bartók and Berg for example. The sonata barely keeps its feet on the solid ground of tonality; and traditional structural relationships, even such as a study of single-movement sonatas by Liszt and Skryabin might suggest, are obviously not of the greatest importance. The dramatic intensity of the sonata makes it entirely appropriate that much of Shostakovich's time between 1927 and 1932 should have been devoted to opera *(The Nose* and *Lady Macbeth of Mtsensk)*, and ballet *(The Golden Age* and *The Bolt)*. Had the cultural climate permitted *Lady Macbeth* to remain in the repertory after its première, Shostakovich's development might well have been very different. As it was, the often frantic concentration carried over from the Second and Third Symphonies must have seemed a major contributory factor to the 'decadence' of the opera. And even though the Fourth Symphony (1935–6) is a much more deliberate and expansive conception than Nos. 2 or 3, it too was felt to be too strongly tarred with the brush of formalism and was withdrawn at the rehearsal stage, not to be heard of again for a quarter of a century.

As is well known, Shostakovich's way out of this crisis was to compose 'a Soviet artist's reply to just criticism' – the Symphony No. 5 Op. 47 (1937). Some Western commentators, in whose veins the blood of democratic liberalism surges so freely, would be overjoyed if it were possible to regard this work not merely as a failure in its own terms, but as a marked decline after the achievements of the more radical, Western-influenced works of the previous decade. Unfortunately for ideology, however, the Fifth, that shameful product of compromise and conformism, is Shostakovich's first major masterpiece, and one of the greatest of all modern symphonies. In it the composer achieved a new clarity and certainty of purpose by simplifying and expanding where he had previously tried to compress and complicate. The Fifth Symphony expresses not the inevitable superiority of Soviet aesthetics, but the particular truth that this particular composer could find his deepest expressive resources only through less experimental, eccentric channels. Not that the work is palely orthodox in form, but it does show a grasp of how traditional features may be adapted, rather than merely copied or stood on end, which is new in Shostakovich's work.[2]

The breakthrough which the first movement of the Fifth Symphony represents was achieved by means of a crucial sacrifice, the abandonment of the attempt to write that 'real symphonic allegro' to which

Shostakovich attached such importance in his own self-critical comments. Just as Prokofiev was only to attain true greatness as a symphonist in works which start with movements which are not merely 'economical' but also have basically broad tempi, so Shostakovich found that breadth and profundity could not be combined, in Beethovenian, or even Tchaikovskian or Sibelian, fashion, with forceful energy. The further challenge was to avoid hyper-romantic self-indulgence in a slow first movement, and here too the Fifth Symphony, with its potentially austere but profoundly moving thematic material, succeeds completely. Central to the originality of the Fifth Symphony's initial sonata-form plan is the new concept of the 'dual theme', whereby a subject which is initially brooding and reflective can organically evolve to a completely different emotional state without changing its basic shape. Thus the thematic process is of fundamental importance: 'this new overall organization of form is achieved by means of closer control of material, which in its turn is dependent on the new-found *adaptability* of Shostakovich's themes.'[3]

The finale is commonly regarded as the weakest movement of the work, and is often described as a crudely turbulent march which achieves an embarrassingly empty apotheosis in an endless belt of D major triads. It has even been claimed that such over-emphasis was a deliberate attempt to expose the essential banality of the Soviet 'paradise' which the work was dedicated to praise. The movement undeniably forms a perfectly logical final stage in the evolution of the symphony from 'darkness' to 'light'. Even if we regard such an ending as organically inevitable, however, we may well prefer the earlier, less optimistic, more introspective music of the first and third movements, which move slowly but never meander. Whatever the relevance or quality of Shostakovich's optimistic perorations, his mastery of the public projection of essentially intimate, personal feelings never faltered, and gradually gained greater emphasis, first through the series of string quartets begun in 1938, and later, in response both to a degree of liberalization in post-Stalinist Russia and to a sense that with increasing age and ill-health he had little to lose, in the outstanding symphonies Nos. 13, 14 and 15. The Symphony No. 14 (1969) is particularly novel in form: a cycle of eleven songs, pessimistic in tone – the subject matter is death – and less conservative in language. Indeed, the concentration and chromaticism of his early music of the 1920s are recalled, though the context is immeasurably more controlled and pertinent, the remarkably abrupt, non-triadic ending inexorably prepared by all that comes before. Concentration and chromaticism are even more satisfyingly integrated in the single-movement scheme of the String Quartet No. 13 (1970). No fewer than five of the earlier quartets (Nos. 5, 7, 8, 9 and 11) are played without a break, though distinctness of the separate stages – in No. 11 (1966) there are no fewer than seven of them – is as important as the underlying unity. Even when the basic form is more conventional, the skill and sensitivity with which Shostakovich shapes it are exemplary (cf. the handling of sonata form in the first movement of No. 2). Yet there is particular satisfaction in observing the way in which the composer returned at a late stage of his career to the issue of strongly unified single-movement symphonic form, an issue which he first tackled in the First Piano Sonata written a mere two years after Sibelius's Seventh Symphony, but which then led to the impasse of the over-ambitious and ill-defined Second and Third Symphonies. The name of Schoenberg has been invoked to account both for the formal plans of the Twelfth and Thirteenth Quartets and for the presence of twelve-note successions – though Shostakovich was still far from 'pure' atonality: the more consistent chromaticism which twelve-note succession involves is used simply to create greater perspective for the ultimate tonal resolutions on which Shostakovich's forms normally depend for their coherent completion.

The increasingly melancholy tone of the later works reinforced the essential romanticism of a style whose strongest roots were in the symphonies of Mahler. Like Mahler's, Shostakovich's wit had a bitter, wellnigh frantic edge to it, and this sardonic, selfconscious trait entered a new phase with the use of quotations (Rossini's *William Tell* overture, some of Wagner's more doom-laden motives) in the Symphony No. 15 (1971). Shostakovich became increasingly willing to quote himself, and to use a musical motto – D, E flat, C, B natural – based on the German transliteration (DSCH) of his initials. This was first consciously employed in what is probably his greatest single work, the Symphony No. 10, Op. 93 (1953).

Its greatness is certainly not the result of structural compression, but of the way in which a natural tendency to expansiveness is not merely controlled, but turned to dramatic – symphonic – account. This is partly a matter of overall structural proportion, with the longest, slowest, most intense movement coming first. In basic outline, this could be a textbook example of sonata form, but it is remarkable how little of it is clearly in the tonic key of E minor or any of its conventionally close relatives. Not only is the main melodic material chromatic, but the entire harmonic motion of the movement involves hints rather than affirmations, implications rather than clarifications. The long first and second subject sections in the exposition enable the music to evolve through the development of smaller thematic units, and the harmonic character is of progress without stability. Ambiguity begins to intensify with the appearance of the second subject (Fig. 17), whose supporting harmony seems designed to contradict an underlying tonic rather than merely to obscure it, and it is not until the return of this second subject in the recapitulation (Fig. 57), differently accompanied, that true stability is reached. Even now, the music remains highly chromatic, but at least the background of E major and, later, E minor harmony is preserved. The coda – which is also the 'real' restatement of the first subject, since the beginning of the recapitulation is skilfully conflated with the later stages of the development – provides the clearest definition of the essential language of the whole work, the tension between chromatic and diatonic factors never more explicit than at the final 'perfect' cadence (Fig. 69) (Ex. 29).

Ex. 29

The second movement, *Allegro*, is an obvious opponent of the first: it is brief, violent, rooted in the key a tritone distant, B flat minor. Even though its main thematic idea begins with the same ascending steps – tonic, supertonic, mediant – as that of the first movement, there is little sense of an argument being continued in a new context. Clearly it is the 'task' of the remaining two movements both to continue these thematic and tonal arguments, and to resolve them. The third movement, *Allegretto*, takes its tonal stance the other side of the basic dominant from the *Allegro*, on C (minor). Once more the main thematic idea begins with the rising steps, but the mood, while still uneasy, is less aggressive, so it is possible to progress naturally to a point at the centre of the movement where a direct reminiscence of first-movement material is heard (Fig. 115). Another prominent thematic element in this movement is the DSCH motive – a permutation of the principal theme's first four notes – and this will be dramatically recalled at the climax of the finale.

The last movement, *Andante – Allegro*, for all its exuberance, is no mere dismissal of the serious issues raised by its three predecessors. First, there is an extended slow introduction of a profoundly tragic character, inevitably highly chromatic but centred in the dominant, B minor. Some of this material reappears during the course of an immense dominant preparation during the closing stages of the movement (Fig. 185), and, together with the DSCH motive, contrives to give a serious dimension to the otherwise triumphant E major ending. Yet even the lighthearted main *allegro* theme rarely remains firmly in its tonic key for long: the contrast of mood between first movement and finale does not imply a change of language, and the consistency with which the chromatic elements in all the themes radiate out into the underlying structural tonal organization is one of the reasons for the work's success. So, while there can be no mistaking the finality and centrality of E in the later stages of the finale, the constant presence of chromatic 'irritation' and brilliantly placed rhythmic cross-accents ensure that there is nothing the least perfunctory about the inevitable outcome.

In Europe several composers have written fine symphonic works, often under the influence of obvious models, but have failed to give the genre a new lease of life. A near-contemporary of Bartók and Stravinsky, Ernest Bloch (1880–1959) had strong roots in Teutonic late romanticism, and his major symphonic compositions – the Piano Quintet No. 1 (1921–3), the Violin Concerto No. 2 (1937–8), the Concerto Symphonique for piano and orchestra (1947–8), the String Quartet No. 3 (1952) – all display a skilled structural sense at the service of material which is rarely sufficiently memorable to warrant such full-blooded treatment. Bloch is best known for his less ambitious but passionately expressive 'Rhapsody' for cello and orchestra, *Schelomo* (1915). The enormous output of the Czech composer Bohuslav Martinů (1890–1959) includes six symphonies and six string quartets, all of the former postdating his strongly neo-classic phase. It is the Fifth Sym-

phony (1946) which a sympathetic commentator regards as 'in a sense
. . . the most classical and perfectly balanced of the symphonies: the
perspectives are precisely judged and the control over detail and its
relation to the work as a whole is complete'.[4] It is a typical example of a
'conservative-modern' symphony: the form was always there for a
sufficiently able composer to employ. But Martinů, for all his fluency
and skill, was less successful than, for example, Prokofiev at imposing a
strongly personal vision on the form, and the result is pleasingly
efficient rather than compulsively memorable.

The five symphonies of Arthur Honegger (1892–1955) belong to the
last twenty-five years of his life and represent a gradual retreat from an
emphasis on dramatic works. The concentrated, contrapuntal energy
of his most characteristic compositions is appealing, and bears out the
accuracy of his own comment that 'a symphonic work must be built
logically; . . . one must give the impression of a composition in which all
is linked, the image of a predetermined structure'.[5] Like most of the
works discussed in this section, they have so far led nowhere, but justify
their own existence, and deserve more frequent performance.

Tonal symphonic form exercised as great a fascination in the United
Kingdom as it did elsewhere. Tippett's work is discussed in Chapter
Eleven, but it was never very likely that he would follow for long in the
stylistic footsteps of Vaughan Williams or Holst. Benjamin Britten was
an even less likely disciple, although his Sinfonia da Requiem (1940),
Spring Symphony (1949) and Cello Symphony (1963) are characteristically well-made responses to the concept, as 'programme symphony',
'choral cantata' and 'concerto'. The inter-war years saw the production
of the two best symphonic works by William Walton (born 1902): the
Viola Concerto (1929) and the Symphony No. 1 (1935). Both are
deeply romantic yet finely constructed compositions, and the very
confidence of their manner makes Walton's subsequent failure to
match them the more regrettable. Walton was no more able to follow
up his success with *Belshazzar's Feast* (1931) in the realm of oratorio.
Several other British composers have remained faithful to tonal symphonic forms since the death of Vaughan Williams in 1958, but none
have achieved a work of major importance or likely longevity.

Of the three American symphonists born in the 1890s – Walter
Piston (1894–1976), Howard Hanson (born 1896) and Roy Harris
(born 1898) – Harris is generally regarded as the best, and his total of
symphonies reached twelve in 1969. Yet it is the Third (1937) which
made the greatest impact, its single-movement form and broadly

diatonic manner inevitably, if superficially, recalling Sibelius. Harris's idiom exploits national roots through the medium of a personal approach to elements of traditional structure. His music is barely known outside America, however, and it may indeed prove to be the case that the most enduring American contribution to the symphony after Ives is that of Roger Sessions, whose twelve-note music is considered in Chapter Nine.

The career of Aaron Copland typifies the problems and rewards of pursuing the tonal symphonic structure in the modern age. Born in 1900, and spending a crucial period of study in France between 1921 and 1924, he seems from his earliest works to have been ideally suited to the task of revitalizing tonal forms without recourse to any extremes, whether neo-classical or 'nationalist'. The Symphony for Organ and Orchestra of 1924 begins delightfully, but its more ambitious later movements are relatively dull. The orchestral Music for the Theatre (1925) uses simple forms in a brilliantly effective way to sharpen the focus of a wholly personal style, whose rhythmic energy avoids mere imitation of Stravinsky and whose delicate lyricism, while obviously 'French', is still given an individual cast. There is a joyful jazziness in places, and little or none of that later, portentously homespun manner which Copland was to cultivate so intensively.

It was the attempt to expand this marvellously instinctive idiom to fill larger forms which was to occupy, and often frustrate Copland in the years ahead. The Piano Concerto (1926) was in many ways an unpropitious omen, with its exhilarating, but ultimately unrewarding confrontation between 'popular' and 'symphonic' elements. The 'Dance' Symphony (1928) is very much better, even if the slow movement seems a little too long. It has great lyric charm, and well-made climaxes generated by rhythmic activity of goodhumoured 'hoe-down' persistence, rather than 'Rite-of-Spring' savagery. After this, the next piece is another disappointment: indeed, the single-movement Symphonic Ode (1928, revised 1955) is in most respects the crudest of all Copland's larger works, especially in its over-emphatic repetition of irregular rhythmic patterns, a technique which palls with great rapidity. In so far as the failure of the Ode may have urged Copland to greater concentration, however, it was worthwhile: certainly the Piano Variations (1930) and the 'Short' Symphony (1933) are far more purposeful, the chromatic elaboration of basic tonal relationships far better controlled. The approach to 'all-thematicism' in the Variations has often been discussed, especially after Copland's much later use of serial techniques (in the Piano Quartet (1950) and other instrumental works of the 'fifties and 'sixties), but the issue of symphonic form as such is not raised by a set of variations, however 'proto-serial'.

Copland's genius as a writer of ballet music was fully displayed between 1935 and 1945, in *El Salón méxico* (1936), *Billy the Kid* (1938), *Rodeo* (1942) and *Appalachian Spring* (1944) – the last a truly miraculous rediscovery of the essential simplicity of his earliest works in terms of a much more confident and personal style. In following it up with the grandiose Symphony No. 3 (1946), Copland dramatized the entire structural issue which his music has faced with startling clarity, for a basic simplicity is here stretched to breaking point by a scheme which almost 'out-Soviets' Shostakovich in its progress towards a diatonic paean provoked by a 'Fanfare for the Common Man'.

This symphony is the last word in great achievements against the grain, for Copland's later instrumental works have displayed as ambivalent an attitude to tonality as they have to sonata form. The single-movement schemes he has favoured – cf. the Piano Fantasy (1955–7), Nonet for Strings (1960), *Connotations* for Orchestra (1961–2), *Inscape* (1967) – may indeed come to be regarded as structural prototypes for composers who wish to retain thematicism while rejecting tonal harmonic relationships. For Copland himself, as his comments on *Inscape* show, the ultimate hope may be for tonality to survive revitalized by a 'fusion' with twelve-note technique: for tonal implications and direction to emerge from twelve-note writing. But there is little sign that such a compromise is finding more general favour.

Chapter 5

Opera

Attempts to argue that opera in the modern age is an anachronism have never carried much purely musical weight. Composers who represent all the diverse styles of the present have felt drawn to some kind of 'music theatre', even if they reject the term 'opera' as such, and even amongst opera composers who retain tonality and remain relatively close to nineteenth-century forms and idioms, ample variety and vitality can be observed.

Both Giacomo Puccini (1858–1924) and Richard Strauss (1864–1949) are generally agreed to have made their major contributions to the medium before 1918. Nevertheless, even with its somewhat perfunctory completion by Franco Alfano, Puccini's final opera, *Turandot*, is the equal of any of his earlier works. It has total conviction of style, firmly established form, and although the exotic sadism of the plot may seem crude for its time, with overtones of oldfashioned melodrama rather than of serious psychological drama, the economy of means and briskness of pace counter the dangers of over-emphasis. No subsequent Italian composer has come remotely near the Puccinian flair and panache: principally no doubt because new linguistic bases for such qualities are extremely hard to establish. Only Dallapiccola has shown how to preserve Puccini's fundamental dramatic devices – even down to the element of sadism – in the very different style of his serial one-acter, *Il Prigioniero*, discussed in Chapter Nine.

Richard Strauss composed eight more operas during the twenty-two years after the première of one of his greatest – *Die Frau ohne Schatten* – in 1919. While *aficionados* will continue to dispute whether this is or is not greater than the first work in which Strauss retreated from the front line of harmonic advance, *Der Rosenkavalier*, few would claim that any of the later operas are as great as either. The one possible exception is *Capriccio*, completed in 1941, which is not only Strauss's own last opera but, in all probability, the last in the line of great romantic comedies which began in 1786 with *Le Nozze di Figaro*. *Capriccio* is closer to *Der Rosenkavalier* than to *Die Frau ohne Schatten*, shunning the occasionally obscure but richly allusive mythic subject matter of Hofmannsthal's most ambitious text. *Die Frau ohne Schatten* provided Strauss with one of his finest characters, Barak – the nearest he ever came to a Sachs. The best characters in the later operas tend to share a degree of Barak's down-to-earth solidity, though Christine Storch in *Intermezzo*, Mandryka in *Arabella* and La Roche in *Capriccio* are all more impulsive, more conscious of being on stage and needing to entertain an audience. Barak's simple, resigned nobility, as expressed at the end of Act I of *Die Frau ohne Schatten*, is never matched again, though the only slightly tongue-in-cheek final stages of La Roche's great monologue in the ninth scene of *Capriccio* run it close.

For all its selfconscious elegance, there is nothing superficial about *Capriccio*. The fact that it is, ultimately, an opera about opera does not exclude the expression of very real human emotions, and the passions of the poet and the composer for the Countess are more important than their devotion to their respective arts. A relatively serious tone for the expression of those passions is not precluded either, though once they have been expressed – and the same is true for the director's hymn of devotion to *his* art – the mood must be quickly lightened, or the passion safely defused, by the highflown lyricism of the Countess's response. The greatest dramatic stroke in *Capriccio* is the postponement of the Countess's own most passionate outburst until the final scene when she learns that she must soon confront her two suitors simultaneously and choose between them. This final scene is nevertheless not about how she arrives at a decision, but about how she regains the equilibrium which makes either a decision, or no decision, possible. She recovers that serene poise which is also the principal musical quality of the entire work.

In general, the conversational episodes and ensembles which occur regularly in the earlier parts of the opera serve to contrast with the more serious monologues and solo sections. Yet, while it is true to say that 'lyricism and parlando . . . flourish throughout', it is less accurate to imply that the opera lacks vigour.[1] It has sufficient vitality for its purpose, and the large-scale Octet in Scene 9 is quite powerful enough a climax, given that it expresses more mockery than hostility, more amusement than anger.

As a tonal composer, Strauss was quite capable of exploiting tensions within and between keys where these were dramatically appropriate: a good example is the dual tonal tendency of La Roche's monologue – C (major or minor) and E flat. In less forthright passages, inevitably, chromaticism becomes more purely a matter of colour, enriching the harmony without creating any lasting doubts about the eventual tonal outcome. A chromatic chord or progression need not positively undermine a tonality in order to enhance expression.

The closing stages of *Capriccio* (from ten bars after Fig. 281) provide an example. The overall tonality of D flat major is by now well

Ex. 30

established and its stability is unlikely to be seriously called into question. As Exx. 30 and 31 make clear, what is so crucial is not so much a low level of chromaticism as a low level of dissonance, with 'unessential' melody notes and 'passing' chromatic chords alike tending merely to poke slight gaps in the prevailing concordant chromaticism. Yet there is fine craftsmanship in the way the next entry of the voice is prepared (Ex. 30).

At the beginning of the example, the music has moved into the supertonic – E flat minor – but before it makes the easy step back to the second inversion tonic chord of D flat, Strauss inserts a gliding gloss over the simple chromatic bass line E flat, F, G flat, G natural, A flat to give the return of D flat just the right sense of resolution. The real point of the slight delay is, however, to enhance the much longer postpone-

Ex. 31

ment of *root position* tonic harmony. During the next nine bars we may not experience disruption, but we do feel suspense, as the harmony floats freely around its tantalizingly tangible goal; and then the voice enters, two bars before the resolution is complete.

The principal chromatic deviations in the remainder of the scene are all sidesteps on to full triads like E major, A major and D major, a semitone away from diatonic chords (Ex. 31). These may reach the discerning ear as 'substitutes' for the 'real' harmony, and even as an aural equivalent of the difference between reflection and reality as the Countess looks into the mirror and asks for an answer 'which is not trivial' to the question, whom shall she choose? The situation itself may indeed seem trivial, judged by the standards of epic myth or psychological naturalism, but the music ensures its memorability.

Strauss apart, Austro-German opera in the 1920s and 1930s presents a lively variety of subject and style. The dramatic works of Schoenberg and Berg are dealt with in Chapters Six and Seven, but with one mighty exception those operas which used tonality were an important part of the postwar reaction against late-romantic idioms and mythological plots. The exception is *Doktor Faust* by Ferruccio Busoni (1866–1924), which he began in 1916 and was still working on at his death: his pupil Philip Jarnach composed a remarkably successful completion to the final scene.

Much of Busoni's music may be criticized for nondescript – or simply inappropriate – material, but *Doktor Faust*, if not free from this fault (notably its presentation of the only significant female character, the Countess), triumphs through its portrayal of the central relationship between Faust himself and Mephistopheles. The force and imagination of the musical invention connected with these characters override the potentially dangerous gulf in the musical language between functional and non-functional factors. The work is less a synthesis of styles than a compendium, where modal counterpoint, impressionistic progressions and almost Straussian late romanticism contribute in turn to a dramatic impact which may be blurred in focus but is all the more intriguing for its very unpredictability. Busoni pulled no punches in *Doktor Faust*. His treatment of the subject is not tinged with any inhibiting reverence for this most resonant of German myths. There is even something ironically Wotan-like about the way Faust cheats the Devil at the end to the extent of ensuring survival through his miraculously resurrected child, and there is a cool, conspiratorial side to Mephisto himself, which suggests affinities with Wagner's Loge. The importance of the purely orchestral music is considerable, but the vocal ensembles and set-pieces show confidence in the adaptation of conventional designs. *Doktor Faust* is a highpoint of late-romantic German opera, but its existence as an epic in splendid isolation is seen in still clearer focus if it is compared with the work of the younger generation during the same period.

Kurt Weill (1900–50) was born too late to become just another German late romantic: indeed, 1900 is virtually midway between the birth dates of Schoenberg and Stockhausen. Yet the hyperromantic tendencies which Weill's remarkable First Symphony (1921) displays were checked by contact with Busoni. 'Busoni challenged this inherent inclination toward the romantic expressionist line of Mahler, Strauss, Schreker and Schoenberg in the course of Weill's membership of his select master class at the Berlin Hochschule during the three years before his death in 1924. From Busoni Weill learned classical restraint and economy of means, although his musical language remained basically true to its Mahlerian roots.'[2] As John Waterhouse has shown, Busoni's influence did not suddenly evaporate when Weill began to write music very different from that which had marked their contact.[3] Even when the obvious differences in temperament and inclination between a man who could produce a *Faust* and one who could create a *Mahagonny* are taken into account, therefore, the links between the two are of decisive importance.

Weill's association with the poet and playwright Bertold Brecht began with *Die Dreigroschenoper* in 1927, the intention being to provide a musical entertainment of immediate and wide appeal (in that, emulating its source, John Gay's *Beggar's Opera*). Weill had already used popular elements in three one-act operas, and the fashion for jazz-influenced style and topical subject matter had already been exploited by Hindemith and by the young Ernst Krenek in his *Jonny spielt auf* (1925–6). Yet *Die Dreigroschenoper*, first performed in 1928, has proved to be the most enduring of all such works. As a portrayal of a decadent society it could hardly be more different from Berg's *Wozzeck* (first performed in 1925), with its compassionate pessimism grounded in deep psychological insight. Brecht and Weill were not concerned with charting the extent to which individual personalities and personal relationships are governed by psychological and social forces. They wished to provoke that political awareness which they believed was present in everyone, though too often remaining regrettably latent. They were not interested in psychological motivation but in political action, hence the need for a simple, direct dramatic style, which would make people sit up, take note and act: hence, musically, the importance of popular idioms.

Of its very nature, however, the collaboration between Brecht and Weill was bound to be brief and unstable. The poet's concept of what he called Epic Theatre was the very reverse of the Wagnerian Gesamt-kunstwerk which the term so easily conjures up: Brecht stressed that Epic Theatre, in seeking to emphasize the independence of text, music and stage presentation, was the opposite of traditional 'dramatic theatre'. Both Brecht and Weill were impressed by what is probably the finest of all anti-romantic, neo-classical 'Epic' theatrical works, Stravinsky's *Oedipus Rex*, for all its lack of purely political relevance, and there is no doubt that Weill shared Brecht's convictions about what Epic Theatre should aim to achieve. The problem was that the poet was deeply suspicious of music which verged on the lyric or romantic, and difficulties therefore arose, for example, in connection with the beautiful 'Crane' duet in their second joint venture, *Aufstieg und Fall der Stadt Mahagonny* (1929); 'its astonishingly delicate lyricism is dangerous from the Brechtian point of view, for it compels the onlooker to identify himself with the feelings of the protagonists. It provides him with sensations instead of "forcing him to take decisions".'[4] (Ex. 32).

Even in *Die Dreigroschenoper*, Weill's musical idiom was not simply of the self-effacing, functional, popular, decision-provoking kind of which Brecht might have unreservedly approved. For all the presence of jazz-derived features, these are not used in a simple documentary sense

Ex. 32

but to further a brilliantly conceived undermining of some of the most cherished features of German late-romantic and modern music. Weill did not simply reproduce the clichés of popular dance music: he 'dissected and reanimated' them with 'extraordinary precision'. 'On a purely analytical level, one finds that the spearhead of his attack on convention is a highly disruptive and almost Mahlerian harmonic style that achieves its forcefulness without any recourse to "contemporary" secundal dissonance. For that reason it attacks the *idées reçues* of modernity as fiercely as it does those of commercial music manufacturers.'[5] Without such ambivalence, it is difficult to believe that the music of *Die Dreigroschenoper* would have survived the decade for which it was conceived. After all, what could be more appropriate for a dramatic work which sought to provoke political and social action on the basis of moral judgments than music which is not merely dismissive but highly critical of decadent conventions?

Ultimately, therefore, Weill's achievement – which ensured an early break with Brecht – was to find a new tension between simplicity and concentration, just as the late-romantic Mahler had explored a new tension between simplicity and elaboration. As soon as poet and composer collaborated on a full-length three-act opera – *Mahagonny* – the inevitably more extended musical treatment was bound to undermine the poet's dramatic intentions. Another problem had already arisen from the simple fact that *Die Dreigroschenoper* had been a success, something which the public could enjoy while apparently remaining impervious to its message. The whole concept of Epic Theatre with music foundered on the failure of the public to distinguish between sensation and stimulus to action. And yet the failure of those works to promote social and political change does not reduce their power as attacks on corruption: perhaps it was their very universality which ensured their immediate practical ineffectiveness.

Even after *Happy End* (1929), which concluded his collaboration with Brecht, Weill remained faithful to the idea of Epic Theatre. *Die Burgschaft* (1930–1), to a text by Caspar Neher, is another social morality with a basically straightforward musical style, but it was far too explicit, for all its vigorous support of a pre-Wagnerian concept of operatic form, to be acceptable in a country shortly to be taken over by the Nazi Party. Weill, the 'radical conservative', went into exile and, in America, became musically a shadow of his former self.

Léos Janáček (1854–1928) wrote only one work before 1914 which is widely admired today, the opera *Jenufa*, and it is in the field of opera that the greater and finer part of his remarkably rich later output belongs. Janáček's style is instantly recognizable, its personal accents making it easy to regard him as a nationalist *par excellence*: and, though the extent to which the rhythms and colours of Czech prose determine his musical processes can easily be exaggerated, it is undeniable that the character of the music is significantly related to that of the language.

Jenufa, though completed in 1903, did not achieve any real success until 1916. *The Excursions of Mr Brouček* also has a long history, from 1908 to 1917, but the last four operas were composed with considerable rapidity, and reflect this in their concentration and brevity.

The three acts of *Káťa Kabanová* (1921) last less than two hours. Based on Ostrovsky's play *The Storm*, it tells how a girl, living in the repressive atmosphere of a small country town, is unfaithful to her husband and driven to suicide when her lover is forced to leave. In basic outline, it may seem little different from the plot of a Puccinian tear-jerker, yet Janáček's powers of musical characterization, of both individuals and their environment, achieve a dramatic conviction in which stylization has no part. There is a simple intensity which can rise to heights of the greatest eloquence even though the expansive lyricism conventionally associated with such an atmosphere in romantic music is normally absent. In purely musical terms, as with the handling of tonality and thematic development, this simplicity may be actual or deceptive. Of all the composers discussed in this book, moreover, Janáček is the least amenable to generalization, so no summary discussion of his procedures can do more than provide isolated instances of techniques which are protean in their variety. For example, he may make the simplest use of dominant preparation when moving from one tonal area to another, as in the extended scene for the lovers in Act II (Ex. 33).

Ex. 33

Alternatively, a dominant preparation may lead into surprisingly remote regions, as at the magical moment of Kátá's first appearance in Act I (Ex. 34).

Ex. 34

This example also shows how such an effect can be heightened by the use of simple thematic variation.

Nowhere is Janáček's musical personality more tangible than in the simple, basically diatonic phrases whose chromatic inflections seem to express a whole world of hope or despair (cf. vocal score p. 27, last line, or p. 133, second line). Nor is there anything more moving in the entire repertory of modern tonal music than those passages in Káťa's final scene (p. 142, *Lento*, and p. 156, *Adagio*) where the harmony seems to be striving for the security of an uninflected G flat or C flat major, but is ultimately defeated, like Káťa herself. The climax of this scene, when Káťa decides to kill herself (cf. p. 161), is also a useful example of Janáček's utterly uncomplicated musico-dramatic technique. The entire passage is only fifteen bars long, and harmonically it moves from A flat major to G flat minor. The thematic motive is in the orchestra, and consists of a short descending figure stated no less than seventeen times in only slightly varied forms. Such simplicity of means inevitably enhances the cumulative effect of the harmonic motion: and even the relatively slight degree of thematic variation merely throws the progress of the harmony into greater relief. A similar technique used on a larger scale can be studied in the crucial scene between Káťa and Boris in Act II (pp. 97–105). The scene as a whole is a marvellous portrait of the vulnerability and essential innocence of the central characters, framed as it is with the folksong-like music for the second pair of lovers, Varvara and Kudriash. Each section is built around the frequent repetition of simple thematic phrases in the orchestra, which the voices occasionally match but which are most important as background to vocal phrases whose every detail – register, rhythm, relationship of repetition to variation – serves to create the greatest romantic intensity.

Janáček's next opera, *The Cunning Little Vixen* (1921–3), is as sharply focused with regard to fantasy as *Káťa Kabanová* is to naturalistic tragedy. Even before the serene beauty of the Forester's concluding monologue, however, the work contains moments of an almost Straussian richness which contrast so extremely with the more *parlando* passages as to create a feeling of aimlessness (at least of harmonic direction) in the latter. Whether or not Janáček himself was aware of the disruptive potentiality of a style with two such different constituents, it is a fact that neither of the last two operas, *The Makropoulos Case* (1923–5) and *From the House of the Dead* (1927–8), contains nearly as much pure lyricism. Their language may be more obviously unified, but the loss of lyric contrast ensures a new, much less instantly appealing austerity, for which the grim subject matter of *From the House of the Dead* is especially appropriate. It may be possible to criticize the way in which Janáček adapted Dostoyevsky's tale of prison-camp life, but the overall effect is of an intensity as implacable and grim as anything in Berg, and the music, while unfailingly powerful, never strains after exaggerated effects.

The emphasis on narration (each act contains an extended monologue for a different character) demands particularly clear structural organization, and Janáček achieves unity without sacrificing inner momentum. The Act III narration may be overlong – its content is almost a Janáček plot in itself – but it accumulates a truly horrific tension, which is released without dilution in the true ending of the work.[6] *From the House of the Dead* is one of the great radical twentieth-century operas in the way it achieves total dramatic conviction through the most intense exploitation of a highly personal musical idiom. Janáček's native tongue may have made it that much easier for him to achieve this originality: but it was his musical inventiveness which enabled him to breathe dramatic life into what might so easily have become large tracts of arid recitative. As (very differently) with Weill, the secret lies in the tension of simple 'units' of harmony and rhythm, which need not behave according to traditional 'rules'. Janáček perfected a language of total coherence and clarity. The blazing diatonic perorations of all his late works may not have ensured the indefinite survival of the tonal system itself, but they summarized the immediate emotional response and the deep humanity of a genius who achieved the aim of all true creative minds: to communicate widely and yet to preserve complete individuality.

One of the most satisfying things about *The Cunning Little Vixen* is the unmawkish way in which Janáček characterized the animals. Ravel's *L'Enfant et les Sortilèges* (1920–5) is another opera from the same decade presenting a fantasy in which animals (and in Ravel's case normally inanimate objects like armchairs and teapots) make use of human speech. The brevity of Ravel's work (it lasts barely fifty minutes) and the use of dance idioms – foxtrot, slow valse, 'valse américaine' – help to ensure an engagingly frivolous tone, while the extreme simplicity of the child's E flat major song (pp. 50–1 of the vocal score) supports David Drew's judgment that the lyrical sections of the opera are among the best things in Ravel's later work.[7] The closing chorus, with the penitent child's cries for its mother, is perhaps a little too saccharine for comfort, but even here the lyric diatonicism spiced with gentle dissonance makes an attractive conclusion to one of Ravel's most spontaneously imaginative pieces.

At the farthest extreme both from Ravel's delicate fantasy and the social concerns of Weill and late Janáček is *King Roger* (1918–24) by the Polish composer Karol Szymanowski (1882–1937). In several respects it is comparable with, though hardly similar to, Busoni's *Doktor Faust*: both are fine works by uneven composers, late-romantic, and therefore, in some sense, 'oldfashioned' in style, though Szymanowski's roots are in Debussy and Skryabin rather than Wagner and Strauss, and both involve a powerful recreation of a literary archetype: in *King Roger*, the *Bacchae* of Euripides.

Roger was a twelfth-century Sicilian king, and the opera tells of his confrontation with two rival forces, representing repression (the medieval Christian church) and liberation (a young, pagan shepherd, the god Dionysos). Given its epic subject matter, the opera may seem surprisingly short – three acts, each less than an hour long – and indeed the emphasis is less on an elaborately explicit plot than on a brief sequence of crucial events in which much remains implicit. In spite of this oblique approach however, it is clear that at the end Roger himself has succeeded in rising above both the stultified traditions of the Church and the dangerously impulsive indulgences of the Shepherd – though these have been the agency of his enlightenment. The last act confirms that the opera is principally concerned with the conflicts within Roger himself, and their resolution is the means of giving full realization to his own personality: the outcome as far as concerns his position as king of a specific country with specific problems is not shown, nor could it be without contradicting the entire dramatic character of the piece. In giving such emphasis to inner rather than outer action, Szymanowski was certainly unfashionable, and even if his approach was in large part simply the result of inexperience (he had composed only one earlier opera, *Hagith*, between 1911 and 1914), *King Roger* still achieves a powerfully convincing climax.

That it does so is because Szymanowski s musical style is equal to the demands of the subject. The drama is projected through an epic lyricism, into which simpler song elements are well integrated, just as the late-romantic harmonic framework can encompass more conventional triadic moments without incongruity. There may be no all-pervading use of functional tonality, but the work relies on the kind of tensions and resolutions which only a language accepting the ultimate primacy of the triad can enforce. Not the least surprising thing about

King Roger is its ending – in contrast to Wagnerian and Straussian precedents – with a triumphant monologue for a *male* singer, Roger himself. Szymanowski never equalled this achievement in his later works, which display a more Bartókian concern to use folk-music-like material in the service of art-music forms. This change of style, which took place when Poland gained political independence after the 1914–18 war, apparently hindered the completion of *King Roger* itself, and although the later music is by no means without power – the ballet *Harnasie* (1923–31), in particular – it is *King Roger*, along with other compositions of the period from 1915 to 1920, like the Violin Concerto No. 1 (1916) and the Symphony No. 3 (1914–16), which represent Szymanowski's best work.

As discussed in Chapter Four, Prokofiev's greatest achievements in the field of instrumental music – principally the symphony – date from after his return to Russia. The blend of lyric and dramatic impulses in the Fifth and Sixth Symphonies produces an epic breadth which does not demand the total elimination of those more sardonic characteristics of the pre-Soviet period. Such a richness of range – equally evident in the full-length ballet *Romeo and Juliet* (1936) – might have been expected to find the same, if not a superior, fulfilment in opera; and Prokofiev's relative failure here could be conclusive evidence that an essentially bitter, tragic core lies at the heart of his often apparently easy-going, good-humoured style – a core which could only find full expression in dramatic subjects likely to be regarded as subversive by Soviet dogmatists. The abundant flair, versatility and originality of the two operas Prokofiev wrote between 1918 and 1927 were construed by his Soviet biographer as evidence of nihilism, involving a 'rejection of the principles of classical operatic form'.[8] Certainly, neither *The Love of Three Oranges* (1919) nor *The Fiery Angel* (1919–27) is a flawless masterpiece, yet the structural problems which remain unsolved were created by the composer's sensible and scarcely unprecedented attempt to devise a dramatic form appropriate to the subject matter.

As a fantastic farce, *The Love of Three Oranges* is probably more effective in its adaptation of the anti-romantic accents theatrically fully in vogue at the time, than *The Fiery Angel* is in its attempt to trump the expressionist music drama. If the first is economically discontinuous, the second seems too protracted, its flamboyant rhetoric becoming tedious and self-parodic. What both works share, with each other and with much that is good in many other early twentieth-century operas, is the convincing realization of an exotic setting, while the importance of diabolic possession in *The Fiery Angel* creates strong links with the entire German romantic tradition, reaching back to Weber's *Der Freischütz*. If the composer's third version of the work had been completed (it would have reshaped the five acts as three, and included two new scenes), the impact might well have been much more powerful and better controlled.[9] As it is, it is difficult not to feel that the Symphony No. 3 (1928), derived from the opera, presents a more satisfying statement of the dramatic musical essence. The opera is 'the work of a symphonic poet, in which a musically conceived atmosphere is tied to appropriate but not always indispensable dramatic presentations. This loose relationship allows dramatic inconsistencies which the overall musical style rarely admits. Taken on this level, the opera falls down at those points where the libretto forces Prokofiev into writing music to fit dramatic threads which are not at one with his original musical concept.'[10]

Prokofiev began his third version of the work after the Metropolitan Opera in New York had indicated in 1930 an interest in staging it (in fact, it was eventually staged in Venice in 1955, two years after Prokofiev's death). Presumably the revision was abandoned at the time that the composer decided, in 1933, to return to Russia. He can have had few illusions about the prevailing Soviet attitude to his earlier music, particularly the operas, and it was not until 1939, with the double success of the Ballet, *Romeo and Juliet*, and the cantata, *Alexander Nevsky*, behind him, that he approached the form with which Shostakovich, with *Lady Macbeth of Mtsensk* (first performed in 1934), had provoked a major political attack.

The omens must have been good. *Romeo and Juliet* was later praised with the words that 'few composers have achieved in music alone, without the aid of a sung or spoken libretto, so concrete and realistic an embodiment of life,'[11] and although at one stage it had been intended to revive Juliet in time for a happy ending, even the stark tragedy of Shakespeare's own conclusion was not interpreted as a symbolic criticism of the capacity of the Soviet state to survive.

'Realism' is also the key term in the Russian eulogies of *Alexander Nevsky*. The inference was clear: Prokofiev was eminently suited to compose a realistic opera rooted in the events of the time – an opera of the kind of which Shostakovich was apparently incapable. With hindsight, it seems regrettable that Prokofiev did not follow up the other possibility in acceptable dramatic themes: Shakespearian tragedy. He actually composed some incidental music for a production of *Hamlet* in

1937–8, but the operatic project which he began the following year was *Semyon Kotko*, a story of peasant life during the civil war which followed the 1917 revolution. It was first performed in Moscow on 20th September 1940 and failed. Nestyev's diagnosis is predictable: the techniques of the earlier operas, which involved 'the rejection of traditional operatic forms . . . were not at all suitable for the writing of a contemporary folk drama'. He was nevertheless prepared to concede that Prokofiev had 'found new, flexible expressive means in the work',[12] and Western authorities have found much to admire in it.[13]

In deciding to use Tolstoy's *War and Peace* as the basis of his next opera, Prokofiev retained the essential nationalist appeal of a 'local' subject while ensuring a more universal interest as well. Yet there is something almost desperate in this eager embrace of the impossible. *War and Peace* might have been an ideal subject for the film-maker Eisenstein, with whom Prokofiev had collaborated so successfully on *Alexander Nevsky* and *Ivan the Terrible*, but it stubbornly resisted the necessary restraints and compressions of operatic form, at least as conceived in Soviet Russia. The sheer determination with which Prokofiev worked at the opera during the last twelve years of his life might for some be the clinching evidence that he was never a true man of the opera house.

The first version of the opera was completed in 1942 and Prokofiev was soon under strong pressure from the Committee on the Arts to revise it. It has been convincingly argued that this first version has 'both a higher degree of dramatic interest and coherence, and much clearer evidence of the strong musical personality of its composer' than the revision:[14] some still rate the 'final' version very highly, while others see it as an eclectic pageant in which Prokofiev's own musical personality tends to be submerged, as the ghosts of Tchaikovsky, Borodin and Mussorgsky gain strength. Prokofiev continued to work on the score, but the authorities were never satisfied. There was a plan in 1946 to perform 'peace' and 'war' on separate nights. Two years later the composer was proposing 'various one-night adaptations of the opera, which more or less gave the authorities *carte blanche* to suppress or emphasize any controversial issues in the plot'.[15] The demoralization which this strategy depicts is indeed tragic, the more so as the composer clearly came to believe that the opera's 'popular appeal' could and should be increased. The result as he left it is nevertheless still a compelling rendering of Tolstoy's epic: indeed, it is perhaps remarkable that so much of true worth remains.

Prokofiev wrote two other operas in the 1940s. *The Duenna*, an adaptation of Sheridan's play (composed 1940, before *War and Peace*, but not staged until 1946), found local favour by virtue of its clear number-opera design and avoidance of caricature in favour of a lyricism recalling that of *Romeo and Juliet*. *The Story of a Real Man* (1947–8) was written at a time when Stalinist repression was at its height. It is a last attempt to dramatize the life of a Soviet hero – a fighter pilot – and in spite of the composer's pathetic statement of intent – 'I intend to introduce trios, duets, and contrapuntally developed choruses . . . clear melodies and the simplest harmonic language possible'[16] – the work had no success and was at once suppressed.

Prokofiev's statement of intent with regard to *The Story of a Real Man* could equally well have been made by Benjamin Britten (1913–76) when writing his first opera, *Peter Grimes*. First performed in 1945 – an earlier operetta, *Paul Bunyan*, had been discarded, though it has since been revived – it was his most substantial composition of any kind at that date, and established him as a composer capable of giving musical life to serious subjects and major issues. Not that the earlier works lack individuality, and the choral variations *A Boy was Born* (1932–3), the Variations on a Theme of Frank Bridge for strings (1937) and the Violin Concerto of 1939 (particularly its final pages) provide the clearest indication of an expressive certainty remarkable for a composer still in his twenties. This aspect of Britten's style owes much to kinship with late romanticism, notably Mahler, and while the early works also display an abundant technical facility and a dazzling sardonic wit deriving from the neo-classical masters, there is at times a simpler lyricism whose origin is, perhaps, more local. Britten was helped to bring these various elements together into a fully mature, personal style by his principal teacher, Frank Bridge (1879–1941), and the first works in which maturity as well as mastery are unmistakably present are all vocal: the Rimbaud cycle *Les Illuminations* for high voice and strings (1939), the *Seven Sonnets of Michelangelo* for tenor and piano (1940) and the Serenade for tenor, horn and strings (1943). All display Britten's abundant capacity for drama as well as lyricism: it was inevitable that he should turn to opera.

Peter Grimes is about an anti-hero, a misfit who longs to conform to social conventions ('society' being represented by the inhabitants of a Suffolk fishing village) but whose instincts and impulses make such conformity impossible. The essentially romantic nature of this theme needs no labouring, though Grimes as a character has few of the attractive, noble qualities of the true romantic outcast: he is not portrayed as a superior being, but as a 'sad case', intriguing and pathetic enough to attract well-meaning sympathy, but too eccentric and, in all probability, too perverse to deserve more than token toleration by a society which can only survive if all its members accept its conventions. Needless to say, society itself is not depicted in the opera as a wholly good and worthy thing. Without approaching the degree of disgust in face of establishment figures which *Wozzeck* displays, Britten and his librettist Montagu Slater provide shrewd and unvarnished portraits of a variety of local worthies, most of whom are motivated by delight in power, on however small a scale, and who turn naturally to persecution of any whose faces fail to fit. The subject, and the opera, succeed principally because these universal issues are given the most convincing natural setting. Britten's genius as a musical illustrator provides a framework of sun, sea and storm which could so easily have become a naive accompaniment to the events enacted. Yet the strong sense of locality – of a particular Suffolk landscape and climate – which the opera possesses does not seem to have hindered its appreciation in many other countries. Britten may in some respects be a latterday nationalist, but his music has a wider appeal than that of any other modern British composer.

Peter Grimes is a motivically unified psychological drama which retains strong links with the traditional number opera, while being more romantic than neo-classical in style. The tonal harmony is typical of the period, balancing functional and non-functional progressions and retaining that clear distinction between discord and concord which has remained Britten's principal expressive and structural device. While it may seem predictable that the chromatic semitone and tritone should be given great emphasis both thematically and harmonically, naive parallels between musical and dramatic symbolism are avoided. Grimes himself is not represented by one key to which all others are opposed, but the work as a whole persistently probes the stability of diatonic harmony and hierarchical relationships. The structural use of clashes between opposing tonal centres is to be expected at more overtly dramatic moments, as in the Prologue to Act I or the Round in the final scene of Act I where Grimes disrupts the stable E flat major and moves the tonality into E major before the chorus regains the initiative. Conflicts also permeate the more lyrical passages, however – even the most beautiful of them all, the short trio for female voices which ends the first scene of Act II.

The trio ('From the gutter') is in three parts, the second and third being variations of the first, and the first itself having an A, A₁, B structure in which each segment is preceded by an orchestral cadential phrase. The character of the music is determined by two types of tonal ambiguity, simultaneous and successive. The simultaneous type is less explicit, concerning the tendency of accompaniment and vocal lines in the A or A₁ segments to pull in different directions. In the first A segment, for example, the accompaniment has triads of C minor, the voices of B flat major, and it is a personal matter whether these are felt to belong together diatonically or to clash (Ex. 35).

Ex. 35

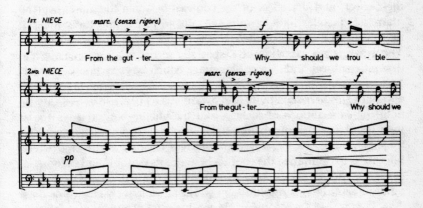

The successive ambiguity is much more explicit, however. The first A section shifts from C minor to D flat major, and this epitomizes the movement within the trio as a whole. Sometimes the shifts within phrases are of a semitone, at other times of a whole tone, as at the end where the final D flat major is arrived at by progression from E flat minor. But the uneasy oscillations of the harmony here are perfectly attuned to the troubled lyricism of the music. Britten's personal voice is perhaps at its clearest in such contexts, where economy of means is the dominant factor, rather than in moments of high drama and elaborate ensemble. Similar passages can be found in plenty in the later operas – the male narrator's superb description of the camp at night in *The Rape of Lucretia* and the ballad in the third scene of Act II in *Billy Budd*. But their effect, and the effect of the contrast between them and overtly dramatic episodes like Tarquinius' ride to Rome and the potential mutiny when Budd is executed, is never more powerful than in *Grimes*. The work is an assertion of a specially fertile association between dramatic subject and musical language which has remained valid for Britten ever since. The vulnerable protagonist is a failure as much on account of greater sensitivity and awareness as because of inability to fulfil the expectations of society, and the vulnerable tonal system is threatened, undermined by the sheer weight of chromatic tension. Yet tonality itself is not destroyed: it survives because Britten's deepest impulse is to dramatize the conflict between its diatonic and chromatic extremes, rather than portray an issue of that conflict. Hence the lack of totally unambiguous resolution in works as sensitively constructed as *Billy Budd* or the War Requiem. Normally the tonal outcome is perfectly explicit, though such explicitness can be given disturbing resonance, as at the end of the Hardy cycle, *Winter Words* (1953), where a bright D major supports an anguished cry for release from the burden of feeling.

It nevertheless seems unlikely that Britten has consciously sought to renew the diatonic-chromatic conflict in every work, or deliberately employed only such subjects and texts as show some concern with social outcasts. The strength of his music lies in the way his chosen language is used, and a symbolic association between sound and subject, however close, will not satisfy unless the sounds themselves are memorable. If it were not for this directly musical appeal, the deep pessimism which often rises to the surface would probably disturb and even disgust many more people than seems to be the case. For all its frequent allusions to Christian imagery, there is little positive hope in Britten's world: there is considerable beauty, and often the music which is involved in expressing fascination with corruption and loss of innocence – especially the operas *The Turn of the Screw* (1954) and *Death in Venice* (1973) and the song cycles *Winter Words* and *Who are these Children?* (1969) – is itself positively beautiful.

As a conservative committed principally to vocal music, Britten has been more skilful at adapting existing forms than in developing new ones: to this extent, the promise of the early choral variations was not fulfilled. He has produced two major works, the Spring Symphony (1949) and the War Requiem (1961), which are in a kind of expanded cantata form, but the latter is surely more genuinely symphonic in its use of a unifying, evolving musical argument, and not even the purely instrumental Cello Symphony (1963) has a more satisfying overall design. In the field of the song cycle for solo voice and orchestra or piano, Britten has favoured related themes or a varied selection from a single poet, rather than attempting to tell a story. English is the favoured language (though he has set French, Italian, Russian and German), images of night, corruption and death the obsessively recurring elements. Britten has achieved great intensity when linking the separate songs of a cycle together, as in the Nocturne (1958) and the *Songs and Proverbs of William Blake* (1965), and also by employing recurring thematic ideas, but the relative loss of continuity in those cycles where the songs are completely separate hardly produces any loss of coherence or expressive power, even when there is apparently no 'logical' scheme of tonal relationships within the cycle as a whole.

It is easy, in discussing Britten's operas, to relate their subject matter to the same central theme as that of the cycles and other vocal works. His main achievement has been to demonstrate both the inexhaustibility of the subject and the variety of ways in which it can be convincingly treated. Britten prefers material which has been created in another form by a great writer: Shakespeare, Maupassant, Melville, James and Mann are among his sources. Yet whether the source is a great writer or merely an efficient librettist, he has demonstrated the versatility of music drama in an age when lavish productions in large theatres have become less and less practicable. The majority of Britten's works for the theatre qualify as 'chamber operas' (in terms of the forces employed). This concern with economy was initially the result of attempting to launch performances of several operas by a new company in the early postwar period, but it has proved to have an attraction for the composer beyond the immediate practical necessity of the late 1940s. The first two such chamber operas – *The Rape of Lucretia* (1946) and *Albert*

Herring (1947) – were well contrasted, but they employ identical accompanying ensembles: thirteen players in all. Of similar dimensions are the arrangement of John Gay's *The Beggar's Opera* (1948) and the 'entertainment for young people', *The Little Sweep (Let's make an Opera)* of 1949. Specific commissions, for the Festival of Britain and the coronation of Queen Elizabeth II, led Britten back to the full-size opera house and larger orchestral forces, but here, too, there is a remarkable contrast between the claustrophobic world of *Billy Budd* (1951, revised 1960) and the ceremonial display of *Gloriana* (1953). The next opera, *The Turn of the Screw* (1954), with its accompaniment for chamber orchestra, its two-act structure and highly unified musical design, involving the linking of scenes by interludes which vary a twelve-note theme, represented another obvious reaction, and is the most clearly transitional of all Britten's major compositions, anticipating features of *Owen Wingrave* (1970) and *Death in Venice*. The explicit tensions between natural and supernatural forces, the inability of Good to conquer Evil, which are the essence of James's chilling ghost story, are paralleled by an increased concentration of musical procedures which focus more directly on diatonic/chromatic conflicts. It was nevertheless not until after his necessarily more expansive and relaxed version of *A Midsummer Night's Dream* (1960) that Britten moved consistently towards a musical language in which tonality could still exist without consistent triadic emphasis or clarification.

The three 'parables for church performance' – *Curlew River* (1964), *The Burning Fiery Furnace* (1966) and *The Prodigal Son* (1968) – represent the ultimate in dramatic stylization and musical compression. Though even the longest – the last – is only seventy-two minutes in duration, they are still more than negatively or residually operatic: distinct elements of aria and ensemble are still discernible, and gesture, regulated by principles derived from the Japanese theatre, makes an unusually strong contribution to the dramatic character of the parables. The sheer starkness of the music, framed by and in large part derived from Gregorian Chant, gives dramatic conviction to the unambiguously moral plot-material, yet prevents them from becoming mere sermons. Not surprisingly, the experience of writing these works for a select group of chosen artists, and his involvement in the preparation of their performances, left an indelible mark on Britten's two later operas, even though these revert to more universal dramatic subjects and forsake church for opera house. *Owen Wingrave* was in fact originally written for television, though staging in the theatre was always envisaged. The plot is an archetypal study of the destruction of the peaceful by the warlike, and Britten attempted what seems likely to be his most ambitious confrontation between twelve-note and tonal features, ending inevitably in a fading ambiguity rather than a grand, healing synthesis. The work is virtually twice the length of the single-act church parables, and at times the 'expanded austerity' of the writing seems to weaken both harmonic direction and dramatic power. Possibly it was consciousness of this which led Britten to give less prominence to quasi-serial elements in *Death in Venice*, though they are certainly still to be found, and as a result a more satisfying overall design can be sensed.[17] *Death in Venice* completes a return from the moralities dominated by religious thought and imagery to a thoroughly secular subject with a sexual element recalling similar undertones in *Peter Grimes* and *The Turn of the Screw*. We should be wary of suggesting that a circle has been completed, however, even though the tonality of A is central to all three operas. *Death in Venice* shows the extent to which Britten, for all his conservatism, has been able continuously to deepen and develop an idiom of the greatest communicative power. Yet what is communicated is, ultimately, a deep sense of insecurity. Even love leads to destruction, and it seems that tonality is clung to only because there is no imaginable existence without it. With Britten, one aspect of the contemporary crisis is expressed in remarkably direct form. The attempt to absorb manipulation of twelve-note thematic shapes into a tonal scheme has apparently failed to exorcise the one or permanently revivify the other. If, therefore, there is a future for tonality outside popular music, it is most likely to lie in the radical return to fundamentals touched on at the end of Chapter Ten.

Part Two

Twelve-note Music

Chapter 6

Arnold Schoenberg

On 7th December 1917, slightly less than two months after his forty-third birthday, Arnold Schoenberg (1874–1951) was finally discharged from the Austrian Army. His first period of military service had lasted from December 1915 until October 1916 and this second short spell had begun in September 1917. The disruption to his creative work was considerable. He was able to write the fourth of the Orchestral Songs Op. 22, in July 1916 (Nos. 1–3 had been composed while he was still in Berlin, between October 1913 and January 1915), but his main project during the war was the oratorio, *Die Jakobsleiter*. He completed the first draft of the text as early as January 1915 and began the music of Part One in June 1917, only to be interrupted by the second call-up three months later. Although he returned to the score as soon as his final discharge came through, and continued to work on it until 1922, the work was never finished. But for the wartime interruptions, the oratorio might stand – complete – as the most mighty and absorbing of transitional works. Certainly there is an element of tragedy in the picture of a genius at the height of his powers forced to let a major work languish while providing a potboiler like 'The Iron Brigade', the march for piano quintet which Schoenberg wrote for a 'festive evening' at his army camp in 1916. From his early years as an orchestrator of other men's operettas to his late years as a university teacher in America, Schoenberg suffered from the supreme frustration: the regular necessity to set his own work aside and perform other tasks in order to support his family. The sympathy for, and efforts on behalf of other composers in a similar plight which his letters reveal are therefore as understandable as his often extreme irritation and impatience with bureaucracy and officialdom in all forms. For Schoenberg, in life as in music, inflexible systems were anathema.

Perhaps the most fundamental of all Schoenberg's creative decisions had been taken ten years before the end of the war – though to describe it as a decision is to minimize the instinctive, impulsive forces at work when he found himself moving away from the traditional tonal techniques he had used so powerfully and imaginatively in works like *Verklärte Nacht, Pelleas und Melisande,* the First String Quartet and the First Chamber Symphony, composed between 1899 and 1908. All the later quibbling – it is still going on – about whether 'atonality' is possible or meaningful is really beside the point, for a situation had arisen in which tonal structures – the relationships between keys and between those types of harmony which had expressed them – no longer seemed to Schoenberg to represent the living language of music. There would be occasions when he chose to revive the traditional tonal structures themselves (e.g. the Suite for Strings of 1934) or when the nature of the material and its treatment in a twelve-note work might suggest that a single note or chord is being given 'tonal' emphasis (*Ode to Napoleon,* Piano Concerto). But the development and use of the twelve-note system was intended, in Schoenberg's own words, 'to replace the no longer applicable principle of tonality'. It established a new principle, and however much importance we may attach to those occasional tonal stresses and triadic harmonies which occur in Schoenberg's twelve-note works, we cannot demonstrate that they represent a continued commitment to the principle of tonality. At most they are references to elements associated with that principle – references usually justified by the closeness of texture and form to the texture and form of tonal works.

Schoenberg explained in a letter how, from about 1915 onwards, he was consciously seeking ways of founding musical forms 'on a unifying idea which produced not only all the other ideas, but regulated also their accompaniment and the chords, the "harmonies" '.[1] If this phrase is surprising, it is simply because he had already achieved such a technique in one of his early non-tonal compositions, the Piano Piece, Op. 11, No. 1 (1909), which, as many analysts have shown, uses a three-note cell to form both thematic motives and accompanying chords. This 'cellular serialism' was, in essence, the technique still being employed a decade later in the first four of the Piano Pieces, Op. 23. In Schoenberg's hands it is a technique of great subtlety and flexibility, which might seem to offer all the balance of unity and diversity which any composer could require. Yet Schoenberg ultimately saw it only as a step along the road to the true method: eventually, he came to feel that short motives should not function as background as well as foreground. Rather, the background should be provided by continually rotating cycles of all twelve chromatic semitones in an order (changing from piece to piece), which would probably have been suggested by a motivic or melodic shape shorter or longer than itself, but which would be to an extent independent of that shape and more capable of projecting and supporting a musical form of the most substantial proportions.

Schoenberg never expected this new method to provide a substitute for the harmonic functions of tonality; many years later he wrote of chord progressions in twelve-note music that 'as such progressions do not derive from roots, harmony is not under discussion and evaluation of structural functions cannot be considered. They are vertical projections of the basic set, or parts of it, and their combination is justified by its logic.'[2] But his musical inheritance and his creative instinct combined to convince him that while an underlying unity was a basic necessity, the diversity of a complex, extended form must be the ultimate goal of any worthwhile compositional technique. On the one hand he was content to be able to 'provide rules for almost everything': on the other his consciously assumed role as the composer of 'really new music which . . . rests on tradition' ensured that only when all twelve notes were given a precise position in a scheme could a form of sufficient power and range be generated. The result at times seems to involve a loss of both the visionary radicalism of the monodrama *Erwartung* (1909) and the elaborately moulded yet undoctrinaire total thematicism of the Piano Pieces, Op. 23, Nos. 1–4. Yet in certain late works (the String Trio for example) both virtues were regained: and Schoenberg was able to show not merely that the new method 'worked', but that he had achieved a new fluency, and a new integration of those traditional and structural textural elements by which he set such store.

The background material for a twelve-note composition comprises the forty-eight versions of the Basic Set: the original or prime version (P-o) and eleven transpositions of it; the inversion (I-o) and its eleven transpositions; and the reversals or retrogrades of all twenty-four. There is still some disagreement as to how this material can best be described, but the twelve-note composer has no choice but to accept that all this material is available. There are, however, no 'rules' which compel him to *use* all of it. Nor is he even compelled to accept the proposition that a twelve-note set is utterly different from a tonal scale, with all the notes of the former being treated with strict equality in contrast to the hierarchical features of the latter. The impulse to formulate the twelve-note method was undoubtedly provided by

Schoenberg's desire to organize the so-called 'total chromaticism' which was the natural product of the nineteenth century's increased emphasis on chromatic harmony. Yet simply because of the way Schoenberg himself composed (it was rather different, as we shall see, for Webern), any sense of the constant and absolute equality of every pitch is virtually ruled out – if not through specific melodic or harmonic emphasis then through the ways in which the twelve-note material itself is used. Such emphases in Schoenberg's music are not necessarily audible: but they are a result of accepting the fact that, of the forty-eight versions of a set, some will bear closer internal resemblances of pitch order than others, and if the form of the work involves hierarchical elements (distinctions between main and subsidiary themes, for example) it will be logical to treat the twelve-note material in a hierarchical manner also.

The practical implications of this can be followed easily enough in the succession of completely twelve-note works which Schoenberg finished in a remarkable five-year creative outburst between 1923 and 1928. There are two movements (the fifth piece of Op. 23 and the central Sonnet in the Serenade Op. 24) which are based simply on single, untransposed twelve-note sets, but in the first work to involve transpositions and inversions – the Piano Suite, Op. 25 (1921–3) – the sets employed are P-o, I-o, P-6, I-6 and their retrogrades. The choice of transpositions at the sixth semitone – the tritone – may seem the consequence of a desire to hint at 'tonic-dominant' relationships, and the occurrence of the tritone G/D flat in all four sets is a hierarchical feature which Schoenberg exploits in several places: see the inner *ostinato* at the start of the Intermezzo and, most obviously, the 'double drone' of the Musette (Ex. 36).

What is important here is not the actual occurrence of these 'common features' or 'invariants' within the composer's chosen forms of the set – the nature of the twelve-note system makes some such invariants inevitable – but Schoenberg's decision to use them. In the Piano Suite the invariants are rendered audible as emphases on specific pitches; in later works, even if single-pitch emphasis occurs, invariance will come to play more of a background role, through the exploitation of certain set-forms, usually in pairs.

The Piano Suite is also highly significant for its use of forms primarily associated with the baroque keyboard suite, and although the music is scarcely neo-classical in the Stravinskian sense, it shows that allusion to the textures of the past was no less important to Schoenberg. There is an expressionistic concentration and forcefulness to the music, nowhere more obvious than in the final Gigue. And when Schoenberg employs canonic imitation most explicitly (the Trio section of the Minuet) it is with strutting, sardonic effect. In several of these early twelve-note works he seems to be expressing savage mockery of his own

Ex. 36

capacity to employ such traditional textures as imitation and such traditional structures as sonata or rondo form. Some have even sensed a bitter admission of failure to develop completely new forms to explore all the potentialities of the new serial method and finally throw off the dead weight of the past. But this is to ignore the tremendous sense of creative liberation which the conjunction of serial technique and traditional structural background reveals. In four large-scale works: the Wind Quintet, Op. 26 (1924), the Suite Op. 29 (1926), the String Quartet No. 3, Op. 30 (1927) and the Variations for Orchestra, Op. 31 (1928), Schoenberg displayed a truly awesome fluency and a remarkable resourcefulness, not simply in using the new technique on a large scale, but in adapting forms originally developed during the tonal period to serve a very different function.

Ex. 37

As a group, these four works triumphantly affirm the central role of thematicism – it is only in the Wind Quintet that the composer's polyphonic dexterity, nourished by the medium itself, seems to have inhibited the generation of striking and colourful thematic material. In the Suite there is even a wittily projected series of serial variations on a simple tonal melody (Ännchen von Tharau). The result is perhaps heavy-handed as a piece of music, but it serves, even at its most incongruous, to prove Schoenberg's willingness not merely to write thematically, but to incorporate a very traditional kind of thematicism into a twelve-note texture. Such direct melodic ideas are more satisfyingly, more coherently found in the Third Quartet and the Variations, however. The Quartet starts with finely controlled lyric melody set off by dynamic accompanimental counterpoints, while the Variations are based on a twenty-four bar theme, mainly in the cellos, whose phraseology and rhythmic character are rooted in the romantic language of the fairly recent past (Ex. 37).

Given such a commitment to thematicism, decisions about form became decisions about thematic treatment. Since Schoenberg's tonal works had shown his ability to intensify and extend the role of developmental processes within the sonata-form scheme, it is fascinating to observe this skill in contexts where the underlying logic of tonal relationships has been replaced by the firm association between thematic ideas and certain versions of the basic set. As early as the first movement of the Wind Quintet, begun on 21st April 1923, Schoenberg had attempted a conventionally proportioned sonata design in which the relationship between exposition and recapitulation is as close (yet as subtly varied) as one would expect in a post-Brahmsian, tonal sonata-form movement. Schoenberg had not merely rejected athematicism: he had chosen to regard sonata form as valid in view of its overriding thematic connotations – valid even when the tonal system itself had been abandoned.

All the movements of the Quintet, the Suite and the Third Quartet establish associations with traditional form, ranging from the expanded binary design of the Gigue (finale of Op. 29) to the sonata rondo of the finale of the Third Quartet. The *precise* associations may be matters of argument – Schoenberg himself disliked the suggestion that the first movement of the Third Quartet was in a straightforward sonata form – but their essential dependence on the statement and elaboration of clearly defined thematic ideas cannot be denied. In many ways the finest and most ambitious of all these works is the large-scale Orchestral Variations (Op. 31), his first orchestral twelve-note work. The opportunity for relatively dense textures demanded a particularly skilful control of serial technique, and this makes one basic decision of the composer's, with regard to the twelve-note material, all the more fascinating. The theme itself comprises three set statements: P-0, RI-9 and R-0, and the two halves, or hexachords, of RI-9 have the same notes (in a different order) as the two hexachords of P-0; the one actual interval which is common to both their first hexachords is the tritone B flat/E, while in their second hexachords it is the tritone G/C sharp. Schoenberg is simply associating sets which have a significant permutational feature in common, something which establishes a degree of unity between them beyond the mechanical transpositional relationship of interval sequence. It is a similar technique to that of the Piano Suite, and its use can be traced in all the intervening compositions. Schoenberg had enjoyed himself as early as the first movement of the Wind Quintet with the 'punning' associations possible between transpositions closely related in the actual order of pitches, but the more far-reaching implications of such relationships took time to work out.

As far as the Variations for Orchestra is concerned, we can extend the area around P-0 and I-9 to include no fewer than six other sets containing that pivotal pair of tritones B flat/E and G/C sharp; these are P-3, P-6, P-9, I-0, I-3 and I-6. Schoenberg's compositional exploitation of their association is already evident in the introductory section of the work, where they predominate, and in the first three variations. Yet the whole work, while involving many rapid changes of set-form, is dominated, not simply by the theme, but by the theme *at its original pitch*. In view of the association of seven other sets around P-0, Schoenberg could have divided the forty-eight possible versions into three sub-groups of sixteen sets each, those sharing their pairs of tritones with P-0, or with P-1, or with P-2. Such comprehensive schematization might be felt to involve the creation of unreal distinctions, fundamentally different from the concept of a basic area which is departed from and returned to (the last thirteen bars of the Variations use only P-0 and its close associates). Nevertheless, Schoenberg did establish a principle for the combination or close association of sets and gave it its first full compositional statement in the same year as the Variations were completed, 1928. In the Piano Piece Op. 33a we have a form clearly derived from the classical sonata or ternary design, though the recapitulation is much compressed. We also have a fixed association between P-0 and I-5 which is grounded in the fact that their first hexachords together provide all twelve notes. This association is fixed and applies to all transpositions (P-1 with I-6, etc.). Schoenberg was to remain committed to it for the rest of his life.

Because of its brevity and simplicity Op. 33a provides a convenient summary both of Schoenberg's adaptation of traditional form and of his newly achieved technique of 'combinatoriality' (Milton Babbitt's term for the fixed-association technique). The ideas are not among the composer's most appealing, but the particularly clear differentiation between the main elements of the first and second thematic groups makes the form perceptible at a very early stage of audition.

As the first few bars show, 'combinatoriality' can involve the juxta-position of set pair as well as their combination. Each of the main subject groups is cast in a miniature ternary form of radically different proportions (first subject $2+7+2$ bars; second subject $5+2+2\frac{1}{2}$) and both have appendages, the first a two-bar transition and the second a four-bar codetta. In the whole of this $26\frac{1}{2}$-bar exposition, only P-0, I-5 and their retrogrades are used. The last thirteen bars of the piece are divisible into five bars of elaboration and eight and a half of recapitulation. The development concerns the chordal material of the first subject-group and 'modulates' away from the basic set-pair, employing P-2 and I-7 (bars $27-9$) and P-7 and I-0 with retrogrades (bars $29-32$). The abbreviated and varied reprise then restores the primacy of P-0 and I-5. The 'sonata-ness' of the piece is as much in the dramatic-lyric alternations as in any more precisely proportioned resemblances to the classical form. We shall see later how in his last String Quartet and the two concertos Schoenberg further refined the process of composing 'serial sonatas'. But his main concern during the period 1928 to 1932 – his last years in Europe – was with another long-established musical form: opera.

Schoenberg's first twelve-note vocal piece has already been mentioned in passing – the Sonnet which forms the fourth movement of the Serenade, Op. 24. In 1925 he composed two works for mixed choir, Four Pieces, Op. 27 and Three Satires, Op. 28. More than two years then elapsed until, in October 1928, he began the first twelve-note opera, *Von Heute auf Morgen* ('From one day to the next'), and that same month produced the first sketch for the text of *Moses und Aron*. From then until March 1932, when the composition of Act II of *Moses und Aron* was completed, he was absorbed by these musico-dramatic projects, though he did turn aside to write a further set of choral pieces, Op. 35, as well as two short instrumental compositions, the Piano Piece, Op. 33b (1931) and the Accompaniment to a Film Scene for orchestra, Op. 34 (1930).

This major shift of emphasis away from the purely instrumental works of the early twelve-note years confirms that Schoenberg was a creative artist whose ideas could not find complete expression in abstract musical forms. For all his resource in the handling of instru-mental designs, and for all his delight in the pedagogic explication of compositional techniques, his need to express ideas through words in the sceptical, often anti-emotional postwar era seems to have been even greater than his desire to express deep inner feelings through the medium of paint on canvas during the heyday of expressionism before the First World War. The attempt to marry a philosophical text and music in *Die Jakobsleiter* had met with frustration, but the 1925 choral pieces, in an obviously less ambitious way, provided an outlet which in turn revived the desire to undertake a more ambitious project. In 1926 Schoenberg completed the first version of his drama *Der biblische Weg*, which he described as 'a very up-to-date treatment . . . of the story of how the Jews became a people'. A further remark could equally well apply to *Moses und Aron:* 'It is highly dramatic . . . and, although its profundities offer the superior kind plenty of food for thought, is vivid and theatrical enough to fascinate the simpler sort.'³ Thus, although Schoenberg finally embraced the Jewish faith only in July 1933, shortly before his arrival in America, his preoccupation with the issues raised by his own race and religion was of crucial importance throughout the 1920s. The path from *Der biblische Weg* to *Moses* is clear. By contrast, *Von Heute auf Morgen* was a fuller working-out of the humorous side of Schoenberg's creative personality, which had already found clear and recent expression in the Satires and the 'Ännchen von Tharau' movement of the Suite Op. 29. The very title suggests another important link with the Satires and with Schoenberg's desire to argue that his own invention, the twelve-note technique, was no modish flash in the pan but a genuine, inescapable and irreversible step forward. His aim, and therefore that of his librettist 'Max Blonda' (alias his wife Gertrud), was 'to show, using everyday figures and goings-on, how . . . the merely modern, the fashionable, lives only "from one day to the next", from insecure hand to greedy mouth – in marriage, but at least equally in art, in politics, and in people's views about life'.⁴

The fifty-minute score, which was completed on New Year's Day 1929, may even be seen as a kind of comic parallel to *Erwartung*. As a case-history of a relationship – and most commentators agree that the plot must have originated in the Schoenbergs' own experience – it shows a particularly keen awareness of the importance which fantasy, role-playing and jealousy can take on even in a well-established marriage. The basic situation, the husband and wife returning home from a party where each has been attracted by someone else, develops into an attempt by the wife to 'win back' the interest of her husband, first by dressing up in an exotic costume, then by flirting over the telephone with her admirer from the party, a famous but fatuous operatic tenor. The husband is by now thoroughly resentful, and the wife, though she has agreed to meet the tenor in a nearby bar, senses that her victory is close. By transforming herself back into the attitude (and costume) of a submissive wife, and helped by the opportune appearance of their small child, she ensures a rapid reconciliation. The final stages of the opera begin with the arrival of the tenor and the woman to whom the husband had been attracted at the party. The married couple survive the mockery of the more liberated, 'fashionable' pair, and the opera ends with a cosy domestic scene at the breakfast table.

The psychological factor is especially evident in lines such as the wife's question to her husband, 'soll ich wieder ich sein?' ('shall I now be me again?') (bars 851–2). One way in which Schoenberg draws attention to it is to associate two linked statements – the wife's 'Man will doch schliesslich auch sein eignes Leben leben' ('can you never lead a life that is your own life?') (bars 294–300) and her later remark 'So will ich schliesslich doch mein eignes Leben leben' ('Thus shall I live at last a life that is my own life') (bars 493–9) – with broad, melodic statements of the opera's basic set (transposed). Yet the musical coherence of the work depends not only on such obvious thematic recurrences but also on the skilful characterization of individuals and situations in such a way that a balance is struck between tendencies to 'recitative' and tendencies to 'aria'. One authority has defined a 'formal scale of recitatives, ariosos and actual numbers', evidence that 'the organization ... can simply be called classical'.[5] In spite of the elaborate orchestration, there is very little purely orchestral music in the opera: the hectic momentum of the comedy requires absolute vocal dominance. Even with such exacting comic requirements, however, there are several moments of great lyric beauty, like the wife's confession of interest in the tenor (bars 177ff.) or, much later, the moment of reconciliation (bars 919ff.). Nor is rhythm uniformly complex from start to finish: waltz patterns and parodies of popular dances emerge from time to time, and the empty-headed tenor is deliciously characterized by simple scalic phrases (first heard in an imitation of him by the wife [bars 198ff.], but coming into their own with his 'appearance' on the telephone [bars 689ff.]. Appropriately a rapid semiquaver figure portraying the anger of the married couple is a clear derivative of the music associated with this potential threat to wedded bliss.

Schoenberg's pervasive contrapuntal dexterity can be found at such incidental moments as the brief four-in-one canon in the orchestra (bar 569) but canon plays a more explicit dramatic role in the couple's anger duet (bars 254ff.) and in the final ensemble for the four singers, ending with an amusing canon at the unison for the tenor and the other woman, which, no doubt intentionally, seems to lie too low for her and too high for him.

The ending is finely calculated to keep both sentimentality and seriousness at bay. Domestic harmony restored, the couple lapse into *Sprechgesang* in a context as different from *Pierrot Lunaire* as from the imminent *Moses und Aron*. The child has the last word, with the question 'Mama, was sind das, moderne Menschen?' ('Mummy, what's up-to-date people?'), and the last notes are a restrained yet luscious orchestral cadence, a true resolution of the earlier discord (Ex. 38).

Ex. 38

The composition of Acts I and II of *Moses und Aron* occupied Schoenberg from May 1930 to March 1932, but only a little of Act III was sketched at this time, and it was never finished. As late as 1950 the composer wrote, 'it is not entirely impossible that I should finish the third act within a year,' and shortly before his death he allowed that 'it is possible for the third act simply to be spoken, in case I cannot complete the composition.' 'Possible', but not essential; it now seems fairly generally agreed that the first two acts alone make a satisfying dramatic whole, whereas merely to speak the short surviving text of Act III would be more of an anti-climax than a consummation, though it may add something to one's appreciation of Acts I and II to know that Aaron is subsequently imprisoned by Moses, and falls dead at the moment of his release. Above all, the image at the end of Act II is surely the most intense and moving portrayal of a desolate and despairing heroic figure since Wagner completed the third act of *Die Walküre* in 1856. The parallels are far from exact, but the central characters are both shown in full realization of their own limitations, and the poignancy of Wotan's 'farewell' music is matched by the less resigned but equally eloquent arches of the superbly fashioned *tutti* violin line that supports Moses' final outburst: 'O Wort! Du Wort! Das mir fehlt!' ('O word, thou word that I lack!') Even if this parallel seems far-fetched, however, it is difficult to dispute Oliver Neighbour's conclusion that 'as the opera stands it says all that can be said in its own terms of man's predicament in face of the unknowable. It is both musically and dramatically complete. Indeed, it is hard to believe that Schoenberg did not know subconsciously, even when he planned it, that Act III is dramatically redundant.'[6]

It is this ending which also clinches the *musical* justification of Schoenberg's decision to make Moses primarily a speaker and only briefly, in Act I, Scene 2, a singer (conversely, Aaron is allowed one brief moment of speech). The philosophical or symbolic basis for this decision seems obvious enough, with the contrast and conflict between Moses and Aaron stemming from Moses' grasp of inner essence and Aaron's of outer representation. Aaron works miracles, while Moses lacks not merely the song but the words which will convey Divine Truth convincingly to all the people. The Tables of the Law stand in opposition to the Golden Calf, and at the end of Act II both are destroyed, yet it is Aaron whom the Israelites follow towards the Promised Land. To imagine a final scene in which Moses sang – even if he had sung throughout – is impossible; or rather, a scene in which he sang could not possibly convey the same degree of deprivation, the same conviction of impotence, isolation and failure. In that Moses' dominant mood is righteous anger (at Aaron's foolishness and at his own inability to prevent it), the heightened speech as notated by Schoenberg is entirely appropriate. But in practice it seems better for the performer to underplay the role: Moses is more convincing as a cold, even remote academic than as a demonic, apparently deranged dictator. Aaron is characterized by long melodic lines of great lyric power, the people by choral textures which may often be polyphonically complex yet which can achieve the direct simplicity of the canon which ends Act I. The orchestra is handled with sovereign virtuosity, most obviously in the wild rout during the Dance round the Golden

Calf, but such hectic elaboration is ultimately purged in the single melodic line which ends the work.

As a twelve-note composition the opera displays interesting hierarchical features. There is some disagreement about the pitch level of the 'real' P-0. Some favour that initiated by the first chord of the whole work (A/B flat/E etc.); others (notably Milton Babbitt) argue that it should start on C sharp, since this is the level at which it is first presented melodically, on Aaron's entrance in Act I, Scene 2.[7] As Babbitt notes, this is the only place in the opera where Schoenberg uses the succession of combinatorial relatives (P-0, I-3, R-0, RI-3), a process found at the start of instrumental works like the Variations for Orchestra, the Fourth String Quartet and the Piano Concerto, though here, for once, the combinatorial pair is not P-0 and I-5, but P-0 and I-3.

Babbitt's essay draws attention to other significant structural features; for example, the reason for beginning Act I, Scene 4 with the Inversion form on D is that this has a 'middle tetrachord' (F sharp/E/B flat/G sharp) in common with the set which ends Scene 3 – the Prime form on C. Of greater aural significance – especially in view of the increasing freedom of note-order within the hexachord in the later stages of the opera – are the larger thematic and textural recurrences at dramatically relevant points. Within Act I, Scene 2, the way in which a lower line of bars 148ff. achieves melodic prominence at bars 162ff. is a good example of the logical manner in which a scene may be structured around thematic recurrence (there is a third 'variation' at bar 187 and a fourth at bar 218).

By the last scene of the first act it is possible to claim that 'by-now-familiar musical materials or clear derivations from them are shaped into an intricate formal mosaic of cross-references to preceding events and within the scene itself.' Material from Scene 2 returns at bar 879 'and it is with this music in the orchestra that the scene closes.'[8]

In the first two scenes of Act II, Aaron's music again refers back to that of Act I, Scene 2, and there is a particularly significant relationship between the end of the long third scene (the Dance round the Golden Calf) and the very start of Act I. The interrelationships between the two acts and the sense in which the whole opera thematically elaborates premises stated in its early stages, are confirmed in the links between the first two scenes of Act I and the final scene of Act II. Conscious perceptions of the strong unifying factors at work in *Moses und Aron* may always be subservient to absorption in the sheer inevitability of the unfolding drama but with familiarity it comes to contribute substantially to an awareness of the superbly controlled intellectual basis of this richly expressive masterpiece.

One further resonance of Moses' defeat and dejection at the end of Act II is its parallel to the feelings of the Jewish people as Hitler came to power. Little more than a year and a half after the completion of Act II Schoenberg and his family arrived in New York, fortunate to have escaped but faced with the inevitable practical aftermath of such an upheaval. The need to earn a living as a teacher and the problems of finding a permanent post absorbed most of the composer's energies until, in 1936, he was established as a professor at the University of California in Los Angeles, and moved into the house at Brentwood Park where he would spend the rest of his life. Here at last he was able to make rapid progress with his first substantial twelve-note instrumental compositions since the Accompaniment to a Film Scene of 1930, the Violin Concerto, Op. 36, and the String Quartet No. 4, Op. 37.

The first work of any kind which Schoenberg completed in America was the five-movement Suite for Strings, a tonal composition intended for student orchestras, which follows on from the two 'concerto-arrangements' he had made in 1932–3: that for cello and orchestra deriving from a harpsichord concerto by G. M. Monn and that for string quartet and orchestra deriving from Handel's Concerto Grosso, Op. 6, No. 7. Like them, the Suite for Strings has points of contact with 'the old style'; the title on the manuscript is actually 'Suite im alten Stile.' Yet Schoenberg's avowedly didactic intention did not demand the mere imitation, much less parody, of an earlier manner. His primary purpose was practical: 'within a harmonic idiom conducive to modern feelings – and without, for the moment, putting students in jeopardy through the "poison of atonality" – I had here to prepare them for the modern technique of playing. . . . But hints of modern intonation, composition technique, counterpoint and phrase structure were also needed, if the student is gradually to acquire a sense that melody, to count as such, need not mean the kind of primitive symmetry, lack of variation and lack of development such as are the delight of the mediocre in every land and among all peoples; rather that here, too, there already exist higher forms, belonging not merely technically but spiritually and intellectually in a higher artistic category.'[9] Such thinking was likely to have been behind all Schoenberg's later non-twelve-note works, whether specifically 'educational', like the Theme and Variations for Wind Band (1942), or not, like the Variations for Organ (1941). Thus his confession that 'a longing to return to the older style was always vigorous in me' was not an admission of neo-classical tendencies, but an explanation of his delight in still occasionally demonstrating that worthwhile tonal compositions could exist alongside twelve-note ones – and share similar textural and structural features.

Schoenberg had composed the first movement of the Violin Concerto before the Suite in 1934, but the work was not finished for another two years, soon after the Fourth String Quartet. Dedicated to Webern, perhaps in response to Webern's dedication of his own Concerto for Nine Instruments, Op. 24, to Schoenberg on his sixtieth birthday, this is Schoenberg's first twelve-note concerto, though it is safe to say that in texture and thematic treatment it profits directly from the Handel and Monn adaptations. The Violin Concerto certainly confirms that, after a seven-year abstention from multi-movement, twelve-note, instrumental composition, Schoenberg was proposing to continue his commitment to traditional forms. Since 1927 the major technical development had been the establishment of the combinatorial relation, with all its consequences with regard to invariant factors within the set-group. The hierarchical employment of the set-group elements in the concerto is indicated by the structural pre-eminence of two sets, P-o and I-5, which are used throughout the first fifty-eight bars of the ninety-two-bar first section of the first movement. They are also present at the start of the finale and end both movements. Parallels with traditional harmonic processes extend further when we examine another pair of sets, P-7 and I-o. As Milton Babbitt has noted, P-7 'is that set which, by a traditionally tested and reasonable criterion of relatedness, carries the work away from the opening area to the most closely related area' (in bar 59). 'This transpositional relation may suggest a parallel with the dominant region of tonal "second subjects," but – be that pertinent or not – this particular transposed form . . . has a singular hexachordal relationship [to P-o] in that it preserves the greatest number of pitches (four) between corresponding hexachords of any set not in the initial complex.' It follows that this relatedness, whatever its associations with traditional tonic-dominant links, 'is determined completely by the . . . intervallic structure of the hexachords of the set'.[10]

The neatness of these tonal-serial parallels can create nothing but confusion if we proceed to assume that the composer intended identity rather than allusion. But all Schoenberg's twelve-note works show that there can be no true analogy between harmonically functional modulation and the change of transposition levels within a set group. Both processes involve departure, both predicate eventual return, but it has yet to be demonstrated that Schoenberg's decisions about when to change transposition levels and which level to move to at any given point were taken with reference to a major functional principle such as decisions about modulation in tonal music involve.

Those critical alike of Schoenberg's suppression of functional tonality and of his 'failure' to evolve completely new musical structures will use the Violin Concerto as evidence to support their case. Yet if the work presents problems of perception, it is less because of the absence of tonal coherence or traditional harmonic progression than because of Schoenberg's belief in the necessity for thematic evolution – the kind of thematic process to which he refers in his remarks on the Suite for Strings. This 'higher form' of melody can certainly be traced in the Violin Concerto. Yet it means that a stage of comprehension centred on the recognition of exact repetition of significant motives or melodic shapes is still a rather primitive one.

A similar situation exists in the Fourth String Quartet, and Anthony Payne's comments on the first movement deserve quoting at length. 'In the first movement . . . one can trace a surface resemblance to sonata or perhaps sonata rondo form, but at the same time appreciate Schoenberg's claim to have freed himself from traditional patterns. . . . This ground plan is firmly signposted by uncomplicated thematic statements, but it is belied by a feeling of continuous growth and development which is typical of Schoenberg's unrelenting temperament. These statements take up very little room, and for the rest of the time he continually devises new shapes and textures. Their evolution from the series ensures their motivic relevance and the rhythm guarantees a more audible unity, but the impression is of continual extension. It would certainly have been possible in theory to make the interludes more dependent thematically on the exposition, rather than solely on the series itself, but Schoenberg's temperament was always opposed to the obvious. If motivic relevance was guaranteed, why overemphasize by thematic reference as well?'[11]

Payne is describing the beginning of a change in Schoenberg's treatment of thematic processes and traditional forms, a change which might seem inevitable in view of the fundamental difference between the harmonic, tonal music from which his own technique ultimately derived, and the non-harmonic world of serial succession. In the String Trio written ten years after the Fourth Quartet, Schoenberg triumphantly unveiled a form – not wholly new, to be sure, but much less backward-looking than any of his earlier schemes – in which his thematic techniques could attain a new range and vitality. His least successful forms in the earlier works tend to be those in which the large-scale sonata scheme is diffused rather than integrated by the evolutionary process. Payne's criticism of the Violin Concerto's first movement has considerable validity: 'Schoenberg uses new material in the 'vivace' central section, but whereas the first of such episodes in the [fourth] quartet achieves a strong forward impulse through the rhythmic layout of the texture, the equivalent episode in the Concerto sounds static and freely episodic.'[12] Whatever the motivic links which result from the use of one basic set throughout, the *Vivace* seems too *thematically* independent of the exposition and varied recapitulation which enclose it. Thematic diversity (and recurrence) are given new purpose in the Trio by being freed from associations with tonally functional structures. Yet the Violin Concerto and Fourth Quartet are works of great sophistication and power. The perceptibility and preeminence of thematic working, which is not so severely evolutionary as to involve the apparent omission of obvious genetic parallels, can conveniently be studied in the shortest movement in either, the Largo of the quartet.

The underlying binary (ABAB) scheme naturally excludes the kind of 'separate development' involved in orthodox sonata form, and on first acquaintance the main fascination of the structure is likely to be on account of the almost 'recitative-aria' relationship of the two main ideas. Schoenberg himself referred to the five-bar unison theme with which the Largo opens as a 'recitative', the rhapsodic character of which is continued for a further ten bars of diverse comments which do not agree on any single thematic or textural way of continuing, or answering, the clear-cut lines of the recitative.[13] Instead, the indications 'ad libitum' and 'rubato' confirm the almost improvisatory, preludial quality of the music up to bar 629 (the bars of all four movements are numbered consecutively).

The second main idea of the movement begins at the *Poco adagio* (bar 630) and is described by Schoenberg as 'a cantabile melody, formulated in the form of a period, antecedent followed by a consequent, very simple and regular, comprising six measures.' (Ex. 39).

As the example shows, this, unlike the recitative, is not a twelve-note melody, not a single horizontal articulation of the basic set. It shares an ascending perfect fifth with the first part of the recitative theme, but in isolation the first bar and a half have an unmistakably 'tonal' cast, the C sharp cadence confirming the diatonic trend of the previous notes.

This tendency is undermined both by the melodic continuation and by the supporting parts, but the 'leading-note/tonic' associations of the phrase are an important aid to recognition in the process which follows. The rest of the first half of the movement (up to bar 663) is concerned with 'varied repetition', elaboration and development of the cantabile melody.

Ex. 39

The second half of the Largo begins with the unison Recitative in free inversion, but its 'rhapsodic continuation' is replaced by what Schoenberg rather unguardedly calls a 'modulatory elaboration'. The thematic content is, obviously enough, derived from the recapitulated recitative, using the same pair of sets: P-10 and I-3. The texture is fugal, with the 'answers' starting on the 'dominant' and inverting the subjects. After the climax of this 'insertion' the return of the second theme is prepared with the help of hints of the exposition's rhapsodic episode (e.g., compare first violin in bars 622 and 678).

The second theme itself returns on the same pitches as at its first appearance, but the continuation differs. 'The deviation from the first

Ex. 40

formulation of this part is far-reaching, because of the difference in purpose. The first time it served as a lyric contrast to the dramatic outbursts of the recitative, which it had to overcome by virtue of its intrinsic warmth. The second time, when the insertion of the [fugal] section has already reduced the tension of the beginning, its purpose is to prepare for an ending.'

The process whereby that purpose is achieved is summarized in Ex. 40. The richness of the elaboration, even in a relatively small-scale movement, is never such as to obliterate the first principles of the idea which is elaborated, and the movement as a whole is a striking example of that typically Schoenbergian blend of spontaneity and intensity, rhapsody and rigour, which is all the more gripping in view of the unambiguously romantic opening. The rhetoric of the recitative can seem disconcerting, but, as Schoenberg himself explained, it is the ideal foil for the rich restraint of the 'subordinate' theme.

The most remarkable feature of Schoenberg's last decade is the contrast between its two most important works, the Piano Concerto, Op. 42 (1942) and the String Trio, Op. 45 (1946). The concerto is the culmination of all that is most recreatively traditional in the composer's handling of twelve-note technique. The single-movement form comprises four distinct sections and to this extent recalls the one-movement schemes of forty years earlier, the First String Quartet and the First Chamber Symphony, though the concerto begins with an *Andante* rather than a hectic fast section. The concerto may initially make a rather more relaxed impression than any of Schoenberg's other twelve-note works, but the melodic breadth of its opening – a thirty-nine-bar theme in the solo instrument – is only one element. More dramatic material appears in the *Molto Allegro* (section two), provoking in turn a still more restrained *Adagio*. The work ends with an energetically good-humoured, rondo-like *Giocoso*, the main theme of the *Andante* reappearing not long before the end (bar 443).

The nature of the keyboard writing itself is strongly traditional in the Liszt-Brahms manner which Schoenberg never completely abandoned. Since this involves much octave doubling and figuration with a considerable amount of internal repetition, the links between the concerto and its nineteenth-century precursors are manifest enough. In all respects, however, it seems like an end rather than a beginning. The treatment of the material shows no loss of invention, but the nature of that opening theme is problematical. With its lilting rhythms and arpeggiated accompaniment it can sound dangerously sub-tonal – perhaps the initial perfect fourth is primarily responsible for this effect – or rather like an attempt to test just how close to traditional functions a twelve-note texture could approach. For some the result is an appealing *quasi-rapprochement*; for others, an uneasy compromise, in which the inevitable appearance of cycles of twelve notes seems to be curiously at variance with the musical impulse, and even to make what is fundamentally a purposeful tonal theme aimlessly atonal.

The concerto was written at a time when Schoenberg was much concerned with tonal composition. Not merely had he finished the

Second Chamber Symphony in 1939, returning to the score after a lapse of thirty years, but, as mentioned earlier, the Variations on a Recitative for Organ, Op. 40, and the Theme and Variations for Wind Band, Op. 43, are also highly chromatic, fundamentally tonal works. Even the twelve-note *Ode to Napoleon*, Op. 41 (1942), is freer in its use of the technique than any of the other late works, and introduces triadic harmonies for illustrative purposes, letting them emerge naturally from a texture – the instrumentation is for piano quintet – in which octave doublings and late romantic figuration are, if anything, even more prominent than in the Piano Concerto.

There is no evidence to suggest that Schoenberg was experiencing some kind of crisis of confidence in serialism as he approached his seventieth birthday. The works composed after the Piano Concerto are in general very different from those of the first American decade, but a change is not necessarily caused by a crisis. It would perhaps be surprising if the Piano Concerto did not reflect to some extent the degree of concern with tonal tradition that the other works of those years display; and as Schoenberg's last large-scale composition in a traditional form, its particularly involved stylistic relationship with the past is appropriate and intriguing. What we do not know is whether Schoenberg wrote nothing else on similar lines because of a sense that the concerto was a kind of conclusion – because of a positive decision not to pursue the kind of *rapprochement* the concerto adumbrates; or whether such thoughts never occurred to him. Certainly the String Trio seems to have owed its origin less to thought than to a particular physical experience: a heart attack, on 2nd August 1946, which almost killed him. The trio was begun only eighteen days later, and finished on 23rd September.

There is a danger of exaggerating the differences, of course. The trio is *not* everything which the concerto is not: it is not athematic, totally fragmented, utterly new in form. For a start, it too is in one continuous movement, with restatement of earlier material rounding the work off. The use of repetition within the five individual sections is the mark of pre-existing structural principles: so too the fundamental lyric-dramatic conflict, though both elements create strikingly new effects simply because of the nature of the thematic material itself. It is here that the contrast with the Piano Concerto is most apparent, for whereas the earlier work begins with ordered, serene melody, the trio starts out in a state of virtual incoherence, searching for thematic stability through a hail of instrumental effects. The trio does not lack melody:

passages in the First Episode and in Part Two are as melodious as anything in Schoenberg; yet these passages occur, not in places pre-scribed by predetermined structural moulds, but simply where they are most appropriate for the continuously unfolding lyric-dramatic conflict in which the work is rooted, as in Ex. 41, from Part Two.

Ex. 41

It is the long-term continuity of the sonata scheme which the trio has most obviously abandoned, but its own short-term confrontations do not add up to an incoherent sequence of arbitrary juxtapositions. There is still a thematic process at work, variation ultimately rounded off by selective recapitulation in the final Part. The trio is not proposing a fully-fledged 'alternative' to the sonata design rejected after the vale-diction of the Piano Concerto, but it does represent a decisive break with some of the most fundamental features of all essentially tonal forms. The twelve-note combinatorial factor is present: but the serial process itself is still in no sense the primary determinant of the form. The new flexibility of thematic evolution is reflected in the reorderings of the set which are brought into play, and the residually hierarchical principle whereby the combinatorial pair, P-o and I-5, return in the closing stages is still employed. But Schoenberg's thematicism is never the slave of prearranged serial schemes and ultimately it is the enlargement of the whole issue of unity and variety in essentially thematic terms which makes the trio so fascinating.

The same concentrated expressive range and structural fluidity recur in Schoenberg's last instrumental work, the Phantasy for Violin with Piano Accompaniment, Op. 47 (1949). The purely timbral tension between the two instruments ensures that in some respects this seems even more the ultimate recreation of Schoenberg's early expressionist impulse than the String Trio. Yet here, too, pure melody (the *Lento*, bars 40–51) can emerge as a powerful contrast to – and a clear thematic relative of – the vehement framing material. As in the trio, the last of the Phantasy's five sections is a varied recapitulation – here, exclusively of first section material. But internal repetitions in the other sections are still a primary factor in ensuring audible coherence.

Schoenberg also wrote some vocal music in his last years. *The Ode to Napoleon*, a setting of Byron's diatribe against tyranny, was a powerful enough war-time gesture, but in many respects *A Survivor from Warsaw*, Op. 46 (1947), for which Schoenberg provided his own text, is more immediate, more economical and more moving. The last pieces of all, a *De Profundis* and a *Modern Psalm* (the latter unfinished), are religious. Schoenberg was, above all, a man of strong beliefs. His long struggle with external circumstances may at times lead us to believe that internally all was certainty and security. Yet the twelve-note method itself is an objectification of tension, a law not to eliminate destructive chaos but to control and filter high emotion. Schoenberg's deeply serious sense of the need to advance without losing touch with the past is of incalculable importance. He rejected revolution yet provided the means whereby music could move away from its most instinctively satisfying element, the sense of key. To some, this is as serious as the loss of oxygen; others have easily adapted to life on other planets, to breathing air which is wholly the creation of our time, but which will survive beyond it.

Chapter 7

Alban Berg

Alban Berg (1885–1935) became a pupil of Schoenberg's in 1904, and developed over the next decade into a composer whose differences from his teacher were of the greatest significance. His first opera, *Wozzeck*, was begun before the end of the First World War, Berg adapting his own libretto from Büchner's play, and it occupied him until 1922: it was first performed, with great success, in Berlin in 1925. On one level it continues the progress away from the Wagnerian heroics begun by Richard Strauss in *Salome* and *Elektra*. Wagner's last music drama dealt with Parsifal, the saviour in spotless armour, the fool who became wise. Wozzeck is a fool who goes mad, a common soldier who saves no one but kills his mistress and, apparently, commits suicide. The three acts together are shorter than the first act of *Parsifal*. The contrast would be complete if Berg had adopted the kind of musical approach which emerged later in the 1920s, in the more determinedly anti-romantic operas of Hindemith and Weill. But the justification for showing so much squalor and brutality is nothing less than the evocation of pity and compassion in the audience. Wozzeck's fate is held up as an object for the observer not merely to contemplate but to regret, and throughout the work, though most specifically in the final orchestral interlude of Act III, the composer expresses his own deep compassion for this pathetic protagonist, driven to self-destruction. This flamboyant gesture has been much criticized, and the musical means by which it is achieved – a build-up to a twelve-note chord which then resolves into a D minor perfect cadence, and the use of overtly Mahlerian material (borrowed from Berg's unfinished symphony) suggests that Berg was involved to a point where it seemed essential to invest the character of Wozzeck with heroic as well as tragic qualities. Nevertheless, in the theatre such extravagance seems all of a piece with the musical attitudes expressed throughout; the final interlude is no arbitrary imposition, but a gesture calculated to ensure that the opera achieves an expressive climax with a sense of revelation: *lux facta est*, but for the audience, not for Wozzeck. In any case, a degree of objectivity is restored in the last scene of all, at the point where sentimentality could overflow and swamp the entire enterprise (did Berg know *Madam Butterfly*, with its embarrassing, climactic use of a child?). The closing scene accurately depicts the vulnerability of the orphan, seen playing with other children when the discovery of his mother's body is announced, without underlining his poor prospects (a contrast here with the end of Debussy's *Pelléas* and its gloomy prognostication: 'C'est au tour de la pauvre petite'). Characteristically, Berg combines resolution – the strings playing soft fifths, G and D, in cadential fashion – with a chordal *ostinato* which decorates and clouds the finality of the ending. Like the much more melodramatic *tremolando* at the end of Act I, this illustrates that balancing of conflicting tendencies which Berg could control so skilfully. In *Wozzeck* the effect is not to suggest that the work is in some kind of 'super-G', but that its fundamental atonality can in fact resolve on to a harmonic entity containing an interval recognizably more 'final' than others. George Perle[1] has identified what he calls a 'primary referential chord' in the opera, consisting of the notes F, G, A, B, C sharp and D (i.e. the second of the *ostinato* chords at the end of the work combined with the cadential G and D), and the possibility obviously exists for the work to resolve, with the F, A and C sharp as 'appoggiaturas', on to a G major triad. In spite of the earlier move into D minor, such a triad would seem an immeasurably crude contradiction of the essentially atonal tensions of the work. Berg goes as far towards it as is consistent with those tensions; so there is a hint of 'tonality' within the actual atonality, a sense of cadence within the undifferentiated *ostinato*.

In *Wozzeck* the intensely 'expressionistic' atmosphere is in fact rooted in clearly defined forms. Act I has five character pieces: Suite, Rhapsody, Military March and Lullaby, Passacaglia, and Rondo; Act II is a Symphony in five movements, and Act III comprises six Inventions, on a theme, a note (B), a rhythm, a six-note chord, a key (D minor) and a constant quaver movement. With such a sequence of relatively short scenes, it may be thought that the internal structure of each could be left free; provided that some sense of overall unity was achieved, contrast between the scenes themselves would easily be established. Yet Berg needed to pass such explosive, grotesque, tragic events through a severely structured formal process. It is difficult to argue that the forms are satisfying in their own right; their justification lies in the way they enable Berg to project the expressive and dramatic content of the opera without lapsing into incoherence. We may not perceive the background structure at all: we do perceive the coherence and fundamental logic to which it gives rise. For all its formidable complexity, *Wozzeck* has the directness and clarity of all great drama.

In his next major work, Berg again constructed an elaborate framework which involved the treatment of traditional schemes in new ways. The Chamber Concerto for piano, violin and thirteen wind instruments (1925) lasts for nearly forty minutes, and its purpose – a fiftieth-birthday present for Schoenberg – demanded something special in intellectual content. Expressively – which is to say, in this context, thematically – the concerto lacks the immediate appeal of the later Lyric Suite and Violin Concerto. What it has in abundance, apart from purely technical virtuosity, is dramatic excitement, for all the carefully plotted symmetries of its design. It shows awareness of the new twelve-note technique without itself being serial, and on the rhythmic level alone is undeniably more elaborately organized than anything by Schoenberg himself.[2]

The first movement is simultaneously a three-part theme with five variations and a sonata design with double exposition, the whole preceded by a five-bar motto which 'translates' the names of Berg (horn), Schoenberg (piano) and Webern (violin) (Ex. 42).

Ex. 42

The second exposition of the theme, which doubles as Variation 1, is for piano solo. Variation 2 ('development' in the sonata scheme) is in Berg's favourite slow waltz time, and deals with the three thematic elements in reverse order (the elements themselves appear in retrograde). Variation 3 continues the development by introducing inversion, the thematic elements now restored to their original sequence; Variation 4, inevitably, uses retrograde inversion. This apparently strict proto-serial organization does not, however, determine every detail of the complex texture: for example, it is possible for a 'prime' version of Schoenberg's motive to appear in the course of the fourth variation combined with its own inversion (bars 166–9). Variation 5 restores the tempo of the original statement of the theme, and can therefore be regarded in sonata-form terms as a free recapitulation. The thematic elements also reappear in their original order, and the variation ends with the soft entry of the violin signalling the start of the *Adagio*.

Each half of the second movement is in three main sections, with the central part of each half further divisible into three, and three times the length of each of those that flank it: thus the five distinct segments of the first half number 30, 12, 36, 12 and 30 bars. This symmetry is further reinforced by the fact that the second half is a free retrograde of the first. (The whole *Adagio* actually contains the same number of bars as the first movement: 240.)

The violin begins the movement with a twelve-note phrase of characteristically stifled intensity, but perhaps the most prominent thematic idea – only freely derived from the Berg-Schoenberg-Webern motto – is presented at the start of the central episode (bar 283). It is restated later in augmentation (bar 303) and, later still, in inversion (bar 314). One final symmetrical feature of the *Adagio* is that the third main section of the first half inverts the material of the first main section. It may have been the experience of composing this movement (apart from anything else, it is totally chromatic), which led Berg away from such severely predetermined practices when he did actually adopt twelve-note technique. The exploitation of such techniques in twelve-note music was more systematically pursued by Webern, in contexts where the contrapuntal essence of mirror symmetries could be more explicitly revealed.

The finale of the Chamber Concerto is a suitably complex blend of sonata and rondo schemes, incorporating thematic features from both previous movements and containing a total of 480 bars, the same as the first two movements put together. The grand total for the whole work is therefore 960.

An even more personal numerical obsession – with the number 23 – finds expression in Berg's next major work, the Lyric Suite for string quartet (1926). Five of its six movements have totals of bars which are multiples of 23: 69 in the first, with the second thematic group beginning in bar 23; 69-23-46 in the third; 69 in the fourth, 460 in the fifth and 46 in the sixth. Tempi may also be related, as with the crotchet 69 principal tempo of the fourth movement, the dotted crotchet 115 of the fifth, and the alternation between crotchet 69 and crotchet 46 in the finale.

Though conceived in homage to Schoenberg, the Chamber Concerto does not, apparently, quote directly from his music. The Lyric Suite is dedicated to Schoenberg's brother-in-law and friend Alexander von Zemlinsky (1872–1942), and the fourth movement contains brief quotations of a theme from his Lyric Symphony, while the sixth movement introduces Wagner's *Tristan* chord-progression (bars 26–7). The Suite is a partially twelve-note work (Berg had first used the method in his second setting of 'Schliesse mir die Augen beide', of 1925); there is no direct evidence that the basic set was consciously derived from either the Zemlinsky or the Wagner quotation, though interestingly enough the Zemlinsky fragment does employ a five-note segment of the whole-tone scale plus an added note (the initial B flat), thereby recalling the 'primary referential chord' of *Wozzeck* (not to mention the main motive of the Op. 3 String Quartet of 1910). It also contains the tritone-plus-major-third unit which can be seen as a permutation of the whole-tone motive, and the same unit also appears within the *Tristan* chord itself (Ex. 43).

Ex. 43

Such speculative associations do not determine the constitution of the twelve-note material, however, and the fourth movement, which contains the Zemlinsky quotations, is not twelve-note at all. (The first and last movements, the outer sections of the third and the *tenebroso* sections of the fifth are the explicitly serial parts.) Each movement employs an intensification of the speed and atmosphere of a predecessor, to form two interlocking 'trichords', thus:

1 Allegretto giovale

         2 Andante amoroso

3 Allegro misterioso
   (Trio estatico)

         4 Adagio appassionato

5 Presto delirando

         6 Largo desolato

While it may well be true that Berg was anxious to employ less grandiose symphonic structures than in the Chamber Concerto, the decision to write the suite could have been the result of this characteristically all-inclusive pattern rather than the result of an initial desire to compose shorter movements in a more heterogeneous relationship.

Ex. 44

The twelve-note set employed in the first movement takes three different forms (Ex. 44). The most rudimentary is that of two scalar hexachords a tritone apart. This makes an easily audible appearance at the ends of both parts of the movement (bars 33–5; 67–8). Next there is an arrangement in two 'cycles' of fifths, which provide the chords in the first bar (a device which foreshadows the arpeggiated opening of the Violin Concerto), and lastly the 'thematic' arrangement of the same hexachords into two all-interval sequences, the second relating as R-6 to the P-0 of the first. Much has been made of the differences between Berg's technique here (and of the substitution processes which provide the new sets for later twelve-note passages in the suite) and the 'orthodox' methods of Schoenberg and Webern, who are supposed normally to employ the same order of notes in the set throughout an entire composition. Of course the difference is aurally striking in the first movement, because of the fifths and scales which are employed: but flexible order within the hexachord was something which had been part of twelve-note practice from the beginning. So it is the way in which such derived orderings are used which is significant, not the simple fact of their existence. In Berg's case they lead away from strict twelve-note practice altogether, until in *Lulu*, 'the texture in general is not dependent on serial procedures but on the assumption of a pervasive harmonic atmosphere based on the preferential employment of certain sonorities, a harmonic background that exists prior to any given series just as the triadic texture of traditional tonality exists prior to any given melodic detail. With Schoenberg and Webern it is the set that presumably determines the harmonic texture, but in *Lulu* a large number of different sets are integrated by virtue of their common dependence on a given harmonic background.'[3]

Such a development is certainly inferable from the partial serialism of the Lyric Suite, but the way in which the work continues Berg's involvement with traditional formal design is probably more important to the listener than its showing an 'experimental' attitude to twelve-note technique. In broad terms the work may not be as ambitiously symphonic as the Chamber Concerto, but its reduced reliance on symmetry and its conflation of development and recapitulation show no loss of confidence, and a welcome gain in clarity. With Berg, there is always the suspicion that personal, programmatic factors override abstract considerations. For example, is not the final *Largo* meant to be a kind of farewell to the musical world of *Wozzeck*, with its approaches to triads of G major or minor and its dissolving coda, another invention on a continuous quaver movement? If so, the farewell to *Wozzeck* is also a farewell to Wagner, though the *Tristan* quotation could have arisen quite fortuitously, since the cello's B flat, A, F (bar 26), which prompt it, constitute the first segment of the movement's basic set (I-5 version). Purely on the level of compositional technique, however, a detailed comparison of the two halves of the first movement – exposition and varied recapitulation – will show just how vital the presence of clearly defined thematic identities remains. Most of the later movements involve substantial amounts of easily perceptible recapitulation, in keeping with their predominantly ternary structures, but only in the third movement, when the repeat of the *Allegro misterioso* is a retrograde of the original, is there anything the least mechanical about the process.

The freest forms and the most intense emotional expression are found in the fourth and sixth movements – those involving the Zemlinsky and Wagner quotations. Perhaps at this stage the way was still open for Berg to move into much more flexible structures in which thematic development and repetition would have played as little part as 'orthodox' twelve-note technique. In reality, however, Berg's last purely instrumental composition was to show more positive reliance on traditionally structured thematic process, filtered through a personal serialism, than that found in the Lyric Suite. Nothing of emotional immediacy is lost in the Violin Concerto, and the overall form is the most satisfying Berg ever achieved.

Berg's next composition after the Lyric Suite was written when he had already begun work on his second opera, *Lulu*. *Der Wein* (May–August 1929), a 'concert aria' for soprano or tenor and orchestra, is a setting of three of Baudelaire's poems in German versions by Stefan George. The entire work has a ternary form, since Part Three (bars 173–216) is a varied recapitulation of Part One (bars 1–87), and the central episode is itself tripartite, the third section (bars 141–172) retrograding the second (bars 112–141). In purely technical terms *Der Wein* qualifies as Berg's first wholly twelve-note work of any substance, but it also confirms his own very personal attitude to the technique, which is developed here with new consistency and confidence.

The basic set itself, like that of the Lyric Suite, has unmistakably tonal associations, so that even if it and its close relatives were used consistently throughout it would be possible to create the effect of a chromatically coloured D minor wherever this was desired. The opening seven bars do just this, employing set forms which share the trichord D, E (or E flat) and F to justify the *ostinato* bass parts (bass clarinet, double bassoon, harp). Berg used invariance in the first movement of the Lyric Suite.[4] In addition, however, as we have seen, he altered the order of pitches within the hexachord to produce specific effects – fifths and scales – though not to underline any potential tonal feeling. In *Der Wein* the reorderings of the basic set and the creation of four subsidiary sets or 'tropes' have the purpose of ensuring the presence of 'a particular kind of tonally-orientated, all-pervasive harmonic and melodic atmosphere'.[5] Such 'development' of the set *itself*, independently of the treatment of material deriving from it, remains an essential part of Berg's serial technique, and the main difference between his and Webern's. (Schoenberg's later use of free ordering within the hexachord and of derived sets, in the String Trio for example, is also a significant acceptance of the value of 'troping'.) It raises one issue: if Berg wanted to write tonally-centred, highly dramatic music in traditional forms, why did he bother with twelve-note factors at all? The answer which the music gives is that he seemed to need both aspects – the partially twelve-note to justify the partially tonal and vice versa – just as in *Wozzeck* the wild emotion needed the strict formal basis. His manipulations of an already tonally-oriented basic set provided a systematically controlled diversification of the properties of that set: three of the four derived tropes of *Der Wein* are less tonally explicit than the original set. So although traditional harmonic elements are admitted – the 'dominant' A major triad at the start of Part Two (bar 89) for example – they are never allowed to cohere in the way they would in a traditionally tonal texture.

There are no quotations of pre-existent tonal material in *Der Wein*, though the presence of an alto saxophone and the prominence of 'tango' rhythm reflect Berg's interest in the sound of popular dance music, already heard in *Wozzeck* and to achieve new importance in *Lulu*. *Der Wein* demands rather less vocal and instrumental virtuosity than any other work of Berg's maturity, and its main value for him may have been to clarify processes which he would elaborate in the new opera. This relative simplicity helps to reveal its character as a late example of the romantic orchestral song, and the underlying D minor creates associations not only with the final interlude in *Wozzeck* but with Schoenberg's sequence of D minor works of twenty years before *(Verklärte Nacht, Pelleas und Melisande,* the First String Quartet). Since, as Willi Reich notes, Berg liked to regard Lulu as 'the female counterpart' of Don Juan, we might almost expect D-minorish tendencies to be carried over into the opera, in homage to Mozart. Yet the relative tonal neutrality of Berg's largest work hints at the possibility that more explicit tonal emphasis of other than a temporary, local kind was only possible for him in simpler contexts, or where there were strongly external compulsions, as there would be again with the Violin Concerto. The hexachords of the basic set of *Lulu* can be reshaped to provide scale segments in B flat major and (with one gap) A or E major, but these relationships are hardly of great structural importance in the opera. As with *Der Wein*, the basic set functions as the source of new twelve-note sequences by means of various selection processes – for instance, the top, middle and bottom lines of a four-chord sequence, or a collection of every fifth or seventh note. Certain thematic elements may have a tonal or even pentatonic flavour, but this is always against a highly chromatic background. Hierarchies of various kinds determine the structure of *Lulu* but there is no overall dominance of a single note comparable to the D of *Der Wein* or the G and B flat of the Violin Concerto.

It is easy to link the subject matter of *Lulu* – the progressive degradation of a prostitute and her victims, ending when she herself becomes a victim (of Jack the Ripper) – with that of *Wozzeck*, and to postulate on Berg's part an unhealthy fascination with such matters, which is itself symptomatic of a decadent cultural epoch. Lulu can be placed alongside Salome, Elektra and Turandot in the gallery of twentieth-century operatic female sadists, who stand for everything that the pure romantic heroine would find unspeakable. Even if the essential point of Wedekind's original plays is held to be that Lulu's lovers are the villains, since she merely becomes what they want her to become, and they, through guilt, will their own destruction, it is difficult to see the work as a simple moral tract urging the virtues of a stable home life and marital fidelity. *Lulu* is not in the least concerned with the more traditionally romantic conflict between nobility and evil, but with honest intensity of experience versus the postures of assumed feeling. The brief final eulogy of the Lesbian Countess Geschwitz over the dead Lulu is moving (and justified), not because any heroic status is claimed for Lulu herself, but because Geschwitz, dying as the prostitute's last sacrificial victim, has been true to true feelings. Her love for Lulu is genuine, and that is what matters, not whether it is 'unnatural' by conventional standards.

'Instrumental' forms still play a part of major importance (and of dramatic appropriateness) in the design, though the structure is less tightly governed by an externally imposed scheme than that of *Wozzeck*. Much of the second and third scenes of Act I, concerning Lulu's conquest of Dr Schön, is organized as a sonata, 'exposed' and repeated in Scene 2 (bars 533–668), developed and recapitulated in Scene 3 (bars 1209–355). The Sonata is preceded, and interrupted, by smaller structural units, some of them vocal character-pieces (Canzonetta, Arioso) and some dance forms (ragtime, 'English waltz') in a design naturally broader, more diverse than that demanded by the concentrated, self-contained sequence of dramatic events in *Wozzeck*. Berg also uses less obviously pre-existent structures where the dramatic design dictates: most notably in the section in Act I Scene 2, after the Sonata exposition, called 'Monoritmica' (bars 669–957). Though most of the prominent thematic motives of the act appear, the basic material is a four-unit rhythm which in the first half of the section (culminating in the painter's suicide) is progressively accelerated: quaver 84, 92, 100, 108, 120, 132, crotchet 76, 86, 96, 106, 118, 132, minim 76, 86, 96, 112, 132 (up to bar 842); the pace is then gradually slackened (though the music is not otherwise palindromic), reaching crotchet 42 (=quaver 84) again at around bar 956.

There are several important correspondences between the first two acts: in Act I Dr Schön replaces the painter as Lulu's husband; in Act II it is Schön's son Alwa, who replaces his father (shot by Lulu). In Act I the most substantial structure – associated with Schön – is the Sonata; in Act II it is a Rondo, which is divided into two main sections (bars 243–336; 1001–96), representing Alwa's 'conquest' of his father's murderer. In Act I the Sonata was interrupted by the Monoritmica and a sequence of other short forms culminating in a palindromic Sextet (bars 1177–208). In Act II the two Rondo sections are divided by Dr Schön's 'aria in five verses', which is itself interrupted by Lulu's song, and by other segments, notably the 'Film Music' interlude (bars 656–718), which, as a palindrome, is an equivalent to the Act I Sextet.

Now that Act III of the opera, so long suppressed, has been edited by Friedrich Cerha, and the score made available, it will at last be possible to begin serious study of the work as a whole. For many years, performances in the theatre ended with the brief extracts from Act III which Berg himself orchestrated for inclusion in the 'Lulu' Symphony. That the work could be such a success on stage even in its incomplete form is some measure of the remarkable affinity between music and 'drama'. For all its complexity, Berg's music communicates through an essentially *thematic* coherence, which establishes the individual characters and also determines the structural process of the work. The brilliantly evocative musical stage-craft, employing every device from melodrama to coloratura, even more than the canons, chorales and variations which make up so much of the musical substructure, confirm that Berg was no mere sensationalist, using a lurid subject to ensure a *succès de scandale*, but a deeply serious composer able to expose motivations and manias undreamed of – or *only* dreamed of – in the world of pre-Freudian romanticism.

The Violin Concerto is a piece of instrumental coloratura organized with all Berg's scrupulous concern with structural proportion. The explicitly tonal or triadic harmonic possibilities of the set (Ex. 45i) render the exploitation of ambiguities all the more necessary, of course.

The prospect of a crowning progression, on the lines of the following (using R-o) was not what induced Berg to use such a set (Ex. 45ii).

Ex. 45

As the end of the concerto shows (Ex. 45iii), it was more satisfying and appropriate to contrive a cadence in which a whole-tone chord (interpretable as a substitute for the 'true' dominant of F major) resolves on to a major triad in one plane, while contradictory whole-tone ascents and descents establish a note (G) which is the added sixth of the 'tonic' triad of B flat, and which, in view of the importance attached to it throughout the work, leaves a doubt in the listener's mind as to whether this may not be a 'true' tonic. In tonal terms Berg may simply have been recalling the final chord of Mahler's *Das Lied von der Erde*, making a double memorial out of this Requiem. In twelve-note terms he was providing the perfect example of how tension between hierarchical features in a set group need not actually achieve explicitly diatonic resolution in order to provide a satisfying ending.

It was on 22nd April 1935 that the eighteen-year-old Manon Gropius died, and the short score of the concerto was finished three months later, on 23rd July. Five months later again, on Christmas Eve, Berg himself was dead, at the same age as Mahler when he died in 1911.

The concerto is a testament, conveniently precise and personal. The form, while substantially different from that of Berg's earlier concerto, shows a similar capacity for the reshaping of traditional schemes: two movements, each in two parts, the slower parts *(Andante* and *Adagio)* enclosing the faster ones *(Allegretto* and *Allegro)* in a shape whose intensifying progression recalls the plan of the Lyric Suite. The *Andante* is a seven-sectioned arch. The introduction anticipates the set in the open-string arpeggios (it also foreshadows the conflict of B flat and G). The three main sections (including a bridge passage) have distinct thematic ideas, the last, as centre of the arch, being the most extended. The bridge is recapitulated in shortened inversion and the remaining sections are abbreviated. The *Allegretto* is another arch form and the first section is itself a miniature arch. The whole movement has a light, dancelike character which modulates into exquisite nostalgia, with the quotation of the triadic folk song just before the coda.

The most violent part of the concerto embodies the greatest extremes. The *Allegro* is a gigantic cadenza, but at the moment when we might expect the most improvisatory elements to dominate, Berg introduces a four-part canon to provoke the return of the opening music of the movement, creating the main climax and completing a ternary shape.

The ternary form of the concluding *Adagio* comprises the introduction and initial statement of the Bach chorale 'Es ist genug', whose whole-tone opening coincides with the last four notes of the basic set; a middle section of three variations (bars 158–213) with a central climax and reminders of the folk tune in its final stages; and a coda (bars 214–30) with a final statement of the whole chorale tune extended by just two bars to achieve the concluding, ambiguous cadence already discussed.

It is typical of Berg that in bar 222 of the coda the instructions 'religioso' and 'amoroso' should appear simultaneously. Other composers after Berg would attempt to evoke essentially Mahlerian moods. Other serialists have continued to explore conjunctions with tonal forms and late romantic expression; but none have equalled Berg's achievement. His expressive extravagance never seems excessive simply because it was moulded and controlled by one of the most skilled musical architects of the age. He established a new tension between freedom and rigour, between volatile romantic expression and strict, often symmetrical structures, the erection of traditionally derived, all-embracing formal schemes acting as a framework and a discipline for material which might otherwise have run riot. Berg's consciousness of the past was as great as Stravinsky's, but his use of quotation and allusion is scarcely neo-classical in spirit. Rather it is post-romantic – the personal memory, the personal nostalgia breaking through the ordered surface which the new techniques imposed as a necessary basis for coherence.

Chapter 8

Anton Webern

'About 1911 I wrote the Bagatelles for String Quartet (Op. 9), all very short pieces, lasting a couple of minutes – perhaps the shortest music so far. Here I had the feeling, "When all twelve notes have gone by, the piece is over".... In my sketchbook I wrote out the chromatic scale and crossed off the individual notes. Why? Because I had convinced myself, "This note has been there already".... The inner ear decided quite rightly that the man who wrote. out the chromatic scale and crossed off individual notes *was no fool*.... In short, a rule of law emerged; until all twelve notes have occurred, none of them may occur again.'[1]

The series of lectures which Anton Webern (1883–1945) gave in Vienna in 1932 and 1933 have survived through the shorthand notes of one of the audience. They present a fascinating picture of a composer wholly convinced of the intuitive rightness of Schoenberg's formulation of twelve-note technique because, as the quotation shows, it matched his own experience completely. Webern himself may have seemed even less obviously predestined to initiate radical innovation than his master. His family background was that of the minor aristocracy, and as a student he specialized in musicology, editing Part Two of Heinrich Isaac's *Choralis Constantinus* (published in the monumental *Denkmäler der Tonkunst in Österreich* in 1909). Those compositions which survive from the period before he began to study with Schoenberg in 1904 – including a good many songs, a ballad for voice and large orchestra called *Siegfrieds Schwert* and *Im Sommerwind*, an Idyll for large orchestra – are naturally enough strongly influenced by the great German late romantics, but from the single-movement String Quartet of 1905 onwards the effect of Schoenberg's teaching – and of Schoenberg's own music – can clearly be felt. The impression made by Schoenberg was of incalculable importance: on the one hand, without his guidance and example it is difficult to believe that Webern would ever have found his way forward as a composer; on the other, Schoenberg's own personality was so strong as to preclude direct imitation: if a pupil had genuine talent and a personality of his own, he would survive and prosper. The differences between the two are indeed profound: but in spite of Webern's less obvious reliance on links with classical and romantic forms and thematic processes he was just as deeply (perhaps more deeply) involved in the reinterpretation of traditional concepts, notably of the way in which unity may be expressed through the use of contrapuntal textures and symmetrical forms. In Webern's own words, 'We want to say "in a quite new way" what has been said before'.[2]

It was natural that Webern should remain closely associated with Schoenberg long after ceasing to be a pupil, and long after establishing that compressed, fragmented style so different from Schoenberg's own. His acceptance of atonality was complete and total – he could see little point in retaining any links at all with something 'really dead'. Yet atonality as such was not a 'law' and the quotation at the head of this chapter shows Webern's own later realization of how the law had been anticipated – necessarily – for it could not have emerged simultaneously with atonality but only through a gradual exploration of atonality. Webern never claimed that he either anticipated or prompted Schoenberg's discoveries. In the lectures he describes visiting Schoenberg 'in the spring of 1917 – Schoenberg lived in the Gloriettegasse at the time, and I lived quite near – I went to see him one fine morning, to tell him I had read in some newspaper where a few groceries were to be had. In fact I disturbed him with this, and he explained to me that he was "on the way to something quite new". He didn't tell me more at the time, and I racked my brains – "For goodness' sake, whatever can it be?"'[3]

During the next six years (1918–23) Webern worked on a succession of vocal compositions, completing the three sets of songs Opp. 13, 14 and 15. These pieces employ a wide-ranging, rhythmically flexible vocal line, with a supporting instrumental texture which occasionally performs an accompanimental function but which more often presents thematic figures of its own. This is contrapuntal music, but it is only in the last song of Op. 15, a double canon *in motu contrario*, that traditional imitative techniques of the kind on which Webern was to rely so heavily in his twelve-note music are found.

Op. 15, No. 5 is rather atypical in another respect, too, for the vocal line employs narrower intervals and simpler rhythms than those of most of the other songs of this period: the opening texture recalls that of the baroque chorale-prelude. Yet neither this nor its successor, the Five

Canons, Op. 16 (1924) for high soprano, clarinet and bass clarinet, are actually twelve-note. None of the vocal phrases present a succession of the twelve chromatic semitones, and most of them contain prominent pitch repetitions (e.g. the Gs in bars 2 and 4). There is also little of that internal motivic repetition (of three or four-note cells) within individual lines, which Webern's methods of set construction made so important in later years. The prominence of the interval of the major third in both main parts at the start may nevertheless reflect that conscious concern with unity which Webern was to explore so creatively through the twelve-note technique, and the pairs of canonic parts both have the same specific pitches in common – a kind of invariance which Webern was to carry over into his combinations of twelve-note sets.

One curiosity about this canon is the change in the interval of imitation between the accompanying parts in bar 7, where the flute's major sixth (bar 6) is answered by a minor sixth (trumpet, bar 7). This must be simply to avoid too E-majorish an atmosphere, which the ear might detect if an E instead of an F were to support the E, F sharp, G sharp ascent in harp and clarinet. The point is significant because it shows that Webern was perfectly prepared to sacrifice strict exactness. He was never a blindly dogmatic composer, imprisoned by laws imposed from outside. Rather, he came to believe that the twelve-note technique was the result of an inevitable historical process which ensured that 'one composes as before – but on the basis of the series'.

We have already seen that in the early months of 1923 Schoenberg was using the new method on quite a large scale – he began the Wind Quintet in April. Webern's instinct led him to try out the technique on his own naturally smaller scale, and the years 1924 and 1925 were largely experimental, the forty-year-old composer seeking ways in which to move naturally from his freely atonal technique to the new twelve-note method. In one sense the distance was small. If we look at one of the 1922 songs – Op. 15, No. 4, for example – we find that the vocal line begins with a twelve-note statement: yet in the remaining phrases internal repetitions seem to have become more and more significant, and the accompanying parts contain prominent repetitions (the B flats and A flats in bars 1 and 2). So this is still a case of all twelve notes being kept freely in play, of the avoidance of tonal tendencies, rather than of the use of a consistent ordering of the notes. We may feel that all twelve notes are more or less equal in importance, but the 'law' whereby they are employed is indefinable save in terms of instinctive rightness. A comparison between this and a simple example of

Webern's early use of the twelve-note method itself is therefore highly instructive. In the autumn of 1924 he composed his Kinderstück for piano solo, the only completed piece from a projected cycle for young players. This seventeen-bar miniature presents six successive statements of a twelve-note set which, while having none of the internal symmetries so characteristic of his mature sets, reveals a significant interest in the interval of the minor second. As a composition this piece is little more than a doodle. Yet it displays a simple progressive form (rather than a ternary or binary shape) which moves from sober to skittish rhythms, from a single line (with typically wide intervals) to a five-note chord at the start of the final set statement. The dynamic range is narrow – between *pp* and *mp* – but a variety of registers is used, only one note, B flat, appearing in the same octave on all six occasions.

Of much greater musical interest are the Three Traditional Rhymes, Op. 17, for voice, violin (viola), clarinet and bass clarinet of the same year (1924) and the Three Songs, Op. 18, for voice, E flat clarinet and guitar of 1925. In particular, Op. 17, Nos 2 and 3 display a virtuosity in the handling of one untransposed, uninverted, unretrograded twelve-note set, which proves just how eagerly and naturally Webern responded to Schoenberg's discoveries. There are no dramatic differences in style and texture between these songs and their immediate non-twelve-note predecessors, and Webern already shows that the twelve-note successions can be submerged into the phrase rhythms of the music rather than mechanically determining those rhythms. There are twenty-three statements of P-0 in the twenty-two bars of Op. 17, No. 2, the longest of which is the first (two bars), the shortest the fifteenth (one beat – the second of bar 15). Here the accompanying trio of instruments share each set statement with the voice in the exact order of notes, so to this extent the piece is a more accurate forerunner of Webern's mature technique than Op. 17, No. 3, where the voice has its own independent twelve-note successions and the instruments supply the missing notes for each phrase in a freer overall ordering (the song actually starts with note 7).

Webern gradually expanded his serial technique to include inversions and retrogrades of the basic set (Op. 18, Nos 2 and 3) and then, in the Two Songs for Mixed Chorus Op. 19 (1926), transpositions of prime and inversion at the sixth semitone (the tritone) – the same transposition level as Schoenberg had used in his first fully twelve-note work, the Piano Suite, Op. 25. These Choral Songs, settings of short poems by Goethe, bring to an end the long series of vocal works which had occupied Webern for more than a decade. Already in 1925 he had composed two short instrumental pieces – the binary-form *Klavierstück im tempo eines Menuetts,* and a movement for String Trio. Both use single untransposed sets – the piano piece nineteen times, the trio thirty-five times (three of the statements are incomplete). Of themselves they are of only minor significance, though the Trio movement turns out to be a preliminary study for Webern's first substantial instrumental twelve-note work, the String Trio, Op. 20 (1927), which is also the first of that remarkable succession of instrumental compositions which dominated the remainder of his output. There were to be more vocal works, too, but the all-important problem of form could only be confronted in instrumental terms: in tackling it, Webern was to achieve one of the most remarkable renovations of traditional modes of thought in the entire history of music.

The discovery of Webern's sketchbooks has yielded the interesting fact that his first three mature twelve-note instrumental compositions – the Trio, the Symphony, Op. 21, and the Quartet for violin, clarinet, tenor saxophone and piano, Op. 22 – were all planned as three-movement works, yet all ended up with only two. This has helped to point up the apparent differences between the kind of overall form which satisfied Webern and Schoenberg. Webern presumably studied Schoenberg's serial works with close attention, yet of his own early essays in the method, only the Piano Piece of 1925, which suggests a knowledge of Schoenberg's Piano Suite of the previous year, has much stylistically in common with the music of the master.

The String Trio is rather a different matter. When Webern came to write it, in the summer of 1927, Schoenberg had completed his first two large-scale twelve-note instrumental works, the Wind Quintet (finished August 1924) and the Suite, Op. 29 (finished May 1926), and he was to finish the Third String Quartet during that same year (it was first performed on 19th September). These compositions demonstrate in the clearest possible way Schoenberg's own commitment to forms and, to some extent, textures, relating quite closely to those of the tonal, thematic music of the classic and romantic periods. Of course Webern himself had a far less impressive early tonal *oeuvre* than Schoenberg, and his only wholly successful early instrumental work to use key relationships was a passacaglia, not a sonata movement. Webern may have sensed that what made Schoenberg's serial-sonata structures appropriate was the type of material invented and the manner of its employment, elements seen in fully-realized form in the remarkable first movement of the Third Quartet, where the second main theme, in particular, has a romantic expansiveness quite foreign to Webern's manner, however intense the lyric atmosphere of some of his songs. Even if more of Webern's forms involve some kind of background relationship with sonata schemes than is often perceived, his instrumental textures tend to employ, or aspire to the condition of, canon, as the most logical way of ensuring the equal distribution of thematic material between all the parts. In general the material is motivic, just as the sets from which it is drawn are subdivisible into units of similar interval-content; the texture is contrapuntal with only rare examples of a melodic line with subordinate accompaniment; and the form likewise will be clearly subdivisible into stages which are most likely to observe the basic symmetry of a ternary form and, on occasion, to invite comparison with sonata or other traditional designs as well.

The trio is the work in which Webern comes closest to a structural basis similar to one of Schoenberg's. Yet even here a Rondo form comes first, and a sonata form second. As the relatively large scale requires, Webern for the first time uses more than a single transposition of his set: in the first movement eighteen of the available forty-eight are employed. Analogies with tonal process are pursued to the extent that the restatement of the principal rondo material in the exposition (bars 16–21) uses the same group of sets as the first statement (bars 4–10), while the entire recapitulation (bars 44–65) repeats the set sequence of the exposition. None of these repetitions is exact with regard to rhythm, register or instrumentation, however, so that in a context where melodic continuity is less evident than motivic interplay, variation becomes the principal structural feature. The music is skilfully shaped on a larger scale by effects like the unmistakable climax (bars 38–40) at the end of the central episode and the carefully balanced contrasts of the tripartite outer sections, leading in the later stages to the neatly engineered cello cadence (F/E, bars 59–60, repeated bar 61), which helps to focus the ear on a fundamental thematic interval.

The rondo contains fifty-four successive set statements: twenty in each of the outer sections, fourteen in the middle. The sonata-form finale is longer and more complex, not least because from bar 40 onwards Webern starts to use two sets in combination. He marks off the various sections of his exposition by tempo modification and rhythmic contrast, while the second subject (violin, bars 41–4) has the phrase of greatest melodic continuity, which is echoed later by the cello (bars 51–4). The exposition is marked for repetition, and is carefully differentiated from the start of the development, yet the very nature of Webern's material tends to invalidate the presence of a *separate* development: motivic interplay (violin, cello, violin, viola from bar 84 onwards, for example) is obvious enough, but in general the constant process of variation overrides the broader structural divisions which grew up in classical music under the pressure of the need for tonal conflict as well as thematic manipulation. There is, however, a full, and fully varied, recapitulation (in terms of sets it starts in bar 115, in terms of structure in bar 118), the first fourteen sets of which are the same as those of the exposition, but which diverges after bar 136, during the transition to the second group.

The Trio is a *tour-de force*, of concentration and flexibility. Yet in comparison with Webern's later works it might seem that the contrapuntal impulse has been inhibited by the use of extended rondo and sonata forms. In the Symphony, Op. 21 (1928), a less hectic atmosphere prevails: all is lucidity and symmetry, and in choosing the most resonant of classical titles Webern stressed the extent to which it could still be relevant to a work in which only certain fundamental structural principles remain valid. Since he now fully understood the principles of serialism, and how he personally could use them to his own satisfaction, he could attempt a far-reaching reinterpretation of the principles of symphonic composition. If tonal symphonic organization was rooted in the concept of hierarchy, for Webern 'considerations of symmetry, regularity are now to the fore, as against the emphasis formerly laid on the principal intervals – dominant, subdominant, mediant, etc. For this reason the middle of the octave – the diminished fifth – is now important. For the rest one works as before. The original form and pitch of the row occupy a position akin to that of the "main key" in earlier music; the recapitulation will naturally return to it. We end "in the same key!" This analogy with earlier formal construction is quite consciously fostered; here we find the path that will lead us again to extended forms.'[4]

The forms used in the two movements of the symphony may not be very 'extended' but each displays a very high degree of symmetry. The useful analytical summaries of the movements provided by Leland Smith[5] reveal groundplans which approach the exactly palindromic, and in his choice of set-types and set-forms Webern demonstrates a concern, not merely with unity, which is unavoidable, but with *similarity*. The symmetrical nature of the basic set of the symphony ensures that P-o and R-6 are identical, thereby reducing the number of set-forms available from forty-eight to twenty-four. The fact that the last interval of the set is an inversion of the first is used as a means of linking set-statements (e.g. P-o to I-3 and I-o to P-9), and the combination of P-o and I-o at the start of the first movement reveals a strong degree of similarity, four of the six pairs of notes being identical in both, though in a different order. Yet the so-called 'precompositional operations' of Webern's later music never amount to merely working out those relationships which would provide the maximum degree of symmetry. If that were the case we would simply be confronted with a predictable succession of palindromes, in which the second half is an exact mirror of the first. Such easy obviousness could not be expected to appeal to a composer of such motivic concentration and subtlety as Webern, for it would in effect eliminate the sense of constantly evolving variation which his best movements possess: 'mirror reflection' is merely exact, unvaried repetition in reverse. So even in the ninety-nine-bar second movement of the symphony, with a theme, seven variations and a coda, and a chain of set forms which goes into reverse at bar 50, comparison soon shows that Variation 5 is a variant of Variation 3, not an exact retrograde of it, and so on. Both movements display a masterly control of the tension between underlying symmetry and continuous evolutionary change. In both there is the return to the set forms from which the movement started out, but this degree of parallelism serves purely as a basis against which the foreground variants are composed. And the more intense, the more dependent on inversion and retrograde the local motivic interplay in a Webern movement becomes, the more important it is that the overall form of the movement, while logical and well-proportioned, should not be naively predictable or obviously pre-determined.

The symphony is important also for its refined and imaginative use of instrumental colour. This was Webern's first work for more than a few instruments since the Orchestral Songs of the First World War period. From now on subtlety of motivic argument can scarcely ever be separated from delicate shading of instrumental timbre: indeed, it was from the intimate relationship between the two that the possibility of serializing timbre was born.

Just as the form of the first movement of Op. 21 implies a strong musical reference to baroque binary form, so that of the first movement of the Saxophone Quartet, Op. 22, 'displays a very real relation to the early classical sonata'.[6] Just as the symphony movement focuses on the tritone A-E flat, so this stresses F sharp-C – a fact Webern is careful to draw early aural attention to by the repetitions in bars 3 and 4. Such apparently hierarchical processes create coherence without ever suggesting even the kind of tonal centrality which some of Schoenberg's twelve-note works imply – the focal notes are never associated with any diatonic relatives.

Webern was to pursue the association between canon and sonata further in later works, but the rondo-type second movement of Op. 22 (the first to be composed) is more in the nature of a glance back at the first movement of the String Trio. Whereas in the first movement of the quartet C and F sharp act as foci without actually beginning or ending any of the sets employed, in the second they initiate and end the movement with appropriate emphasis – an emphasis aided by the combination of P and I set forms at the same transposition level.

It has already been noted that in the Two Songs for Mixed Chorus, Op. 19 (1926), where Webern for the first time employed transpositions of P-0 and I-0, he selected P-6 and I-6, the same level as Schoenberg in the Piano Suite. When Webern returned to vocal composition in the Three Songs, Op. 23 (1933–4) – a return which was in fact a return to composition of any kind, since the Quartet, Op. 22, had been completed three years earlier – he adopted the same grouping of sets: P-0, P-6, I-0, I-6 and their retrogrades.

For the first time, Webern set texts by Hildegard Jone, and all the vocal works of his last decade used her verse. Webern had first met her in 1926 and she and her sculptor husband Josef Humplik became, as Webern's letters to them show, greatly valued friends. The mystical imagery yet simple syntax of the poetry make it an acquired taste, but its appeal for Webern must have lain precisely in the intense simplicity, which is closely akin to the spirit of his music. As Webern wrote to Hildegard Jone in August 1928: 'I understand the word "Art" as meaning the faculty of presenting a thought in the clearest, simplest form, that is, the most "graspable" form. . . . That's why I have never understood the meaning of "classical", "romantic" and the rest, and I have never placed myself in opposition to the masters of the past but have always tried to do just like them: to say what it is given me to say with the utmost clarity.' (Letter 4.)[7]

It was nevertheless not until 1930 that Webern confessed to Frau Jone that 'ever since I have known your writings the idea has never left me of setting something to music' (Letter 17), and three more years elapsed before he was able to report: 'I have been working well. One of your texts is already done. . . . How deeply they touch me. And I am happy to have arrived at this position at last (of making a composition on your words). I have wished for it so long.' (Letter 33.) In September 1933, Webern seemed convinced that the two songs he had composed 'shall remain alone *in themselves* for a while at least. Musically they combine to form a *whole*, in the sense that they constitute a certain antithesis.' (Letter 35.) But on 6th January 1934 he announced that work on a third setting – 'Das dunkle Herz' – had begun, and this, completed in March, became the first of the three published Op. 23 songs. Webern wrote that 'it has got quite long, and in its musical form it is really a kind of "aria", consisting of a slow section, and a faster one ... which nevertheless bears the tempo indication "ganz ruhig".... After a great upsweep in the first part, there is suddenly quiet, peace, simplicity.' (Letter 43.)

The refined allusiveness of 'Das dunkle Herz' is reflected in music of appropriate subtlety and economy. Both parts preserve their initial time signature throughout, and the first treats its basic metre more flexibly than the second (see bars 19 and 22, where triplet patterns are superimposed though even here the primary accent of each bar is preserved). The lyric nature of the vocal line is such as to ensure the subordination of obvious motivic correspondences in the broader sweep of phrases, which evolve in a natural, unforced manner, confirming the spontaneity of Webern's response to his chosen texts.

The vocal line has its own succession of twelve-note sets, but these are not wholly independent of the parallel successions in the piano, which may on occasion 'borrow' a note from the voice or lend one to it. When such interchangeability coincides with the overlapping function – the last note of one set statement acting simultaneously as the first note of the next – intriguing situations arise which must have given the ingenious composer great pleasure. Thus in bar 9 of the first song, the D in the voice part is, primarily, the fifth note in the voice's own complete statement of RI-6; but it also 'completes' the piano's statement of RI-0 and initiates (without being repeated) the next set in the piano part, P-0. Similarly, the C sharp in the voice part on the first beat of bar 33 has a triple function: as note 3 of I-0 (voice), note 11 of R-6 (piano: note 12 is the simultaneously sounded G sharp) and note 1 of R-0, the next set in the piano part! Such interchangeability is reinforced at the end of the song, when the voice with its last note completes the piano's RI-6, leaving the piano to complete the last set begun by the voice, RI-0.

Simultaneously with the Op. 23 Songs, Webern worked on a new instrumental piece, the Concerto for Nine Instruments, Op. 24, which was dedicated to Schoenberg for his sixtieth birthday in September 1934, and here there is a greater sense of his delight in using similarities of interval and pitch order between different transpositions of his basic set, a delight which continues to determine the type of material employed without ever imposing a strictly symmetrical organization on the work. Thus although the concerto's basic material could theoretically be divided equally into those sets whose hexachords contain the same pitches, variously ordered, as those of P-o and I-o respectively, the succession of sets used in the individual sections indicates no desire to exploit such alternations in any systematic way. Similarity is used to great punning effect in the last section of the finale, however, when P-6, RI-1 and R-o (later P-o), all of which share the same four trichords in different orders, are brought together as a kind of 'tonic' group for a free recapitulation of the first section of the movement.

The simplest of Webern's late works is the set of Three Songs, Op. 25, for high voice and piano (1934–5), his last composition for the medium. It was on 9th July 1934 that Webern first mentioned to Hildegard Jone that he was working on the first of the songs, 'Wie bin ich froh.' After the completion of the Concerto, Op. 24, he tackled 'Sterne, Ihr silbernen Bienen,' which was to come third in the final cycle, and reported its completion on 17th October 1934. The final (second) song, 'Des Herzens Purpurvogel,' 'will soon be finished,' he wrote on 9th November.

Ex. 46

While not abandoning the wide intervals so common in earlier cycles, these songs have a directness and clarity which make them particularly attractive. The first and third (the first two in order of composition) use only two set-forms and their retrogrades – P-o and I-2: the last note of P-o, G, is the same as the first note of RI-2, a double function shown by the actual doubling of the note between voice and piano in bar 2 of the first song (Ex. 46).

This is also a good example of what we might term 'anti-combinatorial' technique: not the simultaneous statement of two sets with complementary hexachordal content, but two simultaneous statements of the *same* set-form, RI-2. Such *quasi*-heterophony is unusual in Webern, but actual doublings are frequent enough (cf. bar 11) to suggest that he had no inhibitions about making positive use of them. The third song of Op. 25 has a different sequence of P-0 and I-2, making sophisticated use of Webern's favourite technique of double-functioning; for example, the B flat and C in the vocal line in bars 15 and 16 are the ninth and tenth notes of the voice's statement of RI-2, but the accompaniment is also using RI-2 at this point and simply 'borrows' the two notes without stating them independently.

The middle song of the Op. 25 cycle uses P-5, I-7 and their retrogrades: the same relationship as between P-0 and I-2, but transposed by five semitones. Even here, therefore, there is an underlying symmetry in the cycle as a whole and the return to the original area in the third song is enhanced by the way in which, after the first two notes, the first vocal phrase uses the same notes, at the same register, as that of the first song, though with different rhythm and accompaniment.

In the immediacy and delicacy of their response to the imagery of the text, these songs represent an important element in Webern's later manner, which was to achieve its fullest expression in his last completed work, the Cantata No. 2, Op. 31. Yet he also remained fascinated by the issues involved in achieving a purely instrumental structure which would allow the contrapuntal nature of his material, and the particular properties of the set-forms to which that material gave rise to find the fullest and most coherent expression. One of the most concentrated, extreme results of this process can be found in the second movement of the Variations for piano, Op. 27 (1936), which has received a great deal of attention from analysts on account of the high degree of invariance which it displays – an invariance which anticipates the development of a stricter, more comprehensive serialism, particularly as applied to the register of pitches.

This twenty-two-bar movement is, in effect, a rhythmic 'monody', a succession of single notes with a few pairs of chords as the only 'harmonic' events. Each half of the movement is marked for repetition, and both halves are very similar. Each contains two pairs of sets, one each for the right and left hands of the performer. The four pairs are chosen because they either begin or end with G sharp or B flat. In the first part of the movement it will be observed that eleven pitches always appear in the same octave position. The exception, E flat, occurs in two different octaves, and Example 47 shows that there must be two E flats if the registral pattern is to be inversionally symmetrical around the pivotal A natural.

Ex. 47

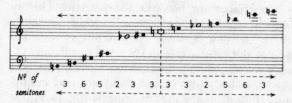

| Nº of semitones | 3 | 6 | 5 | 2 | 3 | 3 | 3 | 3 | 2 | 5 | 6 | 3 |

The pivotal nature of the As and E flats is reinforced by the fact that in all four pairs of sets A coincides with A and E flat with E flat; furthermore, in all four pairs of sets B flat coincides with G sharp, C sharp with F, G with B, E with D, F sharp with C.

All this information might lead one to expect a totally predetermined piece, which is 'set in motion' rather than composed. That it is not is the reason for its particular relevance in a set of variations. The same pairs of notes appear in each of the four pairs of sets: but they never appear in the same order. So, while it is perfectly true that the order is determined by the composer to the extent that he devised this particular set and chose this actual sequence of pairs for this movement, the order of events is aurally unpredictable. The composer's own variation technique is also brought into play in respect of the three-note chords: there are two of these in each pair of sets (four in each half of the movement) and since they always combine and juxtapose different pairs of pitches the surrounding context is kept as flexible as is consistent with the clear characterization of the individual cells and groups by rhythm, dynamics and phrasing as well as register.

This technique derives from that used in the first movement of the Symphony, Op. 21, but Webern never constructed an entire work in this way. As far as the Variations for piano is concerned, certainly, the larger outer movements are more relaxed, and the complete difference in character between the first movement of the symphony and the second of the variations is evidence enough that Webern did not reserve the registrally symmetrical substructure for a particular type of movement. He apparently did not believe that it should achieve the status of a principle, as all-determining and as sophisticated as the pitch-set itself.

The Variations is a fascinating work, yet the String Quartet, Op. 28 (1938), is an altogether finer achievement, meriting the closest study. In the late vocal works, a new lyric expressiveness emerges even in the most concentrated movements, and this quality is also evident in the refined intensity of the quartet, for all its variety of timbre and severity of motivic working. More important, however, the quartet is a highly dramatic, and ultimately symphonic, conception, in which Webern's preoccupation with the tension between symmetry and variation reaches its most complex and satisfying stage.

In essence the work consists of three movements, each tripartite in form, and based on a set which is also tripartite: three versions of the same four-note motive (B [B flat], A, C, H [B natural]). The process of variation is already at work within the basic set: if we chose to analyse the work in terms of a four-note set, the twelve-note prime form (P-o) would consist of P-o, I-5 and P-8. Equally basic to the conception of the work, therefore, are the degrees of similarity between certain transpositions of the set, which reduce the number of possible versions from forty-eight to twenty-four, while also proposing their own continuation or succession. In the first respect, P-o is identical with RI-9, which means it is possible to discuss the set-forms employed exclusively as either P or I forms with their retrogrades; in the second respect, the last 'tetrachord' of P-o can be deployed simultaneously as the first of P-8 – an extension of the kind of overlapping used so often by Webern. Or the last dyad of P-o can be the first of P-10 (not forgetting that the last note of all can be the first of P-9). Moreover, if we pursue the question of overlapping by four notes, and place P-8 alongside P-o,

Ex. 48

we see that while the first tetrachord of the former is identical with the third of the latter, the second tetrachord of P-8 is a retrograde of the first of P-o, and the third of P-8 retrogrades the second of P-o – a high degree of invariance in which P-4 also shares (Ex. 48).

Slightly less close, but more significant in the actual composition of the quartet, is the relationship between sets three semitones apart, e.g. P-0 and P-3, P-9 and P-0. Each equivalent tetrachord in both pairs has three notes in common: for example, the first of P-0 with the third of P-3 and the second of P-9 (Ex. 49).

Ex. 49

Such a network of interrelationships (equally applicable, of course, to all transpositions of P-0) would make it only too easy to achieve a mechanical, anti-musical result. But Webern's genius lay, not in devising these invariants, but in employing them to serve the purposes of a gradually evolving, comprehensible musical discourse.

The 'double function' of the quartet's basic set, as P-0 and RI-9, is reflected in the double structure of the first movement.

VARIATION FORM	TERNARY FORM	BAR NUMBERS
Theme	Introduction	1–15 (minim *c.* 66)
Variation I	First subject	16–32
Variation II	Transition	33–49 (minim *c.* 84)
Variation III	{ Middle section, or	47–65 (minim *c.* 56)
Variation IV	{ Second subject	66–78
Variation V	Recapitulation	80–95 (minim *c.* 66)
Variation VI	Coda	96–112

The main divisions in this scheme are made audible by means of rests and *ritardandi,* as well as by textural differences; the most striking division consists of seven crotchet beats of silence before the 'recapitulation' (Variation 5), which is also more dramatic in character (and faster in tempo) after the relatively relaxed middle section.

The introduction (bars 1–15) is the only part of the movement to use one set at a time, and it exploits tetrachordal overlapping. As Ex. 48

indicates, consistent use of such overlapping would result in a 'loop' of only three sets – P-0, P-8 and P-4 – so having used this loop, and a second statement of P-0, Webern changes the degree of overlap from four notes to two, thus introducing P-10 in bar 11. The main body of the movement is then exclusively concerned with pairings of the type illustrated in Ex. 49.

P-0 and P-3	P-4 and P-7	R-1 and R-4
P-1 and P-10	P-8 and P-11	R-2 and R-5
P-2 and P-11	P-9 and P-0	

The other aspect of serial technique which needs some elucidation is the overlapping of set statements. Variation 1 does not overlap with either the introduction or with Variation 2: its own set pairs overlap by four notes. In Variations 2 and 3 no overlaps are involved, though the actual *texture* of the latter does start before the end of the former (second violin, bar 47). This central section of the seven-part movement is the only one not to employ P-0: indeed, neither of the pairings involved in Variation 3 are used elsewhere in the movement. Variation 4 parallels Variation 1, with overlapping tetrachords. In Variation 5 the interval overlaps are by dyads and finally, in the coda, by tetrachords again. It is in the coda, too, that Webern allows the common pitches between tetrachords (which are the result of combining sets four semitones apart), to become explicit (cf. the C sharps and Es in bars 98 and 99, F sharps in bar 101, Cs in bar 103, etc.).

The form of the first movement can in fact be discussed in a third way, so that the parallel with the tripartite structure of the basic set is closer still. The texture is not merely contrapuntal but canonic: and just as Webern 'submerges' simple serial succession by sharing out the pairs of set statements between the four instruments, so the various canons can change their instrumental locations en route (cf. the Symphony, Op. 21, first movement). In Variation 1 (bars 16–31), for example, the initiating voice is that of the viola, whose three-note interval pattern is echoed by the cello at what proves to be the normal interval distance of three semitones, with octave displacement, and at the durational distance of seven crotchet beats. One would therefore expect the first violin statement to be echoed by the second violin, but the interval pattern (second violin bars 18–19) is 'wrong', and the 'true' imitation at the correct durational distance is in the viola, who therefore changes his role from the *dux* of one pair to the *comes* of the other. The same fate awaits the first violin itself, however, since this echoes (bars 20–1) the second violin statement of bars 18–19. Finally the cello statement of bars 19 and 20 is taken up, again at the fixed pitch and duration interval, by the second violin.

The remainder of this variation (bars 22–32) establishes a more consistent pattern, though purely canonic considerations can be modified by the necessities of twelve-note succession. For example, there is an exact pitch canon between first violin (bars 23ff.) and cello (bars 24ff.), but the distance in crotchet beats between their entries varies, as well as the octave position of the individual notes (Ex. 50).

Ex. 50

In the second and third movements of Op. 28, Webern's canonic wizardry is employed with breathtaking nonchalance. What in the first movement was a tension between twos (the pairs of sets) and threes (the underlying ternary form) now develops explicitly into threes and fours – not merely four instruments but four, simultaneous sets. The double canon of the second movement's outer sections uses trios of tetrachordally overlapping sets: P-1, P-5, P-9 and their retrogrades. (P-1 and R-5 have invariant tetrachords, as have P-5 and R-9, and P-9 and R-1.) The same sets are also employed in the rhythmically more diverse canon of the 'trio'.

In the finale, however, Webern reshapes the association principle of the first movement, so that we start with P-0 combined with P-6 (the tritone at last appearing to assert its basic structural role) and, simultaneously, with both their retrogrades (R-o and R-6). This movement, a scherzo with a double fugue for its middle section, is the playful climax to Webern's synthesis of polyphonic and classical structures. The pointlessness of such concerns in the absence of any specifically harmonic structural determinants will always be argued by some, but it was the essential symmetry of classical ternary form which Webern was adapting, not its dynamic tonal processes. Webern's own view of the lengths to which symmetry should go may be gauged from his own account of the way in which the violin's consequent phrase in the exposition (bars 8–14) reverses the rhythmic scheme of the antecedent phrase (bars 1–7). There is no question of an exact mirror-image.[8] The *concept* of mirroring always stimulated Webern, but the technique of variation drove it into a subordinate position (Ex. 51).

Ex. 51

Soon after completing the String Quartet, Webern wrote, 'I must confess that hardly ever before have I had such a good feeling towards a completed work. It almost seems to me that this is altogether my first work.'[9] Its 'suitability for study', as a compendium of Webern's serial technique in full maturity, should not blind us to its musical qualities, of course, and analytical explorations like the foregoing are worthless if they do not ultimately serve to enhance the experience and appreciation of the music: not just how it is put together, but what it expresses.

In his last completed instrumental work, the Variations for Orchestra Op. 30 (1940), Webern exploited the double-function form of the first movement of the String Quartet on a larger scale. In a well-known letter,[10] he described the blend of variation and 'overture' form, and the result can be laid out in a similar way to the first movement of the quartet:

VARIATION FORM	OVERTURE FORM	BAR NUMBERS
Theme	Introduction	1–20
1st variation	1st subject	21–55
2nd ,,	Transition	56–73
3rd ,,	2nd subject	74–109
4th ,,	1st subject recap.	110–134
5th ,,	Intro./Transition recap.	135–145
6th ,,	Coda	146–180

The later work, since it is not part of a larger whole, contains greater contrasts within itself, and the constant changes of metre and tempo in the first section are an immediate indication of the considerable difference in character between the two compositions.

Certainly Webern continued to explore the implications of a serialism rooted in traditionally-derived textures until his tragic and untimely death (he was accidentally shot by an American soldier). It is appropriate, too, that the last movement of his last completed work, the Cantata, Op. 31, should be a double canon by inversion thrice repeated, each pair of parts employing three sets each. Schematically, this works as follows:

Tenor	I-2	RI-4	R-10
Alto	P-10	P-4	RI-2

Soprano	I-6	I-0	R-2
Bass	P-2	RI-0	RI-6

The basic set is not, in fact, symmetrical or subdivisible in the archetypal Webernian fashion. It does, however, span six semitones (C to F sharp) and if the combinations are set out in simple form it will be seen that in each pair G sharps and Ds always coincide (Ex 52).

Ex. 52

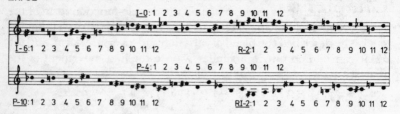

There are other invariants with respect to note order, and overlapping is also involved: by one note only between the first and second pairs, then by three notes between the second and third. This movement, then, is the ultimate expression of Webern's all-inclusive yet freely unfolding serial method. The properties of the material are unfailingly perceived and exploited; the essentially polyphonic nature of a system which has no self-sufficient harmonic properties is rooted in traditional polyphonic textures, giving them new meaning and a renewed thematic importance. The vision and integrity with which all this was done ensure Webern's place among the greatest of all modern masters, as a genius in whom radical and conservative meet and interpenetrate.

Chapter 9

The Spread of Serialism

The irony of Stravinsky's adoption of twelve-note technique is often remarked on, since it came so soon after Schoenberg's death. A deeper irony lies in the failure of Stravinsky's late conversion to win yet more converts to serialism. In both America and Europe the possibilities of 'total' serialism had begun to be ventilated even before Schoenberg's death. In America Milton Babbitt had initiated his uniquely rigorous exploration of serial systems during the 1940s, while in Europe the reluctance of Messiaen to follow up his brief flirtation with the method by a fruitful marriage set a precedent, and the enthusiasm of even his most ardent disciples for a strictly patterned, all-embracing twelve-note process was short-lived. Simultaneously, the early fifties in both America and Europe saw the rapid growth of indeterminate or aleatory music which has provided the most thorough-going reaction of all, not merely against serialism but against the whole idea of a musical composition as something fixed, fully written out, and serious. The fragmentation of the musical spectrum was complete.

In adopting serialism, Stravinsky had to validate not merely the series in his own terms, but also atonality; and, like Schoenberg in his own early exploration of atonality, he had to decide whether and in what sense thematicism could survive. Stravinsky shared Schoenberg's dislike of the word 'atonal', expressing it with characteristic sharpness in *The Poetics of Music*, and somewhat more cautiously in the first volume of *Conversations*.[1] Just as in the *Poetics* Stravinsky was concerned to establish a broader definition of tonality as 'the polar attraction of sound, of an interval, or even of a complex of tones,' so in the *Conversations* he is willing to admit that 'we can still create a sense of return to exactly the same place without tonality . . . form cannot exist without identity of some sort.' It is thematic identity which is structurally more significant in Stravinsky's twelve-note works than the fact that 'the intervals of my series are attracted by tonality'. As the same

177

passage in the *Poetics* asserts, 'musical form would be unimaginable in the absence of elements of attraction,' and it is true that the serial processes may be manipulated by Stravinsky just as they were by Schoenberg to admit pitch-emphasis as that element of attraction (the C sharp in *Abraham and Isaac* is a good example). Yet such an emphasis is of more thematic than tonal significance. Understandable though it is that early commentators on Stravinsky's serial works should have seized on the chance of declaring that at last the great synthesis between tonal and serial had been achieved, the sober remarks of Milton Babbitt, pointing out the incompatibility of the two processes, are ultimately more relevant to Stravinsky's twelve-note works: 'The formal systems – of which the tonal system and the twelve-tone system are, respectively, instances – are, under no conceivable principle of correspondence, equivalent; they are so different in structure as to render the possibility of a work being an extended instance of both unthinkable.'[2]

What Roman Vlad describes, in his analysis of the ending of *Threni*, as 'tonal polarization'[3] is merely the arrangement of sets in combination to achieve a concordant cadence. Even if Stravinsky has 'added together the diatonic implications of the various series,' the result is neither diatonic nor tonal, but polarized to 'resolve' on to this particular interval. Most importantly, since this polarization is of purely local significance (though conclusive), it cannot be held to confirm the tonal direction of the work as a whole (unlike the C of the *Cantata*, the A of the *Septet*). Stravinsky himself was prepared to accept that *Movements* for Piano and Orchestra, the work which followed *Threni*, 'has a tendency towards *antitonality*'. In his own terms, therefore, several of the later twelve-note works are distinctly less antitonal, just as they are considerably more thematic: and even Stravinsky himself is prepared to use the term 'a kind of triadic atonality' to describe the harmonic situation in *Threni*.[4]

Threni (1957–8), with a text from the *Lamentations* of Jeremiah, is not merely Stravinsky's first wholly twelve-note composition, nor is it simply the longest (thirty-five minutes): it is seminal in both form and atmosphere, the former episodic but held together by varied repetitions, the latter elegiac in a manner at once ritualistic and intensely expressive.

The most fundamental unifying factor in the work is the regular occurrence of the Hebrew letters introducing the separate verses of the text. These punctuate the form and articulate the smaller divisions within the larger framework, even though the letters are by no means all set in an identical manner. It is the first of the work's three main parts ('De Elegia Prima') which makes the most substantial use of exact repetition to construct an overall 'rondo' form.

The 'De Elegia Prima' establishes the importance of canonic writing and irregular accentuation, the latter in particular a 'pre-serial' Stravinskian trait, which depends just as much on the reiteration of small numbers of pitches as it did in *Le Sacre du Printemps*. Because of this, it is possible to sense polarization on to F sharp amounting almost to 'tonal centrality' in this part of the work (as the final pitch of P-o, F sharp clearly represents a culmination). Yet however strong such centrality seems in this first part it is not confirmed in the remainder. Only the final section of the 'Sensus Spei' (the second 'movement' of Part Two) gives clear emphasis to F sharp as a pedal in the bass.

Similarly, exact repetition is notably less significant in the two other main parts of *Threni*. Part Two, 'De Elegia Tertia', is itself tripartite, and each part is episodic, with repetition important within the individual episodes. The central section, 'Sensus Spei', thus contains eight distinct episodes, each focusing on a different element set up in connection with each successive Hebrew letter. There is sufficient internal repetition to ensure the distinct thematic character of each episode, however. For example, the section between bars 231 and 245 ('Nun') begins with two two-bar phrases, and these are immediately repeated in varied form before the final seven bars, which are different. Naturally, the derivation of all material from the basic set (though its original identity is not strictly preserved throughout) means that familiarity can suggest ever-increasing similarities of thematic shape to the ear. The perception of such invariants inevitably creates a far richer sense of the work's unity than the simple awareness of virtually exact repetitions will do.

Since *Threni* is longer by ten minutes than any of Stravinsky's later twelve-note works, it is not surprising that substantial repetitions on the scale of 'De Elegia Prima' are not found again. The repetitions therefore seem in retrospect to have more in common with the symmetries of transitional refrain structures like the *Cantata on Old English Texts* (1951–2) and *In Memoriam Dylan Thomas* (1954) than with the more consistently evolutionary later scores, while the essentially episodic organization of the 'De Elegia Tertia' section is an anticipation of some aspects of later developments – notably the quasi-stanzaic form of *Abraham and Isaac*. Certainly the *Movements* for Piano and Orchestra

(1959) presents a remarkable 'alternative' in almost every respect: athematic fragmentation is rife, in spite of some characteristic rhythmic reiterations, and the articulating divisions of the form (five movements linked by interludes) are hard to hear, as is the justification for repeating the 'exposition' of the first movement (bars 1–22).

By comparison, *A Sermon, a Narrative and a Prayer* (1960–1) seems almost artless in its lyricism and rhythmic simplicity. Yet it is not a complete contrast to *Movements*, as the instrumental counterpoint on the very first page shows: there is simply a more appealing expressive range, befitting the return to vocal music on a broader scale.

In the four substantial works which Stravinsky completed between 1962 and 1966 – *The Flood, Abraham and Isaac*, the *Variations Aldous Huxley in memoriam* and *Requiem Canticles* – the structural role of repetition, and of thematic identity, remains of paramount importance. As the longest and most loosely constructed, *The Flood* (1961–2) is nevertheless the only one of these late works to include an example of that most unified and symmetrical of structures, the palindrome, in the fifty-six-bar orchestral movement called 'The Flood'. This is firmly anchored in regular repetitions of a seven-note chord (D sharp/D/C/F sharp/F/B/E) which contains enough semitonal clashes to inhibit any tonal feeling, as does the 'Jacob's Ladder' music which appears four times during the work (bars 6, 179, 496 and 582). On the other hand, the way in which the phrases of the Te Deum near the beginning and the repeat of the Sanctus near the end start out from C sharp (with D sharp and G sharp in close attendance) is more obviously focused, and the two settings of God's words (bars 8off. and 181ff.) inhabit a comparable area.

Abraham and Isaac (1962–3) is a far more concentrated work, though in its acknowledgement of a degree of centrality for C sharp it follows on from *The Flood*. With the concentration goes a vast expansion of the number of available set forms, for Stravinsky here makes use of hexachordal rotations, starting, say, with the fifth note, and continuing with 6, 1, 2, 3, 4, which increases the number of six-note sets theoretically available from 96 to 576. Far from ensuring the complete non-recurrence of any single set and the absolute avoidance both of thematic repetition and of pitch emphasis, however, this technique is so used that *Abraham and Isaac* is still a thematic twelve-note work in which the note C sharp is given clear primacy (F is also emphasized to some degree). Thematic repetition and pitch emphasis are at their clearest in the fourth of the work's ten short sections (bars 105–35), where the hypnotic chant of the vocal line establishes clear links with the melodic style of many much earlier works of Stravinsky (Ex. 53).

Ex. 53

Elsewhere, a more fragmented, less obviously directional vocal line makes this one of his least appealing pieces and notably difficult to perform. Yet in its cool, conscious handling of the multifarious choices open to a composer who rotates his sets systematically it is a *tour de force*.

Like *Abraham and Isaac*, the orchestral Variations (1963–4) has less obvious thematic repetition than *Threni, A Sermon, a Narrative and a Prayer* or *The Flood*. Here, however, there is a broader structural use of varied recurrence, for while the ten sections of *Abraham and Isaac* are all new stages in the thematic process, the twelve sections of the Variations include three which are basically identical in texture and material, though not in timbre. Sections 2, 5 and 11 are all in twelve parts (for twelve violins, ten violas and two basses, and twelve woodwind respectively), so that, even though no thematic process or internal repetition of any kind can readily be discerned within them, they do nevertheless act as clearly recognizable unifying features, set off as they are by the more open texture of the surrounding sections. Other unifying features relate the beginning and the end (compare the chords in bars 2–5 and 137–40), while Sections 7 (bars 73–85) and 9 (bars 95–100) divide into two related phrases. The thematic process of Section 10 (bars 101–17) is particularly clear.

Perhaps it was only in the fifteen-minute *Requiem Canticles* (1964–6) that Stravinsky recaptured an ideal balance between repetition, contrast and variation, making this the most immediately communicative of his twelve-note works after *A Sermon, a Narrative and a Prayer*. The instrumental Prelude is itself a marvellously uncluttered example of the process in action. It is fifty-four bars long, and can be subdivided into four phrases and a coda (the coda restores the harmonic basis of the first phrase, but excludes its melodic material). In the purely tonal sense the Prelude starts out from a brief emphasis on F, establishes a much stronger emphasis on F sharp (bars 20–33), then 'modulates' back to F via D (bars 35–46). Thematically, the second, third and fourth phrases are expanded variations of the first.

Ex. 54

All the other movements can be analysed along similar lines, without for a moment suggesting a mechanical reliance on the processes of the Prelude. In the Lachrymosa, for example, which has six short phrases for the contralto soloist separated by miniature *ritornelli* for three trombones, the vocal phrases finally lose the security of sustained harmonic support, and with it the possibility of any clear pitch emphasis emerging. The instrumental Postlude confirms that, although pitch polarization around a particular bass note may be sensed for a significant part of the work (here, as with the Prelude, there is a movement away from F and back again), it is the thematic content of phrases and the relationship between them which constitute the most vital traditional feature of this music (Ex. 54). Thematicism has replaced tonality as its central *identity*, and variation has replaced modulation as the primary structural agent of meaningful change and progress. In the Postlude of the *Requiem Canticles* what is thematic may be little more than a particular timbre associated with a particular rhythm, but it is enough to create that continuity, that sense of concern with an 'Idea', which is the essential quality of Schoenbergian – and Stravinskian – pitch-serialism.

Of native-born American serialists, the most distinguished exponent of the more traditional, Schoenbergian manner is Roger Sessions (1896-1985). His music is relatively little known, at least outside the United States itself, but it has considerable appeal, confirming in its fluency and clarity that the Schoenbergian example could be followed without pious imitation or purposeless parody.

Sessions was well into his fifties before producing his first twelve-note work, the Violin Sonata of 1953. To a far greater extent than Stravinsky, whose conversion took place around the same time, Sessions had moved towards the technique gradually, and has stated that 'my first use of it was, at the beginning, quite involuntary. I had at various times, for my own self-enlightenment, carried out quite small-scale exercises with the technique, but I still envisaged it as not applicable to my own musical ideas. It was therefore a surprise to me when I found the composition of the Sonata flowing easily and without constraint in its terms.'[5]

Such a natural transition has ensured that in those later works where Sessions uses twelve-note techniques he has been able to continue the exploration of large-scale structures begun earlier. Before 1953 he had already contributed to all the major traditional genres: sonata, symphony, string quartet, concerto, opera; and the serial works reinforce that commitment, notably to the symphony, of which there are now eight, six composed since 1953.

The Eighth Symphony, completed in 1968, is a fine example of a style in which an elaborate evolutionary process, often of considerable rhythmic complexity, maintains sufficient contact with memorable recurrences. The two-movement form – *Adagio e Mesto* and *Allegro con fuoco* – proposes a fairly extreme basic contrast, and the symphonism of the work involves in large part the creation of associations between the movements, preparing an ending which recalls the opening.

Sessions's own straightforward note on the symphony[6] describes the first movement as dividing into three episodes, and a background of traditional ternary design may well be evoked in the third episode with its 'melodic fragments reminiscent of the quieter portions of the opening episode of the movement' and its conclusion with a dark chord which also belongs in the first episode.

Strategic recurrence is also important in the *Allegro*, which follows without a break. As the composer comments, 'the two fast sections which form the main body of this movement are characterized by a three-note motif which ... recurs frequently and in many different guises.' The return to the first idea of the first movement at the end of the second is not in itself an indication of deep thematic associations between the two very different movements of the work, but rather a satisfying demonstration of reversal: the *Adagio* 'prepares' the *Allegro* and the *Allegro* itself can lead logically back to a reminder of the *Adagio* to dramatize the fact that the sheer distance between the two entities can possess its own coherence.

Roberto Gerhard (1896–1970) was born in the same year as Sessions, and studied composition with Schoenberg in Vienna and Berlin between 1923 and 1928. After the Spanish Civil War Gerhard emigrated to England, where he lived for the rest of his life, though he paid several visits to America to teach – and to learn about the more rigorous serial techniques being pioneered by Milton Babbitt. Gerhard's music progressed from the impressionistic nationalism of the Piano Trio (1918), through preliminary essays in serialism (Wind Quintet, 1928) and the expansive synthesis represented by the opera *The Duenna* (1946–7), to the more radical twelve-note works of the 1950s, until the final period in which serialism, while pervasive, is used with sovereign flexibility to encompass a style of the widest resonance: the last melody heard in *Leo* (1969), his last completed work, is a folk tune. Gerhard's openness to the potential of electronic techniques as well as of 'total' serialism never led him to attempt a rigorous fusion of the two. To this extent, he might seem the typical European, using the new to redefine the old, and presents something of a puzzle, particularly to those admirers who would like to explore the precise correlation between theory and practice in his later works.

Gerhard's theoretical writings, and particularly the essay 'Developments in Twelve-Tone Technique'[7] are much easier to read and understand than Milton Babbitt's, but the precise application of theory to practice is more difficult to establish, at least in respect of the correlation of pitch and time sets. In the article Gerhard quotes the pitch set of his First String Quartet (1950–5) and shows how its underlying source set determines the sequence of numbers on which the time set is based. Later he explains how time sets can govern the durational organization of every aspect of a given work by means of relative proportions within and between phrases. Yet analysts have the greatest difficulty in establishing whether Gerhard ever used these properties of a time set in more than an occasional way. Such evidence as is so far available on Gerhard's use of serialism in his later works suggests strongly that, once this theoretically totally consistent universe was conceived, the composer lost interest in it as anything more than a background against which other freer, and often much more traditional, factors could operate. It is therefore likely that the Schoenbergian principle of permutation within the hexachord is of more direct importance than any correlation between pitches, durations and other structural elements in determining the later stages of Gerhard's stylistic evolution.

Four years before the 1956 article, Gerhard wrote his 'Tonality in Twelve-tone Music,' which deals with Milton Babbitt's concept of the source set and its relationship to a 'principle of permutation (within antecedent and consequent) based on a recognition of the fact that beyond the actual series there is an ultimate ground, an abstract archetype – represented by the coupled hexachords – of which the individual series is only one *aspect*, that is, one of the possible permutations. . . . The identity of the series will be maintained in spite of permutation, provided that this takes place exclusively within the constituent units (hexachord, tetrachord, etc.) . . . This seems to me to confirm the view that the fundamental idea of the twelve-tone technique is in fact a new formulation of the principle of tonality.'[8] Gerhard's conclusions are therefore distinctly at variance with those of Babbitt quoted above, and, as will soon be seen, they have encouraged some dangerously vague speculation about the 'tonality' of his own serial compositions.

From 1959 onwards, Gerhard worked exclusively in single-movement schemes, and the works of this last decade – *The Plague*, the Third and Fourth Symphonies, the Concerto for Orchestra, *Epithalamion*, the Second String Quartet, and the five chamber works, *Concert for Eight*, *Hymnody*, *Gemini*, *Libra* and *Leo* – can be regarded as resourceful and consistent continuations of the structural-thematic processes of the late Schoenberg single-movement instrumental works, the String Trio and the Violin Phantasy.

Hans Keller has described the Symphony No. 4 (1967) as a work 'in one movement, but in plenty of sharply characterized contrasting sections which combine the roles of several movements and of sections within movements. Because of these constellations and slow motion sound pictures and, in particular, long notes, the music often sounds athematic, but as the sound begins to make sense, it discloses strict thematicism from the very outset, so much so that there is absolutely nothing in the entire work which cannot be shown to be implied, partly even expressed, in the opening section. Where there are tunes, or snatches of tunes, they hang together in motivic constructions like those of a Beethoven symphony.'[9] These comments are made in the course of an open letter to the composer, and it would have been interesting to read his reply, or at least to discover whether he accepted Keller's terminology. In an introductory note to the recording of the First Symphony Gerhard had described his concern with 'the possibility of evolving a large-scale work as a continuous train of musical invention that would progress – much as a poem progresses – by the strength and direction of its inherent potentialities alone, growing and branching out freely, without being forced into predetermined channels. In other words, I discarded the traditional symphonic frame-work, with its exposition, themes, development and recapitulations. . . . Admittedly the appearance and recurrence of themes provide land-marks that help the listener to find his formal bearings. But today a theme may become a period piece of musical furniture, and it is possible to imagine an infinite variety of land-marks of an entirely different type that will orientate the listener equally well.'[10]

That is an admirably clear statement of the way Gerhard sought to go beyond Schoenbergian precepts, in which thematic recurrence remains crucial. Yet like some of his other analytical remarks, these surely refer to a theoretical ideal rather than a musical fact, and the thematics of the Fourth Symphony can be perceived as a sequence of distinct stages in the evolution of complementary hexachords rather than an indivisible extended 'melody', in the statement of which traditional thematic procedures play no part.

The amount of imitation, *ostinato* and repetition in this symphony is quite enough to create strong traditional associations, and if the work has a weakness, it is in the sense one has of its successive stages occasionally attempting to evade crystallization into 'thematicism'.

More positively, we may respond to an extremely wide range of thematic elements – improvisatory coruscation to lyrical, extended melody – through an awareness of their common serial basis.

As a simple example, we can compare the cadenza-like clarinet entry in the eighth bar of the work – the symphony's first melodic idea – which states two complementary hexachords in close position, each filling out six adjacent semitones, with a passage near the end at Fig. 103, where the first oboe and the violas outline another close-position hexachord (E flat to A flat) and the violins and cellos provide the complementary six notes (A to D) (Ex. 55).

Ex. 55

Examples of such a fundamental process can easily be multiplied: in the passage before Fig. 29 (p. 63), a twelve-note string chord separates out into the hexachords A flat to D flat and D to G. A very different thematic adaptation of the close-position hexachords can be found at Fig. 35, when the violins initiate a typically dense semiquaver passage with A-E; E flat-B flat (descending), while at Fig. 53 the first trumpet presents a new version of the hexachord G-D, with the harps sustaining the complement.

The thematic interrelationships of the work seem stratified according to whether close or open-position hexachords are involved – certainly the connection between the trumpet theme at Fig. 53 and the oboe theme at Fig. 93 is none the less clear for the absence of obvious repetition: it is not merely that 'the identity of the series will be maintained in spite of permutation',[11] but that the links between stages in a thematic process (the series shaped in a particular way) are made explicit.

Hans Keller concluded that: 'while atonality and twelve-tonality permeate the score, so does tonality, open as well as hidden, to the extent of evolving a tonal sub-structure based on functional harmony, whether the composer knows and likes it or not.' Without more details of what Keller had in mind, it is difficult to judge the extent of this tonal basis. While individual thematic cells in themselves may suggest key, they are usually supported by non-tonal, non-triadic chords. For this reason, the tonality of the work must remain a more subjective matter than the thematicism.

Certain similar issues are raised by the music of Luigi Dallapiccola (1904–75), another 'late' convert to twelve-note techniques. While, broadly speaking, Sessions and Gerhard continued to explore the Schoenbergian commitment to substantial instrumental forms, Dallapiccola attempted a still more difficult task, the extension of Webernian lyricism, and the pursuit of that most demanding prize, the convincing full-length twelve-note opera. Both Sessions and Gerhard wrote operas – Sessions, in particular, labouring over his three-act *Montezuma* for more than two decades (1941–62) – but neither has shown such exclusive devotion to vocal forms, or such obvious lyrical gifts in non-operatic vocal music as Dallapiccola.

His advance towards complete acceptance of atonal serialism was as gradual as that of Gerhard or Sessions, and the influence of local, more traditional composers – Casella, Malipiero – was paramount until the mid-1930s. Then, at the Prague ISCM Festival of 1935, Dallapiccola heard the first performance of Webern's Concerto, Op. 24. He wrote: 'We are confronted here with a man who expresses the greatest number of ideas in the fewest possible words. Though I did not understand the work well, it seemed to me to have an aesthetic and stylistic unity on which one could not wish to improve.'[12] This immediate attraction was to a truly 'foreign' music – 'a composition of unbelievable brevity . . . and truly extraordinary concentration. Every decorative element is eliminated.' The impact made by Webern's work was no short-lived phenomenon. Three years later, at the London ISCM Festival of 1938, Dallapiccola attended the first performance of *Das Augenlicht*, which was, in all probability, an even greater revelation, simply because it was a vocal work. He wrote at the time that the twelve-note system is 'a language which contains within itself exceedingly varied possibilities, whose total realization we shall not perhaps live to see'.[13] Yet he did not immediately reject every aspect of his earlier style and plunge into the imitation of Webern. The transitional period, which roughly spans the years 1936 to 1948, contains what may eventually be seen as his finest works, and their quality is the result of positive compromise.

The major works of this period are both operas. *Volo di Notte*, with the composer deriving his own libretto from the book by Saint Exupéry, was composed between 1937 and 1939, and *Il Prigioniero*, again to Dallapiccola's own libretto, between 1944 and 1948. Purely as convincing theatrical presentations of thoroughly modern subjects – the personality of the pilot-explorer, the horror of psychological and political tyranny – these operas, if given the widest circulation when they were new, should have established Dallapiccola as the most important modern opera composer since Berg, and as the obvious continuer of Bergian eclecticism. *Volo di Notte* is a compromise-work in the most obvious sense: it begins and ends tonally (B major – E major) but uses twelve-note processes in between. More obviously Bergian features are the distinct forms used for the different scenes and the use of *Sprechgesang* (Dallapiccola, along with Puccini, had heard and admired *Pierrot Lunaire* in 1924). *Volo di Notte* incorporates material from the slightly earlier *Tre Laudi* for soprano and chamber orchestra, whose reliance on canon is a more explicit link with Webernian practice, and one authority finds the result 'by no means felicitous'.[14]

It is in the smaller-scale vocal works of this period, principally the *Liriche Greche* (1942–5), settings of Italian translations of Sappho, Anacreon and Alcaeus, that the finest expression of Dallapiccola's lyrical gift may be found. In addition, they 'reveal his own personal brand of free serialism in its purest form'.[15] Here, as in the *Canti di prigionia* (1938–41), later to be used in the second opera, Dallapiccola seems to achieve new depth and focus in spite of the flexibility of style: 'no other composer has achieved such a perfect tonal-atonal equilibrium.'[16] This style reaches its apogee in *Il Prigioniero* where 'Dallapiccola's variety of rows and motives, his evocative use of traditional chord structure, his mingled echoes of Verdi, Debussy and Berg, all offend against *a priori* conceptions of serialism; but his right to profit as he chooses from serial discipline is vindicated by the powerful impact the work has continued to make'.[17]

Dallapiccola dedicated the last group of Greek Lyrics (*Sex carmina Alcaei*) to the memory of Webern, and it may be that his very faithfulness to that memory was the principal reason for the relative failure of his later music. It is not solely a matter of form – of trying to do what Webern did on a much larger scale – but of a different kind of compromise. After 1948 tonal reminiscence diminishes and disappears. Within the atonal-serial residue the opposition between 'lyrical' and 'cerebral' elements becomes increasingly marked and, whether the two confront each other or either dominates, the earlier momentum, which the tendency of serially derived harmonies to move towards tonal resolutions had ensured, is no longer to be found. Those critics of Dallapiccola who regard him as one of those who have given twelve-note music a bad name might well wag their fingers and reproach him for not studying Schoenberg rather than Webern, given his desire to write something other than canonic miniatures. Such an over-simplification might nevertheless conceal rather than spotlight the basic issue, which is more rhythmic than harmonic. Whether his last, and only full-length, opera *Ulisse* (1960–8) would be more convincing with the added perspective of tonal harmony is scarcely a realistic question. His earlier operas, which do have such perspectives, are evidently more convincing than the one which does not, but the fact simply helps us to define the style in which he was at his best: it says nothing about serialism as such, or about its potential for compromise or extension.

Milton Babbitt (born 1916) is the most notable of those composers whose theoretical explorations of the twelve-note system have led to radically new techniques. Babbitt's first published work, Three Compositions for Piano (1947–8), appeared when he was in his early thirties. These are still thematic pieces: their continuity is not merely the result of rhythmic and textural factors, but the recurrence of related melodic shapes can be easily perceived in all of them. Even in the first piece, however, a simple kind of serialization of rhythmic patterns is employed, involving units of 1, 2, 4 and 5 semiquavers in Prime (5, 1, 4, 2), Inversion (1, 5, 2, 4), R and RI forms, and this, in combination with the pitch serialism, helps to fix the piece in the Schoenbergian tradition of 'developing variation' (i.e. variation and development of a specific thematic idea). Constant variation of every element, to exclude thematic process, was not long in coming, however, and various other applications of serialism to the time factor were tried out: for example, the attack-point set in which the distance (in semiquavers) between instrumental attacks relates to the distance in semitones between the first pitch of a given pitch-class set and its eleven successors. The opening of Babbitt's Composition for Twelve Instruments (1948) shows the association between a P-2 attack-point set and the initial pitches of the twelve different pitch-class sets in use (one for each instrument) (Ex. 56).

There may still be a degree of melodic continuity in such music, and one must emphasize that even in much later works – for example, the String Quartet No. 3 (1969–70) – certain phrases will stand out as more melodic than others, simply by virtue of longer note-values and *legato* phrasing: since Babbitt's works involve the deployment of all musical characteristics in specific relationships, total fragmentation is as unlikely to occur as total continuity. But such moments of melodic emphasis will be no more thematic in the traditional sense than the fragmented textures. Babbitt is quite explicit that, for example, the single, eighteen-minute span of the Third Quartet 'does not instance any cherished surface "formal" pattern created by conjoined repetitions'. There is recurrence beneath the surface: 'there is a fundamental and – I trust – helpful articulation into four "parallel" sections, created by the pitch structure, for – to within familiar transformations – the

Ex. 56

P–0 : 0(C♮) : 1(C♯) : 4(E♮) : 9(A♮) : 5(F♯) : 8(A♭) : 3(E♭) : 10(B♭) : 2(D) : 11(B♮) : 6(F♯) : 7(G♮)

P–2 : 2 : 3 : 6 : 11 : 7 : 10 : 5 : 12(0) : 4 : 1 : 8 : 9

linear dispositions and ordering of the pitch-classes, the linear consistency of aggregates and the order of aggregate progression of these sections are identical.'[18] It is the problem of perception which such deeply submerged continuity entails which has led to the belief that Babbitt's work 'appears to have extended the musical universe in a multitude of directions and respects and has taken it near to the bounds of human conceptual and perceptual capacity, while taking it near as well to the heights of contemporary intellectual accomplishments.'[19]

Inevitably, in view of the demands accurate performance of his works makes, Babbitt has been much involved with electronic techniques: his own account of the attempt to perform his *Relata I* for orchestra (1965) is a classic revelation of the apparently unbridgeable gap between the traditional symphony orchestra and the total serialist.[20] Babbitt has probably communicated most directly through his vocal works, notably *Philomel* for soprano, recorded soprano and synthesized accompaniment on tape (1963–4). Even now, however, his own achievement is difficult to disentangle from his enormous influence as a teacher, an influence unfortunately more easily observed through analytical articles than through the publication or performance of music by his pupils. By giving prime emphasis to the serialization of rhythm, duration, dynamics, register and so on, commentators have too often diverted attention from the fundamental rethinking of compositional process which this may involve. Babbitt's control of serial relationships is such that, in the Third Quartet, 'triadic harmonies' can occur without remotely suggesting any kind of tonal basis: thematic restatement, thematic characterization of any kind, are as unlikely to occur in Babbitt as a diatonic progression is in a Webern serial piece.

This is a measure of the degree to which Babbitt has advanced beyond the first generation of twelve-note composers, and a measure of his greater remoteness from those traditions to which they still acknowledged a basic allegiance. Even the last Webernian link, canonic imitation, is jettisoned. There are, of course, plenty of serial composers today who retain imitation and with it the thematic process, yet none of them is established as a figure of central importance. The athematic serialists have their athematicism in common with many 'experimental' composers who have reacted against strictness and control in so many different ways, while the true heirs of Schoenberg's compromise are likely to find themselves lumped together with the surviving believers in tonality as the decadent adherents of reaction. So if composers born within fifty years of Schoenberg himself have achieved considerable freedom in either accepting or adapting the principles which he established, those who are younger still are likely to take an even less respectfully academic view of serialism. Part Three of this book will show how most of the important younger composers have found it impossible to ignore twelve-note techniques, even though they will almost invariably seek to adapt them to their own purposes, often achieving startling new effects.

Part Three

From Past to Future

Chapter 10

The Radical Aesthetic

Convenient categorization of the mass of composers, from Satie to Stockhausen, who are neither consistent upholders of the traditional tonal forms nor totally committed to the twelve-note technique, is virtually impossible. Basic distinctions can still be made between stylistic features and techniques, but in most cases it is the confrontation between different, if not opposing, tendencies which has produced memorable music: increasingly, to be a radical is to be an eclectic. The distinction which has been suggested[1] between 'avant-garde' and 'experimental' music is an attempt to clarify the confusion, even at the risk of over-simplification: 'avant-garde' composers are those who continue to build on the traditional foundations of European music, however remote their actual techniques may be from those of the best-known classical and romantic representatives of that tradition, whereas 'experimental' composers have rejected that tradition, however hard they may occasionally seem to find it to avoid the parody and distortion of what they have determined to put behind them. In these terms, all those composers so far discussed who are not obviously conservative are closer to the avant-garde camp than to the experimental, and many of those who remain to be discussed may be considered as experimental in intent but avant-garde in practice. It is at least already fairly easy to distinguish between those whose experimentalism is wholehearted and those who are prepared to compromise with (potentially 'conservative') avant-gardisms.

The most obviously experimental music has arisen in response to those radical movements in the other arts known as Dadaism and Surrealism. In 1924 André Breton's Surrealist Manifesto defined Surrealism as 'thought dictated in the absence of all control exerted by reason, and outside any aesthetic or moral preoccupation'. The primacy of instinct over intellect might have been expected to promote purely intuitive, improvisatory artistic expression, and as far as music is concerned, such elements have indeed been brought into prominence, especially since 1950. Yet it is far from being the case that the avant-gardist is all self-regarding intellectual manipulation while the experimenter is pure unsullied instinct. The crucial distinction is in basic attitude, rather than in the methods whereby those attitudes are given musical expression.

The essence of the experimental attitude can be sensed in John Cage's description of Erik Satie (1866–1925): 'He despised art. . . . He was going nowhere.' Cage inevitably stresses those tendencies of a more extreme kind which he finds in the French composer, to be interested in whom, he claims, 'one must give up illusions about ideas of order, expressions of sentiment, and all the rest of our inherited aesthetic claptrap'.[2] But Satie's experimental attitudes are expressed through techniques which cannot be so conveniently or narrowly defined.

With Wagnerian single-mindedness, Satie produced an *oeuvre* of consistently anti-romantic characteristics. From the *Sarabandes* and *Gymnopédies* (1887–8) to the ballet *Relâche* (1924) his compositions have a disconcerting simplicity. Cool restraint or sardonic humour are expressed with an instinctive disregard for the conventions of continuity or integrated contrasts which serious music had evolved over the centuries. Satie is not merely a composer of light music, however, and his earlier works are by no means so austere as to be completely inexpressive. The distortion of basically traditional processes of chord-progression, phrase-structure and form removes pieces like the *Gymnopédies* from any direct dependence on traditional associations; even if such associations are to a degree unavoidable, they remain peripheral and highly ambiguous. Yet even to use the term 'distorted' implies a conscious intention on the composer's part which can hardly be proved. The music is reticent in the extreme: it establishes consistency of style by simple repetition, but it is music in which the will, if not the personality of the composer scarcely obtrudes at all. This, in Cage's terms, is the archetypal example of music which doesn't 'do' anything to a listener. For Satie, the 'absence of emotion' is a means of expressing the spirit of 'humility and renunciation' which the modern composer, in his view, should cultivate. It was therefore natural that in the later years of Satie's life his compositions should have aspired, not to the hyper-romantic condition of a philosophy or religion, but to that of furniture: something which we use and take for granted. This *'musique d'ameublement'* should not be listened to with the intense concentration due to a Brahms symphony or a Wagner music drama, but merely heard as part of the background of ordinary life, contributing to it 'in the same way as a private conversation does, a painting in a gallery, or the chair on which you may or may not be seated'.[3]

Such an attitude indicates that Satie would probably have endorsed Cage's view that 'no music could ever be as interesting as life itself'.[4] Even so, far from regarding all Satie's late pieces as 'furniture music', it is possible to argue that because of their 'radical economy' they make the most stringent demands on listeners.[5] In both the ballets *Parade* (1917) and *Relâche* – the title means 'no performance' – the juxtaposition of different types of usually very simple material is disconcerting, yet can still be felt to add up to something more than an arbitrary succession of separate events, the order of which could be shuffled at will. And the symphonic drama *Socrate* (1918), for all the rhythmic uniformity so deplored by Stravinsky, lives up to its title in that the narrative process is both consistent and coherent by conventional musical standards. That Satie has been a great influence on later experimentalists is evident, and their view of him is not so much inaccurate as one-sided. He may have despised romantic art for its philosophical pretensions and exaggerated gestures – so did Debussy – but he never despised technique as a means of ensuring that a work for which one individual took ultimate responsibility could make its points directly and precisely.

Edgard Varèse (1883–1965) was studying at the Schola Cantorum in Paris when Satie embarked on a three-year course there at the age of thirty-nine in 1905. The only surviving piece by Varèse from this period is the brief Verlaine setting, 'Un grand sommeil noir' (1906), though a *Rhapsodie Romane* for orchestra and an opera *Oedipus und die Sphynx* were lost in a fire, and Varèse himself destroyed the orchestral work *Bourgogne* as late as 1960. The loss of these youthful works is unfortunate, but it was only after his move to America in 1915 that Varèse began to achieve maturity as a composer. He lived for another half-century, well into that era of electronic music which he had foreseen and foreshadowed. He was therefore physically, practically closer to experimental music which, between the wars, was pursued more consistently in America than in Europe. Yet it is questionable whether Varèse's own most radical works are as genuinely experimental as those of Satie, and it is significant that Cage's enthusiasm for Varèse is distinctly less wholehearted.

Cage diagnoses a 'need for continuity' which fails to 'correspond to the present need for discontinuity'. Yet he is prepared to concede that 'more clearly and actively than anyone else of his generation, he established the present nature of music', which 'arises from an acceptance of all audible phenomena as material proper to music'. Cage's main criticism of Varèse is that he is 'an artist of the past. Rather than dealing with sounds as sounds, he deals with them as Varèse'. So, in *Déserts* (1954), a work in which orchestral music and taped sections of 'organized sound' alternate, 'he attempts to make tape sound like the orchestra and vice versa, showing again a lack of interest in the natural differences of sounds, preferring to give them all his unifying signature'.[6]

These are shrewd points, for it is possible to regard Varèse as a composer who, even if he wanted to, was unable to throw off the 'burden' of traditional musical processes, and who therefore remained, however reluctantly, committed to the continuity of which Cage writes. Varèse himself could admit that 'the very basis of creative work is experimentation', while refusing to accept that the finished work itself could be described as experimental. 'I offer a "finished product": it is for the audience . . . to make the experiment of confronting a new work'.[7] So, while the finished product came to contain a far greater range of 'audible phenomena as material proper to music', the very concept of a work of art as a finished product, fixed and immutable save for the shades of interpretation, reduces its experimental status in the eyes of those for whom such traditional principles of structure are anathema.

Between 1918 and 1936 Varèse completed a series of compositions which are remarkably original and remarkably successful. The personal nature of these works – Varèse once commented, 'I don't like looking over my shoulder' – naturally does not exclude all influences. Debussy and Stravinsky are of particular importance, but Varèse's debt to them is as much structural as stylistic. Melodic lines which evolve through internal repetition are an 'impressionist' feature which transfers directly to Varèse's more scientific, crystallographic interests. Yet such evolutionary processes, the presence of which makes it dangerous to assume that Varèse's structures are in some sense inorganic, had to find their place in a satisfactory form. Just at the time when the great European masters, nationalist, neo-classical and twelve-note alike, were rediscovering or reinforcing sonata form, Varèse began in earnest to question the whole nature of musical continuity. Speaking in later years of Debussy's *Jeux*, he commented that in it 'we find a higher state of tension than in any work before it', and the exploitation and control of high tension dominate his own most characteristic works. The terminology with which he described his techniques in 1936 is also explicitly linked to such considerations: 'taking the place of the old fixed linear counterpoint, you will find in my works the movement of masses, varying in radiance, and of different densities and volumes. When these masses come into collision, the phenomena of penetration or repulsion will result. Certain transmutations taking place on one plane, by projecting themselves on other planes which move at different speeds and are placed at different angles, should create the impression of prismatic aural (auditory) deformations.'[8]

With such preoccupations, it is hardly surprising that Varèse later spoke of neo-classicism as 'deplorable'.[9] Yet he praised the discipline provided by the twelve-note method, and never showed the slightest sign of wishing to adopt the indeterminate techniques of those composers to whom he was invariably regarded in the last years of his life as most spiritually akin. Whatever Varèse's final position with regard to experiment, it was arrived at gradually. There was no sudden, blinding revolt, no rejection of every pre-existing compositional technique, but a radical re-examination of them, leading to new conclusions.

Varèse's first American compositions were *Amériques* (1920–1) and *Offrandes* (1921), but the four-minute work for wind and percussion called *Hyperprism*, completed in 1923, is his first fully realized statement of radical intent. The title presumably means 'intensifying a prismatic function', and therefore implies a basic unity strongly refracted by surface contrasts. While it is not difficult to perceive that the interval of the major seventh possesses a primary thematic function which unifies pitch procedures throughout, the sheer diversity of tempo and thematic shape within the short single movement is ultimately disruptive rather than integrative. The final *Allegro molto* may indeed summarize the intervallic emphasis of the work with various piled-up transpositions of the major seventh, but it still seems structurally arbitrary: something stuck on. Here, the term 'inorganic' is certainly justified, and the music is, if anything, closer to the disconcerting juxtapositions of a Satie ballet than to the dynamically inter-connected units of *Jeux* or the Symphonies of Wind Instruments. Thematically, too, the contrasts between single-note reiterations, a sinuous flute melody (after Fig. 2) and an initially chorale-like brass phrase (Fig. 4) emphasize the dangers of producing too episodic a scheme in the attempt to elaborate very simple basic elements without completely submerging them. In *Octandre* for seven wind instruments and double bass (1923), Varèse composes three separate movements and then establishes thematic cross-references between them, with some slightly incongruous results in the third, with its *quasi*-modal opening and miniature *fugato*. Nevertheless, his concern to achieve a new form which does not involve the absence of all unifying factors is still more evident.

With *Intégrales* (1924-5) Varèse returned to the ensemble of wind and percussion and the single-movement scheme. It is longer than either *Hyperprism* or *Octandre*, but Varèse's control of form and thematic process is much more assured, and the surface thematic diversity is here more firmly projected from the fundamental unifying factors.

The opening section of *Intégrales* – *Andantino* – is an exposition involving much repetition of a thematic idea which is little more than a reiterated monotone. The music here verges on the static, in spite of constantly changing time signatures, but in view of the frequent changes of tempo in the middle of the work, this is an appropriate foundation. After a somewhat slower second section, marked *Moderato*, in which the monotone of the *Andantino* with its two-note anacrusis remains the central thematic feature, the tempo changes, first to *Allegro*, then to *Presto*, and the material becomes more conventionally melodic. With the establishment of a slow tempo (crotchet 58), which dominates the rest of the work until the coda, melodic material is related to monotone material in a manner which is truly 'integral', and allows for explicit reminiscences of earlier moments (Ex.57).

Ex. 57

The coda, which starts as a *Presto*, also looks back, confirming that Varèse has been able to achieve a satisfactory balance between 'evolutionary' and 'recapitulatory' factors in a work which is thematic without obvious adherence to traditional structural proportions. There may be a short-breathed phrase structure in places – the tendency to reach climaxes rapidly, then restart, is even more evident in the longer, orchestral *Arcana* (1926–7) – but *Intégrales* is a rare example of a work composed in the mid-1920s which is both truly radical and convincingly coherent. Even if a critical interpretation is preferred which gives greater prominence to more radical elements, interpreting the title as a reference to the retreat from the exclusive, well-tempered scale into the integral world of instruments capable of a true pitch continuum, filling the spaces between the semitones, it can scarcely be claimed that *Intégrales* represents a total break with the European past.

The battery of percussion which *Hyperprism*, *Intégrales* and *Arcana* employ is the most obvious evidence of Varèse's experimentalism, the interest in new sounds as such, since without new instruments the composer was forced to exploit new combinations and unusual selections of existing instruments. In *Ionisation* (1931) Varèse wrote for percussion alone, and the whole piece up to the coda uses unpitched instruments (the siren, strictly speaking, is an exception, though its

Ex.58

pitch is in a constant state of change). 'Ionisation' is another scientific term, denoting the 'electrophoresis', or migration, of electrically-charged particles. In the composition, the particles are rhythmic cells, or 'sound masses', and even in the absence of pitch a thematic process can be observed. *Ionisation* has even been analysed (by its dedicatee and first conductor, Nicolas Slonimsky) as a sonata-form movement, and the basic pulse (crotchet 69) remains stable until the somewhat slower coda, when pitched percussion (piano, bells and glockenspiel) enter for the first time.

Varèse's next composition, *Ecuatorial* (1934), saw his first use of electrically-generated sound, with a pair of Ondes Martenot. As with *Ionisation*, the phrase structure as such is far from revolutionary, and the vocal line contains significant amounts of varied repetition (Ex. 58). After *Ecuatorial*, however, twenty years were to elapse before another substantial work – *Déserts* – was completed, and that would use pitch without 'themes', and organized sound on tape alongside live orchestral sound: only *Densité 21·5* (1936) and the *Étude pour Espace* (1947) were composed during the intervening period.

Speaking of Varèse's last finished work, the *Poème électronique* (1958), Stockhausen noted that 'anyone living today – Varèse was at the time living in New York – is confronted daily with the hurtling together of all races, all religions, all philosophies, all ways of life . . . of all nations. In works by the musician Varèse this bubbling of the cauldron is aesthetically portrayed . . . New York, that prime blueprint for a world society, is without question an indispensable experience for the contemporary artist. Ideas one might have about possible integration, about a coherent unification, or about possible syntheses of the influences issuing from all parts of the globe, all these must be tested against living experience if they are to lay claim on any truth.'[10] These remarks are also relevant to *Déserts*, which occupied Varèse from 1950 to 1954, and which is in the most basic sense a portrait of an urban desert. *Déserts* may indeed be a deeply pessimistic work, a commination of the whole of modern civilization: it is also the logical outcome of the more radical tendencies in Varèse's earlier works. Like them, it has vital organic features: a 'continual process of expansion, penetration, interaction and transmutation accounts for the immense sense of growing organism in the entire score, and illustrates Varèse's concept of "sound as living matter"'.[11] What is remarkable – and remarkably avant-garde – about *Déserts* is that this 'organic process' has now ceased to be in any traditional sense a thematic process. At last Varèse's own term, 'sound mass', seems precisely right to define the 'idea, the basis of an internal structure'.[12] The successions of sound masses which surround the taped episodes of organized sound in *Déserts* present a process in which single pitches are successively brought into focus. Even in this athematic context, a residual degree of hierarchy survives, and nowhere more simply and clearly than at the end, when a 'rich but subdued' horn E flat, prolonged through the last two bars by piano, vibraphone and flute, forms a clear point of focus, even of resolution (Ex. 59).

The danger of exaggerating the structural function of a series of pedal notes in a thematically featureless pitch texture is obvious. Yet in its tendency to *Klangfarbenmelodie*, *Déserts* invokes association with such pioneering essays as Schoenberg's Orchestral Piece, Op. 16, No. 3, composed in 1909. The athematicism of *Déserts* recalls those statically conjoined blocks of sound matter employed in the early stages of

Ex. 59

Intégrales, and the alternation between live and taped sound, with their radically different associations, may heighten one's sense of discontinuity. Yet Cage was surely right in claiming that Varèse was attempting to make the tape sound orchestral and vice versa: the object was to bring the new world of concrete and electronic sound into the orbit of the old, and mediate between them, not to use the new to demonstrate the redundancy of the old.

The experience of composing *Déserts* must have increased Varèse's desire to invent a purely electronic work, and the 1958 Brussels World Fair provided the opportunity, with its Philips Pavilion designed by Le Corbusier for the simultaneous presentation of projected visual images and 'organized sound' through 425 loudspeakers. The diversity and realism of many of the sounds employed categorizes the *Poème électronique* as *'musique concrète'* (a term coined in 1948 by the French musician Pierre Schaeffer for recorded sound material which, even if electronically modified, originates in nature or man-made environments), rather than true, studio-generated electronic music, but it remains the fulfilment of a vision which, while radical in impulse, was never content with totally abstract sound manipulation. By the time the *Poème électronique* was first heard, Stockhausen and others had progressed beyond *musique concrète* (useful though its principles were to remain) into the purer, less anecdotal world of electronic synthesis: Stockhausen's *Studie I* was composed during the summer of 1953. Yet far from dismissing Varèse's work as oldfashioned or amateurish, Stockhausen paid it a warm tribute: 'Varèse is alone in his generation in having composed a work of electronic music and furthermore in having heralded in this *Poème* a modern formulation of compositional relationships whose true significance can only today be recognized: namely the sequential presentation and superimposition – even though sometimes abrupt and unmediated – of events of a heterogeneous nature.'[13]

In 1958 Varèse was seventy-five, and any discussion of such work as survives from the last years of his life is inevitably tinged with speculation about what he might have achieved had the electronic techniques available to him in the 1950s been on hand when he first envisaged them more than thirty years before. As it is, the last works seem like a retreat, or even a pessimistic confession of disillusionment, since neither *Nocturnal* for soprano, chorus and orchestra (1961), only a fragment of which could be edited for publication, nor the later, still unavailable *Nuits* for soprano and chamber ensemble (1965) use any electronic elements, and the prevailing atmosphere of *Nocturnal* is sombre and doom-laden. For all the fragmentary nature of these works, enough remains to indicate that Varèse's career as a whole cannot be considered as a simple forward progress starting with ruthless rejection of conventions and reaching its consummation in the eager, exclusive exploration of new electronic sound worlds. Perhaps his greatest single work is *Ecuatorial*, that enigmatic prelude to the long silence, a passionate, primitive prayer for survival, which in its simplicity and seriousness is utterly remote from the kind of radical experimentation which was shortly to gain ground in America. Perhaps the most daunting thing for Varèse in his last years was not the complexity which rapid developments in technology had brought into the world of electronic music, but the sense – shared by Boulez, Ligeti and others – that composers were insufficiently equipped to develop the new technical possibilities to the full: that one lifetime, even in the twentieth century, would not be enough.

In October 1918, three years after Varèse had arrived in America, Charles Ives (1874–1954) suffered the heart attack which was a crucial factor in his abandonment of further creative work. Instead, he began the complicated task of sorting and editing his many manuscripts, and arranged for the private publication of certain pieces. Performances were still slow in coming, however, and during the interwar years it was publication which won Ives such recognition as he received.

Elliott Carter was an early acquaintance and admirer of Ives – they first met in 1924, when Carter was only sixteen – and Henry Cowell (1897–1965) published several of Ives's works in his New Music Edition. As early as 1912 Cowell the composer had begun to question received beliefs as to how traditional instruments like the piano could be exploited, and to employ highly discordant tonal clusters for which he devised a new kind of notation. In 1919 Cowell completed a short book called *New Musical Resources* which, although pre-dating many of his most influential experimental pieces like the 'Mosaic' String Quartet (1934), an early example of so-called 'open' form, is a remarkable anticipation of the spirit of root-and-branch questioning of accepted ideas about music which only became widespread after 1950.

New Musical Resources was not published until 1930, but it was in the late 1920s that Harry Partch (1901–74) wrote the first draft of what was to become a still more radical attempt to create a genuinely new music: *Genesis of a Music*. This enormous, rambling tome provides both a critique of the entire history of musical theory and composition from Partch's own very personal viewpoint, and a primer in the new techniques of 'Corporeal Music', which reject Equal Temperament and are rooted in just intonation with a scale of forty-three steps to the octave. What makes Partch such a consistently radical figure is not his rejection of an old tradition but his determination *not* to create a new tradition. His own compositions are not intended to provide 'a basis for a substitute tyranny, the grooving of music and musical theory into another set of conventions. What I do hope for is to stimulate creative work by example, to encourage investigation of basic factors, and to leave all others to individual if not idiosyncratic choice. To influence, yes: to limit, no.'[14]

In discussing musical instruments which attempt 'better intonations', Partch ruefully noted that they tend to survive only in museums. Now that all perceptible inflections of pitch can be achieved electronically, the odds must be that his own instruments – even those with such evocative titles as the Marimba Eroica and The Spoils of War – will also finish up alongside Bosanquet's Enharmonic Harmonium and General Thompson's Enharmonic Organ (both to be seen in London's Science Museum): that is, unless their visual, dramatic potential, undoubtedly so superior to that of any electronic equipment, wins them survival. Partch's own compositions have also shown little potential for attracting frequent performance. So however predisposed one may be to approve of a composer who uses titles like 'A soul tormented by contemporary music finds a humanizing alchemy' (*The Bewitched*, Scene 4), the effort involved in learning the special techniques can only reward those who sympathize deeply with the aesthetic philosophy and view of history underlying those techniques.

Partch was never tested by success, but John Cage (born 1912) has shown remarkable resilience in the face of exposure to the full glare of acclaim as a cult figure. In the musical scene since 1945, Cage stands at the opposite pole from Milton Babbitt, the only ground on which they meet being the use of electronic techniques. It is therefore ironic that, while Babbitt has done more than any other American composer to build on twelve-note foundations, it was Cage who actually studied with Schoenberg, between 1935 and 1937. Earlier, Cage took lessons from Henry Cowell, who did much to stimulate an interest in non-Western ideas; and this interest, later to embrace aspects of Buddhist philosophy, did much more to mould Cage's development as a composer than the harmony-oriented, post-Renaissance assumptions of Schoenberg.

Cage soon gained attention as an explorer of new sound sources, carrying on from what Varèse had achieved in *Ionisation* at a time when Varèse himself was virtually silent. One of his earliest characteristic works is the *First Construction in Metal* for percussion ensemble (1939), and in the same year he also produced *Imaginary Landscape No. 1* for two variable-speed gramophone turntables, frequency recordings, muted piano and cymbal. This is not only a genuine precursor of electronic music, but also employs what is probably Cage's most familiar modification of a traditional sound-source, the 'prepared' piano. In view of the Dadaist expectations aroused when audiences see a pianist plucking the strings, using drum sticks, inserting screws, pieces of paper and other objects to deaden resonance, or simply tapping on the instrument's closed lid, it is important to remember that Cage's most substantial composition for prepared piano, the seventy-minute Sonatas and Interludes (1946–8), involves quite rigorous rhythmic structuring. It is in fact only since 1950 that the experimental concept with which Cage is principally associated has been fully established and explored. 'Indeterminacy', as this is most commonly called, has been defined in many different ways, but in essence it involves a shift of emphasis away from the idea of a musical composition as a sequence of permanently fixed and fully realized elements to an approach which seeks a significant degree of freedom and flexibility in the structure and notation of a composition. It was only with the liberation of music from the principle that every performance of a particular piece will be substantially the same, however revolutionary the language employed, that experimentalism achieved a new breakthrough. That breakthrough, though variously anticipated during the first half of the century, did not finally achieve a wide following until the postwar period, at a time when many composers were disillusioned with 'total' serialism.

Indeterminacy encouraged greater spontaneity through performer participation in actually determining both the course of events in a work and the content of those events, and it was soon possible to observe parallels with those surrealistic dramatic happenings often known collectively as the Theatre of the Absurd. The more imprecise, graphic methods of notation likewise resemble abstract or surrealist art more than traditional musical notation. These more extreme manifestations of musical indeterminacy have inevitably tended to receive the greatest publicity, and to create the assumption that the entire movement is more destructive than constructive. Yet the most common and fruitful kind of indeterminate or aleatory element has been that which permits a performer to select the number of segments in a work and the order in which they appear. This allows the interpreter a more positive role than he has in much other modern music, where the technical difficulties are such that the most he can hope for is an approximate reproduction of the 'correct' pitches and durations; but the role of the composer is not usurped. For Cage himself, however, a more radical approach was necessary: if music was to aspire to the condition of furniture (in Satie's terms), if the now decadent distinctions between Art and Life were to be eliminated and, the concept of composition as something more valuable than any other human activity to be discredited, then the authority of the composer as decision-maker must be undermined, and the traditional idea of a concert as an event in which clearly distinct hierarchies – composer, interpreter, listener – are preserved, should be destroyed: in this Reformation, the first 'monasteries' to be wiped out were therefore concert halls. Cage first attempted to cast off the responsibility for creative decisions by such random procedures as employing the *I Ching*, as in his *Music of Changes* for piano (1951). Later he came more and more to favour Dadaist activities like the *Theatre Piece* (1960) and *Musiccircus* (1968), in which his role is confined to that of an initiator of events which are likely to possess certain characteristics but in which the gulf between what is 'notated' in the 'score' and what takes place at a performance is, intentionally, immense: it is in that gulf that freedom from traditional shackles, and therefore the experimental essence, lie.

Cage himself has always been perfectly willing to discuss his motives, and even to make 'compositions' out of his lectures – as in *45' for a speaker* (1954), the seventh minute of which is laid out as follows.

Ex. 60

7' 00"	Composers are spoken of as having
	ears for music which generally
	means that nothing presented
	to their ears can be heard by them.
	Their ears are walled in
	with sounds
10"	of their own imagination
	Of five aspects
	observe
20"	*two.*

The highest purpose is to have no purpose
at all. This puts one in accord with nature
in her manner of operation. If someone comes
along and asks why? there are answers.
30″ However there is a story I have found very helpful. What's so interesting about
technique anyway? *What if there are twelve tones in a*
row? What row? This seeing of cause and effect
is not emphasized but instead one makes an
identification with what is here and now. He
40″ then spoke of two qualities. Unimpededness and Inter-
penetration.

The relationship of things happening
at the same time is spontaneous
and irrepressible.
50″ It is you yourself
in the form you have
that instant taken.
To stop and figure it out
takes
time.

His writings are full of recurring themes: 'I attempt to let sounds be
themselves in a space of time . . . I do not object to being engaged in a
purposeless activity;'[15] and 'more and more in this global electronic
world that we are living in, I think this experience of non-knowledge is
more useful and more important to us than the Renaissance notion of
knowing ABCDEF what you are doing.'[16]

Perhaps the archetypal experimental composition (leaving aside the
argument that the most experimental thing of all would be to compose
nothing) is Cage's *4′ 33″* (1952), the score of which 'bears the numbers
I, II, III, each marked "TACET" and each given a duration in
minutes and seconds which together add up to four minutes, thirty-
three seconds. A secondary part of the notation tells the performer that
the piece may be done on any instrument, for any length of time. Since
"tacet" is the notation which informs a player that he should play
nothing during a movement, the performer of *4′ 33″* is asked to make no
sounds in the three timed sections.'[17] It is obvious enough that the
whole 'point' of this piece lies in its contradiction, graphic and dramatic, of what normally happens at a concert when a pianist enters and sits
down at the piano. In these terms, it may irritate or amuse: after all,

those decisions which the composer *has* made are still very important. Such precise timings are obviously a parody of a composer's normal concern with durational relationships within a piece, but they at least ensure that the 'joke' is bearably short. More fundamental aesthetic issues are nevertheless raised when the whole question of what is heard during those 4′ 33″ is considered: audience shuffles, laughter, traffic outside the hall, air-conditioning systems and the like. 'Any sounds which might be heard . . . are of no consequence in themselves; the real interest of the piece is in the concepts which underlie it (that "silence" does not really exist, reversal of the roles of performer and listener etc). . . . In much Experimental Music, style, in my sense of a coherent musical language and discourse, has been painstakingly destroyed. All that remains are ideas and concepts, which on closer examination begin to appear positively reactionary in their implications.'[18]

It is nevertheless appropriate that Cage's most consistent trait should be unpredictability: so he may still occasionally produce a composition which, surrealist connotations notwithstanding, is not merely a matter of letting unforeseen sounds occur by accident. *Cheap Imitation* (1969) 'consists solely of the melodic line of Erik Satie's *Socrate*, using the I Ching to determine the mode and transposition of each bar or half-bar. There is no counterpoint because the entire work (which, like *Socrate*, is in three movements and lasts about twenty minutes) is monodic; . . . it is wonderful to come upon a piece which makes a unique effect with such subtlety that one is scarcely aware of it happening. . . . I am sure of the lesson which this piece can teach us – that perhaps it is the simplification rather than the elaboration of musical language which is now the most fruitful way forward.'[19] Cage's affectionate and characteristically personal tribute to his most admired precursor may therefore also represent his recognition that what other experimental composers have been doing increasingly since 1960 has genuine musical value, in spite of its remoteness from the more extreme manifestations of Dadaist 'play' and Buddhist 'will-less-ness' alike.

In general, there has been a retreat from chance and from the 'happening': 'perhaps a reaction against indeterminacy was inevitable: the music of LaMonte Young and Terry Riley, Steve Reich and Phil Glass . . . shows a many-sided retrenchment from the music that has grown from indeterminacy, and draws on sources hitherto neglected by experimental music. This music not only cuts down the area of sound-activity to an absolute (and absolutist) minimum, but submits the scrupulously selective, mainly tonal, material, to mostly repetitive, highly disciplined procedures which are focused with an extremely fine definition (though the listener's focusing is not done for him).'[20] Further evidence of such retrenchment is provided by another American experimentalist, Christian Wolff (born 1934), who senses that 'practically everything's been done now. There are just a few bizarre things that haven't been thought of. . . . There's a desire now to come back and get reconnected to what most people have been trained for. I think it's perhaps more a desire to relate to music which can reach a larger public and which has clear-cut technical demands.'[21] Often the motivation for the new simplicity is political, as in Wolff's own *Accompaniments* and *Changing the System*, so it is not surprising that experimental techniques which had their origins either in the consciously frivolous, apolitical aesthetic atmosphere of the years immediately after 1918, or else in the eager absorption of Eastern religious philosophies, should no longer seem so relevant: today it is Mao rather than Buddha who is the most important Eastern inspiration.

The music of Riley (born 1935), Reich (born 1936) and Glass (born 1937) — known variously as minimalist, systemic, process or repetitive — is certainly a more positive kind of experimentalism, often involving the sensitive interaction of an ensemble in a group performance, than the isolated snook-cocking of a work like Cage's *4′ 33″*. This music involves a creative response to certain areas of Western tradition, especially pre-Renaissance music, as well as to those aspects of non-Western music more concerned with the sustaining and contemplation of a single state than with determined progress towards a goal. 'Gradual changes in time' — Reich's phrase — therefore assume tremendous structural significance, and for this reason it might be assumed that this is music for participation rather than relatively passive listening. Yet more extended, comparatively recent compositions like Reich's *The Desert Music* for chorus and orchestra (1983) and Glass's operas, notably *Akhnaten* (1984), have proved very successful with audiences. These works in relatively conventional genres are evidence of a move away from the more extreme, least evolutionary kinds of repetitive music. Yet there remains a clear distinction between the ways in which Reich and Glass use the elements of tonality and any full revival of the functions and processes of traditional tonal harmony. In this respect the minimalist composers have remained true to their experimental principles.

Chapter 11

Three Individualists

Michael Tippett (born 1905), Olivier Messiaen (born 1908) and Elliott Carter (born 1908) are all highly regarded for their integrity and individuality. They have little enough in common with their most prominent fellow-countrymen and virtually nothing, in terms of style, with each other, beyond an ability to shape and direct highly ornamented melodic lines in the context of substantial musical forms. It is the extent and direction of their stylistic evolution which justifies bringing them together under one heading. All three began as relatively conservative, tonal composers; since 1945 all three have moved away from any overriding reliance on tonality and traditional formal designs, even though neither Tippett nor Messiaen has severed all links with triadic harmony. Their development is evidence of the remarkable impulse which, even before the principles of serialism were at all widely understood, led to an increasing dissatisfaction with attempts to shore up tonality, and an awareness that 'atonality' did not automatically imply the use of discontinuous athematicism. In the mid-1940s all three composers were younger than Schoenberg had been when the twelve-note method was formulated, yet their independence of the Viennese tradition and their instinct for working broadly, on a large scale, may well have been sufficient to convince them that the consistent employment of serial techniques would not be compatible with their expressive aims. Both Messiaen and Carter adopted highly comprehensive forms of discipline with regard to pitch organization, but in general the actual order of pitches and intervals at every stage has not been dictated by any system. Tippett, the eldest of the three, is the least radical, and in spite of instances like the twelve-note theme in *The Knot Garden*, associations with music of an earlier time tend to be more obvious in his case.

In strong contrast to his younger English contemporary, Benjamin Britten, Tippett matured slowly as a composer, and his early interests –

especially the instrumental music of Beethoven – have proved to be of
lasting importance. Long study and severe self-criticism combined to
ensure that the first works which have been allowed to survive date
from the late 1930s, but the last of these, the Concerto for Double String
Orchestra (1939), is not merely evidence of a newly matured composer's freshness of style and sophistication of technique: it is one of the
finest works for the medium ever written, and one of the best British
compositions of the century.

Ex. 61

Ex. 61 (contd.)

The concerto is, in the broadest sense, neo-classical: a modern re-creation of older stylistic elements which are, in fact, pre-classical. The flexible rhythms and vigorous contrapuntal textures recall the English madrigals and fantasies of the sixteenth and seventeenth centuries, transmuted through a jazz-inspired exuberance and a pervasive modality suggested by folk music itself and by modern British composers influenced by its idioms. The uninhibited melodiousness and radiantly diatonic sheen of the texture at the end clearly proclaim a composer committed to positive statement, and even if nothing were known about Tippett's involvement in amateur music-making, or his pacifism, it would be possible to assert with confidence that this was the work of no ivory-tower composer (Ex. 61).

Yet the sheer passion of Tippett's commitment to ideas, as well as his openness to musical inspiration, has created problems of transmission and translation which he has had to fight hard to solve. In the oratorio *A Child of our Time* (1939–41), the timely theme of racial persecution could be expressed in music of maximum directness – hence the incorporation of Negro spirituals. But when Tippett moved on from public to more private concerns in his first opera, *The Midsummer Marriage* (1945–52), the subject matter and its mode of verbal expression became more complex, risking both incongruity and incoherence. The dramatic theme is still a very simple one: maturity, fulfilment and the ability to relate to others can only be attained through self-knowledge and self-acceptance; and Tippett's music is fortunately capable of illustrating how such a state can be attained much more directly and convincingly than his words or stage directions. The richness and spontaneity of the musical language employed in the opera – and in the two major instrumental works of this period: the Symphony No. 1 (1944–5) and the String Quartet No. 3 (1945–6) – proved that the Concerto for Double String Orchestra was no happy accident: the manner presented through such an appropriate medium in the concerto was capable of considerable extension and enrichment, and it found its apotheosis in *The Midsummer Marriage* with its satisfyingly positive conclusion depicting the joyful union of two self-knowing, unselfish people.

Only a composer with supreme confidence in his musical language could use it to express such supreme confidence, and for most of the next decade Tippett's music was dominated by the principle of the ultimate, positive major triad. The Piano Concerto (1953–5) and the Symphony No. 2 (1956–7) both reflect the richness of the world created for the opera, though in the symphony the lyric impulse yields its pre-eminence to a more forceful rhythmic profile and sharper thematic outlines. A transition had begun, and *King Priam* (1958–61), Tippett's second opera, reveals the elements of a new manner: the ultimate possibility of tonal resolution is finally stifled by a curious, disembodied cadence (Ex. 62). Instrumental colours and groups alternate and conflict in mosaic-like rather than development contexts, and the lyric impulse is compressed and burnished to yield a new, uncompromising clarity.

Ex. 62

Tippett's use of tonality had been no more imitative of classical and romantic practice than that of most other modern masters, but he could only abandon his reliance on the expressive power of the triad as the embodiment of positive resolution at the risk of entering a different, darker world of expression. In the years after the completion of *King Priam* the implications of this new situation were worked out with characteristic single-mindedness and resource.

Tippett changed direction at a remarkably late stage in his career. For Messiaen, as for Carter, it was the late 1940s, rather than the early 1960s, which were the crucial years, at which time he had been prominent as a composer for twenty years. When the short organ piece *Le Banquet céleste* (1928) and the Préludes for piano (1929) were written, Debussy had been dead for only a decade, and Messiaen has acknowledged Debussy as his most important musical forebear. Yet he would probably condemn Debussy's way of life and lack of serious Christian concerns. For Messiaen it is not enough to be a religious composer: he sees himself as a *theological* composer, dedicated to the task of reconciling human imperfection and Divine Glory through the medium of Art.

Such an aim might easily have led to the cultivation of a popular, or at any rate highly conservative, style. Yet Messiaen has never been concerned to provide liturgical material for average choirs, organists and congregations, and his approach – the use of relatively radical techniques to express an unquestioning acceptance of Catholic dogma – contrasts strikingly with that of equally didactic Communist composers, who use conservative techniques to express supposedly revolutionary social and political concepts. In a revealing interview, Messiaen has voiced his detestation of most aspects of modern life, both social and political, and has summed up his view of the present in terms of a pervading 'bad taste'.[7] He much prefers the idea of the great Assyrian or Sumerian civilizations of the past. It is logical, then, that his music should exploit certain aspects of non-European music, and also involve such a purely natural, non-human, musical phenomenon as birdsong.

Just as Debussy was particularly influenced in his formative years by French and Russian masters (Massenet and Mussorgsky, for instance), so Messiaen's early works owe something to both the sensuous religiosity of Gounod and Franck and the erotic mysticism of Skryabin. The influence of Debussy was paramount, however, and although Messiaen once believed it was no longer possible to compose operas, he claims that

Pelléas et Mélisande has influenced him more than any other single work. Messiaen has shown himself well able to continue and intensify the rapt, contemplative moods and the timeless reticence so characteristic of much of *Pelléas*. He is by no means exclusively attached to understatement, but the more bombastic effects which occur from time to time do not always seem organically integrated into the overall scheme: one is more aware of contrast between meditation and jubilation than of transition from one to the other.

The technical importance of Debussy's example is far-reaching, and Messiaen responded to it with that keen analytical intelligence which has made him much sought after as a teacher. In particular, his system of pitch modes, whereby seven different scales and those transpositions of them which do not merely present the same pitches in a different order can be used to produce 'non-functional' tonal harmony, represents both an extension and a codification of Debussian chromaticism, whose own relationship to systematic modality was so fruitfully ambiguous.

A simple example of the expanded tonality which these Modes of Limited Transposition make possible is taken from the seventh movement of the *Quatuor pour la fin du temps* (1941) (Ex. 63). This passage uses the first version of Mode II, the nature of which excludes the occurrence of conventional cadential progressions; although several tonic triads may be deduced, none of their dominants or subdominants are available. Even so, the phrase-structure of this extract is conventional, with the second three bars a sequential repetition of the first a minor third lower, and the final six bars an extended sequential repetition, another minor third lower. And although no 'pure' triads are employed, in each phrase there is a clear distinction between relatively tense or dissonant chords – those including the clash of a minor second – and the less tense added sixths with which each phrase ends. These 'resolutions' enable the successive tonalities of A major, F sharp and major and E flat major to be hinted at rather than firmly established, but at this stage in his development Messiaen still retained a fundamental allegiance to tonality as an essential structural force.

Messiaen shares Debussy's dislike of sonata form and love of metric flexibility, though his view of rhythm 'as arising from an extension of durations in time rather than from a division of time'[2] is a new factor of great importance. Debussy also had a notably ambivalent attitude to Wagner, and Messiaen in turn has established certain Wagnerian associations through his interest in the Tristan story. Messiaen has made it clear that this archetypal account of the strengths and weaknesses of human love attracts him only to the extent that, even at its greatest, human love palely reflects Divine Love, thus providing a link between life and death, man and God. In a trilogy of works composed between 1945 and 1949, Messiaen provides an elaborate treatment of this 'theology of love.' The song cycle *Harawi* (1945), the *Turangalîla*

Ex. 63

Symphony (1946–8) (Turangalîla is the Hindu word for love song) and the *Cinq Rechants* for twelve unaccompanied voices (1949) are a formidable theologico-aesthetic statement, but they are also a stylistic turning-point. As the symphony shows, Messiaen was content to employ quite simple structures, often involving the alternation and repetition of self-contained sections, on a very large scale. Already, too, there was a notable variety of material, ranging from florid ornamental lines deriving from transmuted birdsong to a rhythmic 'series' and simpler, chordal, triadic themes. Messiaen may have sensed that the expressive and structural weight being placed on these triadic 'resolutions', not only in the symphony, but also in large works like the *Visions de l'Amen* for two pianos (1943) and the *Trois petites Liturgies de la Présence Divine* (1944), was not sufficiently justified in a purely linguistic sense; or he may simply have decided to give the more complex harmonic elements already present greater prominence, just as birdsong and chant-like thematic material, densely harmonized, began to oust more traditional melodic phrases. The end of the war meant for many European composers the chance to discover serialism: for many it was to lead to conversion, and even for Messiaen, at a time when his pupils included young firebrands like Pierre Boulez, it demanded serious consideration and left permanent effects.

It was in a Paris dominated by the neo-classicism of Stravinsky that the young Elliott Carter studied from 1932 to 1935. As a friend and admirer of Charles Ives, Carter could never have felt as close to the great European tradition as either Tippett or Messiaen, yet he was equally cautious about imitating the exuberant and often chaotic experimentation of Ives, with his dense atonal polyphony, his constant quotations of hymn tunes, popular songs and other borrowed material, ranging from *Sir Roger de Coverley* to Beethoven's Fifth Symphony. Carter opted for discipline and clarity, so that during the 1930s and early 1940s he seemed to be treading a path roughly similar to that of the leading American neo-classicist, Aaron Copland. Yet this cautious beginning was the foundation of one of the most complex and imaginative stylistic transformations in twentieth-century music. Messiaen's religious beliefs continued to shape his musical subject matter after the dogma of serialism had failed to compel his adherence; Tippett's voracious absorption of literary, philosophical and psychological imagery stimulated more far-reaching musical explorations than a musical language framed by triadic rhetoric could contain; and Carter, too, was decisively influenced by extra-musical factors: 'Before the end of the Second World War, it became clear to me, partly as a result of re-reading Freud and others, and thinking about psychoanalysis, that we were living in a world where . . . physical and intellectual violence would always be a problem, and that the whole conception of human nature underlying the neo-classic esthetic amounted to a sweeping under the rug of things that, it seemed to me, we had to deal with in a less oblique and resigned way.'[3]

After his return to America in 1935 Carter's style in works like the ballets *Pocahontas* (1939) and *The Minotaur* (1947) resembled Hindemith and Stravinsky as well as Copland. As long as he remained committed to some kind of tonality these were likely to remain his most basic influences, yet they did not inhibit the evolution of a vigorously confident manner nor the use of substantial forms. The Piano Sonata (1945–6), for all its tonal framework, is far from palely neo-classical, and suggests an almost epic imagination, a confrontation of major expressive issues of the kind acknowledged in the above quotation. Elsewhere, Carter has defined the neo-classic aim as to make music 'anti-individualistic, to sound almost machine-made', and the basic impulse in his move away from such concerns after 1946 was a desire to rethink 'the rhythmic means of what had begun to seem a very limited routine used in most contemporary and older Western music'.⁴ So it was to African, Indian, Arab and Balinese music that he turned, as well as very un-neo-classical Western composers like Skryabin and Ives. 'The result was a way of evolving rhythms and rhythmic continuities, sometimes called "metric modulation":' a further result was the abandonment of neo-classical structures with their 'static repetitiveness', and with the loss of traditional forms came the loss of tonality itself. The parallel with Messiaen's increasing involvement with aspects of Eastern culture needs no stressing.

All these tendencies and tensions are found in the fine Sonata for Cello and Piano (1948), a transitional work in which only the second of the four movements uses key signatures. This was apparently written first – the first movement certainly came last – and the key signatures are the result of a musical character described by Carter as 'a breezy treatment of a type of pop music, [which] verges on a parody of some Americanizing colleagues of the time. . . . . It makes explicit the undercurrent of jazz technique suggested in the previous movement by the freely performed melody against a strict rhythm.'

The Cello Sonata is remarkable for its anticipation in admittedly simple form of many of the basic features of the later radical masterpieces. Thus it begins and ends with 'extreme dissociation' between the two instruments: the cello plays 'a long melody in rather free style, while the piano percussively marks a regular clock-like ticking.' As Carter says, these differences of character are 'one of the points of the piece'. They are nevertheless differences which are so far from being immutable as to be interchangeable, and the whole work ends with the cello using the ticking rhythm and the piano recalling the expressive melody. The drama of changing characters is significantly exploited at the end of the second movement, when the piano 'predicts the notes and speed of the cello's opening of the third', and also at the end of the third movement, where the cello 'predicts . . . the piano's opening of the fourth'. In the simplest terms, then, the texture of the sonata is concerned with mediation between relative dissociation and relative association, a process which can be clearly observed in the first movement itself. 'Association' begins at the point where the piano

Ex. 64

echoes the last three notes of the cello's first long phrase, and reaches unity of character and rhythm at the climax just before what can still be defined as the recapitulation (Ex. 64).

After the completion of *King Priam* in 1961, Michael Tippett began to work out the implications of his new style in the most direct way by using music from the opera in two further works, the Piano Sonata No. 2 (1962) and the Concerto for Orchestra (1963). *King Priam* is a heroic tragedy, and its study of men caught in the web of violence and conflict is as intelligent and compassionate as – perhaps – only someone dedicated to non-violence could achieve. To this extent it has more in common with *A Child of our Time* than with *The Midsummer Marriage*, but the purely stylistic innovations – the juxtaposition, repetition (usually in varied forms) and combination of specific types of material and colour – raised purely structural issues which stimulated further exploration. The Piano Sonata No. 2, a single ten-minute movement, uses eight different types of material (including motives from Act II of the opera), alternating and intercutting in a sequence which, when set out diagrammatically, might seem highly arbitrary, yet which creates a satisfying psychological progression in performance. The great danger of this kind of form is that it might produce an episodic succession which fails to cohere into a larger unity, particularly when tonality is lacking. There may seem no decisive reason why *one* sequence of events should be preferable to any other, yet Tippett's instinct ensures essential coherence; as he himself has commented, 'the formal unity comes from the balance of similarity and contrast'.[5] It may be that works which exploit contrast more explicitly than continuity are inherently less satisfying: they move forward as much by contradiction as by reasoned argument – hence the contention that such 'block' forms are anti-developmental. Tippett avoids a static effect through the sheer dramatic excitement engendered by the unpredictable interaction of easily identifiable thematic elements; the sonata's material ranges from highly dissonant and percussive chords to a lyrical, quasi-tonal melody which recalls the world of the Piano Concerto and *The Midsummer Marriage*. It is certainly possible to dispute the assertion that the work is atonal, for the composer's technique of repeating material at the same pitch, and of allowing occasional chords to approximate to triadic formations, can create at least a residue of tonal feeling, even if, as in *King Priam* itself, the ending avoids any obvious sense of resolution.

After pursuing these techniques on a larger scale in the Concerto for

Orchestra, and creating a particularly striking contrast between the florid melodic continuity of the central *Lento* and the more disparate, variously coloured elements of the flanking movements, Tippett returned to vocal composition in a work which is extremely difficult to perform yet is one of his most remarkable. *The Vision of St Augustine* for solo baritone, chorus and orchestra (1966) is a three-part setting of a text which combines Augustine's own words with quotations from the Latin Bible and other sources. Augustine was deeply concerned with the meaning of Time – and Eternity – and Tippett prefaces his score with T. S. Eliot's line 'and all is always now', adding in his introductory notes that 'we cannot in this temporal existence experience a true present'. Time-structure is of fundamental importance to the work, and the page facing the first bars of the score sets out the fourteen tempi (ranging from crotchet *c.*56 to dotted crotchet *c.*168) which operate during its course. *The Vision of St Augustine* projects a great melodic and thematic richness which is fully equal to its ambitious 'programme'; and this richness, and an ease in the handling of a 'new' idiom, display satisfying links with the ecstatic lyricism of Tippett's earlier manner. The new style achieves its clearest definition, and most ambitiously proportioned form, in conjunction with fundamental features of the old.

Tippett's third opera, *The Knot Garden* (1970), is another parable of the need for self-knowledge and an account of its attainment by a diverse group of characters (including a musician and a psychoanalyst), whose stylized environments and inter-reactions are projected through music as economical and as expressively intense as that of *The Vision of St Augustine*. The text is not without a characteristic awkwardness: jarring quotations, slang, high-flown imagery, jostle together in an idiosyncratic mixture which is nevertheless vindicated by the sheer force of its need for just this particular dramatic form and musical setting.

The progress of the characters towards positive self-realization is dramatized through music of extraordinary imagination, often hectically disjointed, but equally capable of the simplest lyrical phrases. Arias, ensembles and brief orchestral interludes provide a framework of precisely the right degree of formality, and the music is often disruptively critical of both formality and convention, as in the hysterical coloratura of Denise's long scena (Act I, Scene 13) (Ex. 65).

Equally ambiguous is the role of tonal stress, with the note B exercising an underlying force which rises most obviously to the surface in Act II with the quotation of Schubert's song 'Die liebe Farbe'. This technique of reminiscence is carried further in *Songs for Dov* (1971), an offshoot of the opera in the form of an extended cycle for one of the characters, and is also crucial to the Symphony No. 3 (1972).

Ex. 65

While even less tonally explicit than *The Knot Garden*, the symphony is closer to the opera and also more remote from traditional formal types than is the Third Piano Sonata (1973). The first of its two parts presents a polarity between the concepts of 'Arrest' and 'Movement', terms used by Tippett to imply 'a compression of energy and an explosion of energy; both positive'.[6] These entities alternate five times each, getting progressively longer until the fifth recurrence of the 'Movement' material is cut short to make way for a combination of the two elements (Fig. 87). The remainder of Part One is a *Lento* in which there is a change of polarity. Tippett speaks of the elements as representing Discontinuity and Continuity – discontinuity in the sense of the constant repetition of rather static shapes. The repetitions of the viola melody which represents Continuity grow shorter until, on the fifth and last appearance, the original thirty bars are reduced to two.

The movement ends, not with the two elements combined, but with a sixth reference to the Discontinuous material.

The first part of the symphony therefore involves two very different kinds of opposition but a similar means of simple structural intensification in each case: a more convincingly symphonic procedure than that of the works written immediately after *King Priam*, with their greater number of short contrasting segments. Part Two is more sectional in structure, beginning with a turbulent *Allegro molto* 'which is a play of five contrasted "musics" (metaphorically, like a juggler with five different objects in the air at once)'. Apparently Tippett originally intended to follow this with a sequence of purely instrumental Blues, but his inclination to parallel what he has called the 'abstraction' of Part One with the 'dramatics' of Part Two led him inevitably to vocal music. In that the four of his own poems which he sets are 'songs of innocence and experience: two and two', the structural dualities of Part One may have generated the dramatic contrasts of Part Two. Further dualities involve the quotation and distortion of the finale of Beethoven's Ninth Symphony (Tippett's fourth poem recalls Schiller's *Ode to Joy*) as a kind of goad to Tippett's own propulsive style, and the contrast between the transfigured Blues idiom of the first three settings and the 'original' Tippett of the last – complete with references to Part One of the symphony. Yet the grand affirmation which ends Tippett's text – 'We sense a huge compassionate power / To heal, to love' – is still not matched by the sort of transcendentally lyrical peroration and triadic resolution most memorably achieved in *The Midsummer Marriage*. Instead, a sequence of orchestral chords (alternately loud and soft, and all discords) intone a 'coda' in which alternative gestures seem frozen into immobility. The power is sensed: it cannot yet be used.

The Third Symphony employs the symphonic principle in a highly personal way. The Third Piano Sonata is, at least in outline, more traditional, for its three continuous movements are, respectively, a 'fast sonata-allegro, i.e. . . . a statement of contrasted materials', a slow set of four variations on a theme comprising 'a succession of seventeen elaborate chords', and a fast finale which is 'an ABA-shaped toccata'.[7] In place of the shifting contrasts and cumulative superimpositions of the symphony, Tippett adopts more formal, symmetrical procedures which may well have been suggested by the visual mirror-image of a pianist's hands moving inwards and outwards between the extremes of the keyboard. Thus 'the independence of the hands is explored chiefly in the outer fast movements and the unity in the middle.' In the slow movement, each of the four variations transposes the basic sequence of chords up a minor third, 'thus returning in Variation Four to the initial level'. Then, in the finale, the central section repeats the first in mirror form. Such a comprehensive rediscovery of traditional structural features is satisfying, since, far from displaying a dilution of Tippett's musical language, the Third Sonata is characteristically forceful and eloquent. For a composer with Tippett's associative mind, it has never seemed that compositions which proceed entirely 'by statement' (like *King Priam* and the Second Sonata) would prove permanently attractive. The dramatic nature of that opera suggested a musical approach which has had a powerful effect on Tippett's style, but his finest music is more wide-ranging and ultimately more appealing.

Messiaen's short piano composition *Mode de valeurs et d'intensités* (Mode of durations and dynamics), written in 1949, is often loosely described as 'totally serial', but the title itself suggests that the piece presents an extension of Messiaen's own modal techniques. It does not even follow the Schoenbergian principle of fixing the twelve pitches in sequence; as in all Messiaen's earlier modal works, the notes of the mode need not appear in any specific order: some may be omitted altogether, others used as often as the composer desires. More significant in terms of serialism in this piece is the association between certain registers, durations and dynamics. The keyboard is divided into three regions, which themselves overlap to a considerable extent. The lowest region has the longest durations (quaver to dotted semibreve), the highest the shortest (demisemiquaver to dotted crotchet), but some durations recur in two or three regions. Messiaen employs twelve different durations and twelve different types of attack (including 'normal'), but only seven dynamic markings (*ppp* to *fff*) – a more realistic arrangement than the twelve, ranging from *ppppp* to *fffff*, adopted by some composers.

As a reaction to the delayed exploration of serial music in Europe in the late 1940s, this piece, along with its close contemporaries *Cantéyodjayâ*, *Neumes rythmiques* (both 1949) and *Île de Feu* I and II (1950), has undeniable historical importance. We know that, 'as early as 1944, during the course of his discussions of Berg's *Lyric Suite* in his composition classes, Messiaen spoke out against the tendency of the second Viennese school to experiment exclusively with pitch structures while adhering to traditional conceptions of rhythm and form:'[8] yet Messiaen's style was never likely to turn permanently in the direction of such highly unified pattern-making. Twelve-note pitch serialism has had a permanent effect on his later music, but his only orthodox twelve-note piece is the fifth movement of the *Livre d'Orgue* (1951), and his use of various kinds of rhythmic motives, modes and series, which predates *Mode de valeurs et d'intensités*, is more a result of his continuing interest in Eastern music – principally the 120 deçi-tâlas of Sharngadeva – than an outcome of Western pitch-serialism as such. The major works of the 1950s, with their increasing concentration on the atonal polyphony of birdsong and the colours of tuned percussion, are consistent in their rejection of any all-embracing serial system: *Réveil des Oiseaux* (1953) derives its material entirely from thirty-eight different birdsongs, and the gigantic seven-volume *Catalogue d'Oiseaux* (1956-8) synthesizes elements as potentially disparate as tonality, modality (of pitch and rhythm) and twelve-note sets in free permutations. *Chronochromie* (1960) is characteristic in its presentation of highly complex textures in terms of simple formal outlines involving much repetition, and in *Et Exspecto Resurrectionem Mortuorum* (1964) the emphasis on more monumental thematic outlines and simpler rhythmic patterns was primarily the result of a conception which envisaged open-air performance – the work is scored for wind, brass and metal percussion. Each movement is prefaced with a biblical quotation and the finale – 'and I heard the voice of a great multitude' – is a rare example of a Messiaen movement entirely founded on a regular pulsation. An almost unbearable tension results from this inexorable reiteration. The bonds of the small form were burst, and Messiaen embarked on three works on a much larger scale than anything since the *Turangalîla* Symphony of twenty years earlier.

La Transfiguration de Notre Seigneur Jésus-Christ (1963–9) is an oratorio in two seven-part sections, or septenaries. Once again all the essential stylistic elements are present: the repetitive forms, the chant-like monody, birdsong, Greek metres, colour chords. In this work there is also a greater use of tonal concords, most explicitly of all in the massive chorales which end the two septenaries. The simplification of thematic outline and rhythmic pattern which *Et Exspecto* displayed is therefore extended here to harmony, and it is confirmation of the sureness of instinct with which Messiaen composes that these triads should sound like a rediscovery, not a retreat, proclaiming his ability to integrate and control the most diverse elements without incongruity.

Such integrated diversity is also to be found in Messiaen's first major organ work for almost two decades, the nine *Méditations sur le Mystère de la Sainte Trinité* (1969) and in the huge *Des canyons aux étoiles* (1974) for solo piano, horn and orchestra. With their references to the text of the *Summa Theologica*, the *Méditations* present a parallel summation of Messiaen's musical language, covering the widest range from simple tonal and triadic progressions to the metrically complex, anti-tonal textures of the 1950s and '60s. Yet the summation itself generates a new technique, for Messiaen has ceased to be entirely content with a musical language of explicit symbolism, and has devised an actual alphabet of pitch and duration in order to translate specific words into tones. The partial use of this alphabet is evidence of its experimental nature. With it, Messiaen associates musical figures for grammatical cases and also for the twin concepts of 'being' and 'having' (the latter an inversion of the former). Such 'translations' of texts occur only in two movements, however, and of greater musical importance to the work as a whole are the motto themes representing various aspects of God, the presence of three tritones in the principal version of which suggests that Messiaen is impervious to the traditionally diabolical associations of that interval. As a contributory stylistic aspect of the composition as a whole the alphabet exists on one extreme of a spectrum which is primarily notable for structural simplicity, the avoidance of extended contrapuntal textures, and for the admission that modality can engender tonality.

The seventh movement is particularly suitable for detailed study in that it brings together virtually all the important features of Messiaen's style. The composer has described it as falling into three parts, the outer sections an Introduction and a Coda which unfold the same basic sequence of events, three in all.

The first segment of the Introduction presents a series of seven chords with durations of 6, 7, 5, 8, 9, 11 and 13 semiquavers respectively. Messiaen explains that the chords employ pitches from two modes of limited transposition, 3^2 and 3^1. Combined, these modes provide all twelve chromatic semitones, and only the first of the chords belongs exclusively to either mode (3^2). Other *Méditations* use the third mode more systematically, especially with regard to the triadic elements present in its first and fourth transpositions.

The second segment of the Introduction, *Oiseau de Persépolis*, is a characteristic episode of birdsong – an unidentified bird which Messiaen heard at Persepolis – continuing the irregular rhythmic motion of the first segment, and with much internal repetition. The Introduction then ends with a pedal B (the dominant of the E major which will end the whole movement), over which four dense 'horn-chords' are heard; the first belongs to Mode 3¹, the second and third blend 3¹ and 3², and the last, a dominant aggregate in E major, belongs to 3².

The Coda of this seventh *Méditation* is one of Messiaen's typically varied recapitulations. The opening chords have the same sequence of durations as those of the Introduction but the pitch sequence is reversed, so that the notes of the Introduction's first chord appear in the Coda's last, and so on. The second section – *Oiseau de Persépolis* – begins with the identical pair of double statements, continues differently, but returns to the original material in the last group of demisemiquavers: the cadence in the Coda is a transposition (down a perfect fifth) of that in the Introduction. Segment Three adds an E to the original B pedal, and this time the horn-chords resolve on to a pure E major triad. All the chords in this final segment of the Coda belong to Mode 3¹ (Ex. 66).

Ex. 66

These outer sections of the seventh *Méditation* are either harmonic or monodic in character, but the main body of the movement is considerably more complex, and closer in style to the more radical works of earlier years. It is a trio, with the thematic material concentrated in the middle voice. This material 'translates' a sentence from Aquinas – 'the Father and Son love, through the Holy Spirit [the love which proceeds] themselves and the human race' – in the following way (Ex. 67).

229

Ex. 67

Père	8-note theme (begins as 'Being')
Fils	8-note theme (inverts 'Père': begins as 'Having')
Aiment	10-note theme ('aimer': to love)
Père	repeated
Fils	repeated
par	motto for ablative case
Saint Esprit	Prime and Retrograde of 'God' motto
Amour	'Aimer' theme repeated
Procédant	each letter 'translated'
Père/Fils/aiment	repeated as before
Race Humaine	each letter 'translated'

par/Saint esprit	repeated as before
Amour	as before
du	motto for genitive case
Père/du/Fils	repeated as before

This thematic statement involves considerable internal repetition, and the texture is completed by decorative counterpoints, each of which is organized in a different way. The right hand is exclusively occupied with birdsong – the Moroccan Bulbul – which, while thematic in its own terms, is not related by the incidence of its internal repetitions to the text. The pedal part involves a rhythmic *ostinato* which, while apparently not a specific deçi-tâla (these can be found elsewhere in the work), uses a rhythmic series of the following semiquaver values: 5, 5, 4, 4, 3, 3, 2, 2, 1, 1, 1; followed by a longer value, the duration of which varies on each appearance. This series appears six times in all, with extended, irregular pauses between each statement.

The overall effect of this trio is therefore to suspend any sense of regular rhythmic succession or tonal direction. In terms of the movement as a whole, it is a contrast, but it clearly carries the meditative essence, suspended in both space and time.

It was with the Second String Quartet (1959) that Elliott Carter finally established those stylistic principles which were the logical result of the process of exploration begun in the mid-1940s. This quartet is not merely atonal; 'dependence on thematic recurrence ... is replaced by an ever-changing series of motives and figures having certain internal relationships with each other.' The single movement is symmetrically divided into nine sections: an Introduction and Conclusion frame four principal movements which in turn are linked by cadenzas for viola, cello and first violin respectively. The four main movements are each dominated by a single instrument, each of which is given a particular expressive character and its own repertory of speeds and intervals. Thus the *Allegro fantastico* focuses on the 'whimsical, ornate' first violin, with its predominant minor thirds and perfect fifths: the *Presto scherzando* on the 'moderating influence' of the second violin, with emphasis on major thirds: the *Andante* brings forward the 'almost lamenting' viola (the tritone), and the *Allegro* the 'romantically free' cello (perfect fourths). 'The separation of the instrumental characters is kept quite distinct throughout the first half of the work but becomes increasingly homogenized up to the Conclusion, at which point the separation re-emerges.'[9]

The opening of the quartet (Ex. 68) shows the way in which the character and intervallic material of each instrument is defined. It will be clear that the overall form of the work does not sever all links with the traditional four-movement sequence, just as the decision to define material in terms of certain intervals is still, in the broadest sense, 'thematic'. As far as the listener is concerned, Carter is exploiting one of the most basic of all perceptions – the ability to distinguish between the primary intervals, and he is using that fundamental fact as the foundation for his highly dramatic scenarios, which involve the conflict and interaction of 'thematic' elements in a state of constant transformation.

Ex. 68

The basic, dynamic concept of diverse elements gradually coming to fusion, then diffusing to the point of maximum diversity again, is also the groundplan of the Double Concerto for Harpsichord, Piano and

Two Chamber Orchestras (1961). This time, the available intervals are divided into two groups, and since each interval is associated with a certain metronomic speed, a further level of differentiation between the groups becomes possible. As with the Second String Quartet, the single-movement form has a *quasi*-symmetrical layout, with the Introduction and Conclusion presenting the material in a state of maximum differentiation while the two ensembles come closest to fusion in the central *Adagio*.

In the Piano Concerto (1966) there is again a division of the available material into two, between a 'concertino' comprising the piano solo and seven other instruments and the 'ripieno' of the rest of the orchestra. The work is in two movements, the first stressing the similarity between the material of both groups, and the second the dissimilarity, a process which obviously shuns the more symmetrical scheme of the Double Concerto, with its return to the original diversity after the greater homogeneity of the central *Adagio*. The Concerto for Orchestra (1969) has a form which elaborates the basic scheme of the Second String Quartet, with its four distinct 'temperaments', one for each instrument. The Concerto for Orchestra has four main movements, each at a different speed, each featuring a different combination of instruments. Instead of following one another, however, the four movements interpenetrate throughout, each coming into focus successively, but always against the background of the other three.

This may seem the ultimate in polyphonic complexity, but the Third String Quartet (1971) develops the simultaneous statement of different movements a stage further. Here the basic duality (first violin and cello, second violin and viola) is exploited to the extent that 'the two duos should perform as two groups as separated from each other as is conveniently possible, so that the listener can not only perceive them as two separate sound sources but also be aware of the combinations they form with each other'.[10] The first duo plays four 'movements' or types of material, initially (and always *quasi rubato*) in the order *Furioso* (A), *Leggerissimo* (B), *Andante espressivo* (C) and *Pizzicato giocoso* (D), which alternate to form this sequence: A B C D B A D C B D A C A. The second duo, 'playing in quite strict rhythm throughout', has six 'movements', which move through a different sequence. Each of the ten 'movements' emphasizes a particular interval, with the eleventh interval, the major second, being used as 'connective tissue',[11] and the polyphonic process is such that each of the Duo I movements is heard at some stage in combination with each of the Duo II movements.

Clearly only a composer of phenomenal ability could hope to shape such complex processes to musical ends. In following through the principles first fully deployed in the Second String Quartet to such lengths, Carter has inevitably left far behind the immediately comprehensible impact of such transitional works as the Piano Sonata, the Cello Sonata, the First String Quartet and the Variations for Orchestra (1955). Since he has affirmed that 'while I believe that music should be continuously surprising, I believe it should be so in the sense that whatever happens should continue an already perceived ongoing process or pattern', and declared his business as a composer 'to be sufficiently aware of the probable predictive expectations of the listener who has grasped the process I have begun',[12] it is not possible to accuse him of writing only for himself. Just as performers have come to terms with music which was thought to be unplayable a few years ago, so listeners – especially those who can sense the way in which the spatial and structural principles of the music reinforce that concern not to be *evasive*, of which the composer has spoken – will doubtless find the music both increasingly satisfying and increasingly exciting. Carter, like Tippett and Messiaen, is at once a deeply serious and a hearteningly spontaneous composer. The positive exuberance which is such a large part of all their work is one of the best signs we have that the musical future, though likely to owe little enough to the well-tried techniques of the past, need not necessarily involve a total rejection of all its most cherished qualities.

In the past decade these three composers have continued to flourish, with an energy and vision belying their age. Perhaps the most consistent signs of mellowing have been in Carter, the most 'extreme' in earlier years. While not succumbing to the seductions of a rediscovered tonality, he has shown that his hard-won musical language can adapt to the needs of vocal music. Of three substantial vocal works the last, *In Sleep, in Thunder* (1981), to poems by Robert Lowell, is the most fully realized example of Carter's new lyricism. Freely flowing melodic lines project a sure sense of direction, despite the absence of any clear-cut motivic processes. This development has been paralleled by an increased emphasis on more playful, comradely qualities within the still close-knit, fiercely argued textures of Carter's instrumental works. *Triple Duo* (1982), *Penthode* (1985) and the String Quartet No. 4 (1986) all confirm the resource and flexibility, as well as the continued vitality, of those principles of generation and continuation forged by Carter in the 1950s.

For both Messiaen and Tippett the past decade has been dominated by a single *magnum opus*. At first Messiaen's might seem the more arresting, since it employs a genre he has rejected for so long. Yet his opera *St François d'Assise* (1983) is, in both form and style, very much the outcome and fulfilment of what went before: it is more a series of tableaux than a developed drama of character and situation. The sheer conviction and originality of Messiaen's materials enable him to use similar ideas and effects from work to work in ways that might seem self-indulgently repetitive in a lesser talent. So the opera confirms the ritual, ceremonial core, uniting nature and humanity, that powers all Messiaen's works: that, and his commitment to a mode of form-building that prefers juxtaposition to through-composition.

Such a mosaic-like approach to construction can also be found in Tippett's major works of this period, his fourth opera *The Ice Break* (1976) and *The Mask of Time* for voices and instruments (1983). The highly personal overview of issues in politics and philosophy embodied in *The Mask of Time* is a more generalized but no less urgent continuation of the concerns evident in *The Ice Break*, which itself grew out of the Symphony No. 3. Mosaic or not, *The Mask of Time* is not a mere assemblage, but adds up, through its accumulating stages, to a magnificently modern statement (questioning, ambivalent) about the place of man in the universe. There is, in all Tippett's recent compositions, including the Triple Concerto (1979) and the Piano Sonata No. 4 (1984), an increased openness to fruitful explorations of associations with the earlier phases of his own development. 'Tonality', as Tippett first conceived it, is still kept at bay, but — as in the later Messiaen — its consequences, and its components, can often be detected, in ways which never for a moment reduce the remarkable individuality of the result.

Chapter 12

Seven Europeans

The early works of Witold Lutosławski (born in Poland in 1913) display a wide range of influences from among those modern composers who retained an ultimate commitment to tonal emphasis. Of their very nature, however, these influences were likely to stimulate further exploration rather than mere imitation, and the music of Szymanowski and Bartók was of particular importance in providing Lutosławski with ideas about how he might develop a more personal, more radical style.

Well before the Polish political 'thaw' of 1956, Lutosławski had encountered some of the recent music of Western European composers like Boulez and Stockhausen, and witnessed both the eager involvement with 'total' serialism and the speedy reaction into degrees of indeterminacy. Yet Lutosławski's own reaction to these two phenomena was principally determined by his awareness of what remained potent in his own earlier idiom. Thus, although he soon became what can be very loosely described as a 'twelve-note-aleatory' composer, it was with clear consciousness of the limitations of both orthodox serialism and Dadaist indeterminacy. With regard to the former, and its extension into total serialism, Lutosławski believed that, because of the inaudibility of its essential processes, 'it places the experience of a musical work outside the realm of human sensibility'; and the latter likewise becomes futile as soon as it reaches the point where the composer himself cannot 'foresee all possibilities which could arise within the limits set beforehand'.[1]

Since the Five Songs (1956–8) Lutosławski's structures have been built around 'elementary' twelve-note chords containing 'one, two or three types of intervals'. Such chords 'have for me a distinct, easily recognisable character, while twelve-note chords comprising all types of intervals are colourless – they lack a clearly defined individuality. Elementary twelve-note chords enable the use of strong harmonic contrasts, a possibility which is denied, for example, in the serial technique. . . . The only thing that links me with this technique is the almost continuous flow of the twelve notes of the scale.'[2]

Lutosławski came closest to orthodox serialism in the *Funeral Music in memoriam Béla Bartók* (1958), parts of which use a melodic twelve-note set containing only two different intervals – minor second and tritone. Even at the beginning, however, this set is presented in two different orderings, and it is the climax of the work 'based on chords comprising all the twelve tones' which 'are gradually drawn towards the middle register where they form a unison',[3] which is a clear adumbration of the technique which Lutosławski has since developed and expanded. In the much later Preludes and Fugue for 13 solo strings (1972), for example, the Fugue ends on a two-interval twelve-note chord (built from major seconds and perfect fourths), the last of twelve twelve-note chords which help to define the structure of the movement (Ex. 69).

Ex. 69

Three years after the *Funeral Music*, in the orchestral *Jeux vénitiens* (1961), Lutosławski used 'aleatory counterpoint' for the first time. The term is exact, for it is the contrapuntal relationship between simultaneously played parts which is no longer strictly controlled by a uniform metrical process. Instead, a period of time is defined either by gestures from the conductor, by signals from other players, by listening for other players to start new material, or by 'space-time' notation, which allots a certain amount of space on the page to an approximate duration, usually marked in seconds. The individual performer then repeats the group of notes provided for the period in question, and during that period there is no fixed co-ordination between the several performers. 'This treatment of the element of chance consists above all in the abolition of classical time division, which is consistent for all members of an ensemble. . . . [It does not] affect in the slightest degree the architectural order of the composition or the pitch organization.' 'Differences arising from the independent playing of particular members of the ensemble have no influence on the whole form or on its particular stages. In composing my piece I had to foresee all possibilities which would arise within the limits set before hand. This, in fact, consisted of setting the limits themselves in such a way that even "the least desirable possibility" of execution, in a given fragment, should nevertheless be acceptable. This guarantees that everything that may happen within the previously set limits will fulfil my purpose.'[4] Lutosławski has nevertheless relaxed this principle in the Preludes and Fugue, allowing that 'any number of Preludes in any order can be performed with or without a shortened version of the Fugue', and this, while still far from total freedom, may indicate that he is increasingly conscious of potentially troublesome links with traditional, through-composed, symphonic forms. Increasing the 'mobile' element does not necessarily reduce the dramatic potential of a work. Yet just as Lutosławski's technique centres not solely on twelve-note chords but on the relationship between such chords and the opposite – a single-note tonal emphasis – so his forms involve an attempt to balance, if not to integrate, 'closed' and 'open' factors.

The *Trois Poèmes d'Henri Michaux* (1960–5) is a choral and orchestral work which is one of his most ambitious and successful achievements, welding the various stylistic tendencies into a coherent and satisfying unity. Though there is considerable elaboration of detail, as befits the often expressionistic character of the texts, the underlying structure is clear and simple, the overall threefold scheme reflected in the constitution of the individual movements. Even more striking is the conviction with which a single note – F sharp – is brought into focus in a way which does not evade the connotations of a 'resolution' and yet which avoids anything remotely suggestive of traditional tonal harmony.

Lutosławski's own ideas about the whole question of devising appropriate large-scale forms for works in which aleatory and fixed sections co-exist, are expressed in his fascinating essay about his Symphony No. 2 (1965–7).[5] His approach is characteristically practical: 'the limitations which the old instruments impose on the contemporary composer are gallingly restrictive,' but, while waiting for the day when adequate new instruments (whether electronic or not) will appear, the best way in which to make old instruments sound 'in a fresh and stimulating way' is to use 'a very restricted and strictly controlled aleatoricism.'

Such aleatoricism has the major advantage of making the music simpler to play, but this ambivalent attitude to existing instrumental resources is still matched by mixed feelings about traditional 'closed' musical forms. Lutosławski believes that forms which were at their peak in the baroque and classical periods 'are today cultivated mostly in their ossified and degenerate form': yet even if sonata form, rondo and so on cannot be validly revived as such, 'a long process of evolution' may still be ahead of the closed-form principle. Lutosławski's own works are 'inseparably bound with the closed form', and, for the Symphony No. 2, he decided to use the traditional title, not because the work has anything in common with 'the classical or the neo-classical form', but because 'it is a work for symphony orchestra composed in a large closed form'.

The symphony has relatively little tonal feeling, and as such is a distinct contrast to the Cello Concerto (1970) which came immediately after it, though the climax of the second movement does reiterate E flat and F, the pitches which begin and end the entire work. Detailed analysis shows that the thematic working involves the evolution of three-note cells into twelve-note units as part of a highly sophisticated process which can surely be regarded as an important adaptation and transformation of serial procedures. Above all, there is a satisfying relationship between progressively evolving details and the dramatic, logical totality which justifies the description of the second movement as 'one of the most powerful symphonic arguments composed in the twentieth century'.[6]

Only when this thematic process is under-characterized, and tends to sound more like a counterpoint of *ostinati* than an on-going argument, is Lutosławski's music less interesting. The use of 'aleatory counterpoint' can make a texture sound less thematic and more random than is in fact the case, in spite of the clear structural divisions which are always apparent. Yet, while it may be that any use of the aleatory principle is more disruptive of traditional responses than Lutosławski would accept, there can be no denying the attractiveness and integrity of his attempts to achieve a positive *rapprochement* between them.

Lutosławski's mature style is rooted in the most positive kind of compromise: one which is not imposed from the outside but grows out of particular musical predispositions and concerns. Iannis Xenakis (born 1922) is a very different kind of composer, even though his music may seem to involve the same underlying need to integrate the 'fixed' and the 'free'.

Xenakis was Greek by birth, and although he moved to France in 1947 he was still able to claim in 1966 that 'I am always rediscovering in the civilisation of ancient Greece the germ of the most advanced ideas of contemporary life'. At eighteen, after a youth 'saturated' with 'classicism, antiquity, philosophy, poetry', he became directly involved with the anti-Nazi resistance; from 1940 to 1945 he lived a very different kind of life, and, as with Henze and Stockhausen, who were both conscripted at an early age, its influence was profound. 'In my music there is all the agony of my youth, of the Resistance, and the aesthetic problems they posed, with the street demonstrations, or even more the occasional, mysterious, deathly sounds of those cold nights in December 1944 in Athens. From this was born my conception of the massing of sound events, and therefore of stochastic music.' On this basis, the desire to create a completely new world *on* the ruins of the old, rather than *from* those ruins, becomes understandable, and Xenakis evidently believes that the evolution of a truly modern music has barely begun.

Mathematics has a vital role to play in that evolution, and here Xenakis's early training and practice as engineer and architect are crucial. For more than a decade after arriving in France and for several years after ceasing his musical studies with Honegger, Milhaud and Messiaen, Xenakis worked with Le Corbusier. He admits that 'if one approaches music in the same way that I approach mine, it marches with and intermingles with mathematics. ... [Yet] music has to dominate mathematics. ... [Mathematical logic] is a working tool, a universal language, an achievement, happiness, a joy in the abstract game. Obviously there is something else in music, be it a sheen or an embellishment that mathematics does not have. Don't ask me to define music solely in mathematical terms. These two "arts" cannot be identified with each other, cannot be placed one above the other, only they fuse, having certain aspects in common.'[7]

LOUVRE *droit d'entrée*

European total serialism of the 1950s, in which,
of precise calculations sounded utterly imprecise
he used his mathematical skill to develop a
it was possible 'to attain the greatest possible
nological sense) and the minimum of constraints,
[8] This 'stochastic' principle is derived from the
as defined by Jacques Bernouilli in 1713. The
nation of the law instances the tossing of a coin:
sult is unpredictable within the obvious limits of
ssibilities. Continue to toss it, and the number of
creasingly tend towards equality: 'the law of large
, the more numerous the phenomena, the more
eterminate end.'[9] So 'Large number' or 'Stochas-
provision of limits for sound aspects (for example,
npered semitones) and of a formula to determine
oices within these limits: the calculations may be
carried out manually or automatically.'[10]

It has been argued that 'with Xenakis the music can be happily
listened to in complete ignorance of the theory: for the logic of its
operations is axiomatically the logic of the listener's every mental
process,'[11] and the composer's own attitude to the problem of comprehension displays both arrogance and optimism. With reference to
one of his programme notes, which cites Poisson's Law and includes
several algebraic equations, he says: 'If the listener doesn't understand
any of it, it is first of all useful to show him to himself as ignorant.
Because the laws which I cite are universal ones and treasures of
humanity, real treasures of human thought. To be unwilling to know
them is as uncivilised as to refuse to recognise Michelangelo or
Baudelaire. Furthermore, these formulae, which ten years ago were the
property only of the specialist, are now the common property of the
average student of elementary mathematics. In a few years' time they
will be in every schoolboy's satchel.'[12]

The presentday listener may nevertheless do better to note the
composer's further remark that stochastic laws 'are the laws of the
passage from complete order to total disorder in a continuous or an
explosive manner'.[13] Two of the stochastic works which use identical
basic material can scarcely *not* be heard other than in terms of contrasts
between relatively regular and irregular patterns. The works are
ST/4-1, 080262 and *ST/10-1, 080262*, both completed in 1962. The
titles mean the first piece of stochastic music for four and ten instru-

ments respectively, using calculations made by computer on 8th February 1962.

Ex. 70

Example 70 shows two extracts from ST/4 (for string quartet), displaying the extreme contrast between constantly changing durations, dynamics and pitch patterns, and a far simpler texture which includes a descending chromatic scale with regular note values and a uniform dynamic level. Such contrasts are a fundamental feature of stochastic works: *Morsima-Amorsima (ST/4–1, 030762,* for violin, cello, double bass and piano) begins with extreme diversity of register, duration and dynamics, with relatively rapid pitch succession, but after six bars a much sparser texture ensues; the rest of the piece alternates these two basic elements.

Xenakis has also used Game Theory, another branch of mathematics, in several compositions; the orchestral *Duel* (1959) and *Stratégie* (1959–62), and also *Linaia-agon* for horn, trombone and tuba (1972). Here, too, 'there is no abrogation of the composer's function, as with "aleatoric" music where you get either partial or total abrogation, which is absurd.'[14] Yet the most important technique which Xenakis has developed since the first stochastic works is his so-called 'symbolic music,' which derives from certain concepts in the field of symbolic logic. 'Xenakis's symbolic music has more the nature of a translation into sound of theorems of set theory,'[15] and his technique in works like *Herma* for solo piano (1961) and *Nomos Alpha* for solo cello (1965) certainly resembles a highly personal expansion of the serial principle, now related not to the thematic and textural practice of late nineteenth-century German composers but to the mathematics of set theory.

As Paul Griffiths's analysis of *Nomos Alpha* implies, even comprehension of the mathematical principles does not ensure that the resulting musical processes can be aurally detected: 'the listener's attention is directed towards the general features of events, such as various types of *tremolando, glissando* or *pizzicato,* rather than to pitch and rhythmic aspects.' For the moment, then, the listener may be no better off than in relation to the detailed organisation of those serial works which Xenakis so scornfully dismissed when embarking on his stochastic exercises. And if the listener is obliged to compromise to the extent of accepting that his perceptions of this particular universe may be severely limited, so the performer may be forced to compromise between the ideal and the possible. Peter Hill has even suggested that there is an implied compromise between accuracy and inaccuracy built in to Xenakis's apparently precise notation.[16]

The music of György Ligeti (born 1923) is much more immediately approachable and appealing than that of Xenakis, which may reflect the distance between talk of Poisson's Law and the remark that 'many of my pieces have an underground connection with *Alice in Wonderland*'.[17] Ligeti was born in Romania but studied in Hungary and taught at the Liszt Academy in Budapest from 1950 to 1956. There the accepted modern style was, inevitably, closer to Bartók than to Webern, but just as, in Poland, Lutosławski's idiom had begun to change even before political upheavals gave such changes impetus and legitimacy, so from about 1950 onwards Ligeti had begun to explore alternatives to the prevailing national-cum-neo-classical manner.

The brief liberalization which preceded the savagely repressed Hungarian uprising in 1956 enabled Ligeti to hear some of the most recent and radical Western European music, and when he arrived in Germany soon after the revolt was crushed he took refuge in Cologne, first with Herbert Eimert, the pioneer of electronic music, and then with Stockhausen. In 1956 increasing enthusiasm for aleatory procedures and electronic techniques was leading many younger composers away from serialism. Like both Lutosławski and Xenakis, Ligeti could see no point in continuing Schoenbergian or Webernian types of twelve-note technique, and his rejection of the European variety of total serialism, as found in Boulez's *Structure Ia*, was complete.[18] He did write two electronic works, *Glissandi* and *Artikulation* (both 1958), but soon abandoned the medium as too limited and primitive for his purposes: a third electronic piece, *Atmosphères*, was planned but eventually became a purely orchestral work.

For all its relatively primitive qualities, Ligeti's first mature orchestral composition, *Apparitions* (1958–9), already displays that 'desire to search back for a fundamental simplicity in the musical idea itself',[19] which is at the root of his subsequent development. *Atmosphères* for orchestra (1961), the successor to *Apparitions*, is often likened to a transcription of an electronic piece from which not merely theme but motion itself has been eliminated: though 'built on very clear proportions with a certain construction', it belongs to a period when 'rhythmic patterns and harmonies and intervals were boring for me, and therefore I destroyed them'.[20]

It was perhaps inevitable that at a time of such hostility to the traditional resources of compositional construction Ligeti should have tested aleatory techniques. *Volumina* for organ (1962) rejects precise notation in favour of graphic representation, yet the sequence and overall duration of sections remains fixed, and Ligeti was soon to conclude that 'for me a work of art is a finished and defined thing. It has nothing to do with everyday life.' Cage and his associates believed 'that life is art and art is life . . . my artistic credo is that art – every art – is not life. It is something artificial.'[21] This phase produced one piece of pure farce, the *Poème symphonique* for 100 metronomes (1962), and two scrappy and monotonous studies in vocal agility, *Aventures* (1961) and *Nouvelles Aventures* (1962–5). Yet concurrently Ligeti composed the

Requiem (1963-5) and here, once again, textures originate from a very specific and tightly controlled polyphony or 'micro-polyphony'. Since then it is increasingly the contrast between rhythmic and harmonic elements which are positively articulated, and those which are both more diffuse and less explicitly defined in time and register, which serves as the structural foundation of his compositions. These concerns are most obviously reflected in the splendidly evocative title *Clocks and Clouds* (1972-3), a vocal work referring to an essay by the philosopher Karl Popper.

Ex. 71

Apart from the opera based on *Le Ballade de Grande Macabre* by Michel de Ghelderode, a forerunner of 'absurdist' playwrights such as Artaud and Ionesco, all Ligeti's other recent works have been instrumental. Exploration of 'cloud-like' textures have been of particular importance, and nowhere more so than in the orchestral piece *Lontano* (1967). This begins in 4/4 time at crotchet 64, but the composer makes it clear that a rigid pulse should be avoided and one does not hear a regular succession of such beats: the polyphonic entries all take place within quintuplet, quadruplet or triplet subdivisions of the beat (Ex. 71).

Given that these entries generate dense cluster-chords which change their internal constitution almost imperceptibly, the pervasive cloudiness is manifest, but too predictable a uniformity is avoided by imaginative instrumentation and skilful handling of the underlying dynamic fluctuations, which ensure that the piece is more than a static musical 'sky-scape'. *Lontano* is very much a study in cloud-formation, but textural contrast is not totally excluded, taking the principal form of certain *simultaneous* attacks on sustained harmonies, as with the string chord at Letter H, and the entry of most of the instruments on octave Ds at Letter X. In neither case, however, do these assertions of uniformity lead to clear, regular accentuation: the clouds are never transformed into clocks.

The Double Concerto for flute, oboe and orchestra (1972) is another example of Ligeti's fastidious craftsmanship and sensitivity to slight but telling timbral variations. Moreover, it confirms that his techniques can best be discussed in terms of *process* rather than of *argument*. The music evolves by means of expansions and contractions, successive or superimposed contrasts, which involve clearly audible, structurally satisfying distinctions between simple and complex textures and the use of narrow registral areas. The whole work moves from the 'cloud' of the beginning, where a narrow pitch-area (the major third, D flat to F) is filled in and gradually expanded by means of instrumental entries and changes of pitch, which are individually barely perceptible and rhythmically avoid any clear demarcation of time into regular successions of beats, to the more 'clocklike' rhythmic unisons of the later stages, where the rapid succession of crotchet beats is emphasized by alternations between different subdivisions: the very opposite of the work's initial unsynchronized attacks.

Like Lutosławski, Ligeti makes much of the regular repetition of specific rhythmic and intervallic patterns, as well as of material which sounds more conventionally thematic. Yet Ligeti's recent scores are wholly determinate, with every slightest rhythmic detail precisely notated. The preference for highly ornamented or sustained material rather than fragmented, isolated elements is also an important feature in giving the music a positive expressive impact. The process may not be strictly systematic, but it is logical and coherent.

The Italian composer Luciano Berio (born 1925) developed independently of the kind of political upheavals that affected Lutosławski, Xenakis and Ligeti. Though his very earliest work was tonal and romantic (cf. the 1948 song in *Recital I*), he soon progressed, under the guidance of Dallapiccola, to an exploration of the twelve-note technique. Among his serial works are *Chamber Music* (1952), settings of James Joyce, who has exercised a great and lasting influence, and *Nones* (1954), an orchestral piece from a projected cantata on W. H. Auden's poem of that name. Berio's last wholly serial work was *Serenata I* for flute and fourteen instruments (1957), but just as he had shown flexibility in his approach to the twelve-note principle – *Nones* actually uses a thirteen-note set – so his later music retains links with the basic practice of keeping the twelve notes in regular circulation: more a matter of expansion and transformation than of rejection.

In 1955 Berio joined Bruno Maderna (1920–73) in setting up an electronic studio at the Milan radio station, and a year later he produced his first tape piece, *Mutazioni*. Berio was never likely to become an exclusively studio-bound composer, however, and the years 1958 to 1960 display an impressive broadening-out of stylistic principles and technical resources. *Tempi concertati* for flute and four groups of instruments (1960) actually incorporates a transition from fixed to free rhythmic relationships, ordinary notation gradually being replaced by a scheme in which 'the absolute rhythmic values are not indicated but rather the relative time proportions'. Small segments of material are provided which can be started at any point, then read forwards or backwards, and there are other segments from which elements may be selected by the performer (cf. Berio's preface to the score).

Even more significant, in view of Berio's subsequent development, is *Différences* (1958–9), in which for the first time he uses both live performers and pre-recorded sound – that of the instruments which are also used live: flute, clarinet, viola, cello and harp. The result is often highly complex, yet the complexity is precisely controlled.

These developments provided Berio with an expansion in expressive

Ex. 72

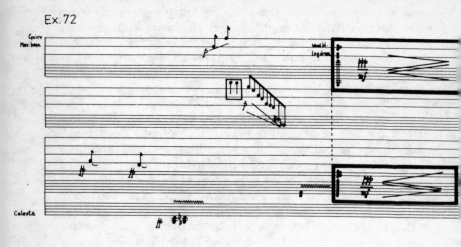

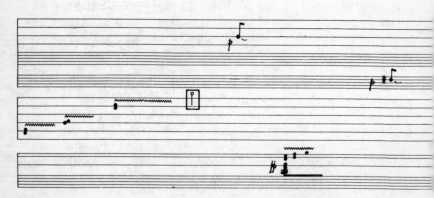

resources which he has explored in a wide range of works, many of which are vocal and often, in varying ways, dramatic. The first of these, *Circles* (1960), is also the simplest and shortest, using small forces (female voice, harp and two percussionists), no electronics, and the work of a single writer, the poet e.e. cummings. There are five movements, and the text of the second reappears in the fourth, though

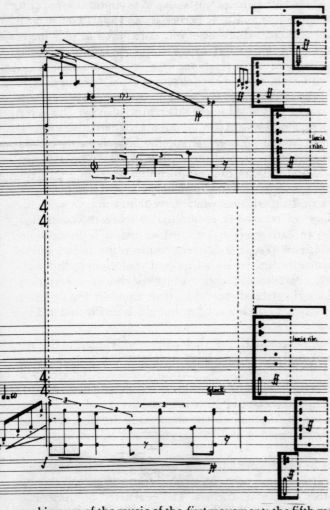

making use of the music of the *first* movement: the fifth movement uses the same text as the first, and there are also clear points of contact between the music of both. Yet of greater interest than Berio's apparent flirtation with arch form in *Circles* is the balance between fixed and free elements, particularly in the sphere of rhythm: the central movement is both the freest in its notation and the most expressionistic in mood, but

249

even here regular rhythmic successions play a crucial part (cf the bar in 4/4 on p. 30, where both percussionists play in rhythmic unison) (Ex. 72). The work is a vehicle for Cathy Berberian, and apart from using a wide range of vocal techniques the singer is required to play finger cymbals, claves, glass and wood chimes, to clap, to beat time and to use three different locations on the platform.

Compared to *Circles*, most of the later, larger pieces seem diffuse. *Epifanie* (1961, revised 1965) has twelve short movements, five of them vocal, which can be performed in ten different sequences. This is the only one of Berio's major works to permit such alternative choices, several of which appear to override specific links between certain pieces, and the result is 'an undeniable lack of coherence' between orchestral and vocal sections, each of which uses a text by a different writer.[22] Berio's search for new dramatic forms has led him into more explicitly theatrical experiments which have things in common with the 'happenings' of composers committed to more thoroughgoing indeterminacy. In *Passaggio* (1963) a speaking chorus is divided into five groups which are placed at different points in the auditorium in order to dramatize the fact that the attitudes of 'conformity, selfishness, mental laziness and defence of taboos' which the chorus expresses are likely to be shared by the audience.[23] On stage, a solitary female figure represents resistance to these attitudes, but she is finally defeated by them.

Like *Epifanie*, *Laborintus II* (1965) employs a wide range of literary source material, and this is associated with both live and electronic sound, and with the use of specific musical quotations. Longer than either *Epifanie* or the later *Sinfonia*, it rather overdoes both the 'little girl' vocal effects (the result of using the Swingle Singers) and the reliance on spoken narration. Indeed, the best moments of the work are those where the voices are silent and instrumental and electronic sounds interact.

Fixed forms in which symmetrical factors are prominent represent the opposite extreme from open forms which provide several equally valid alternative structural schemes. The symmetry of *Circles* has already been mentioned, and in the five-movement *Sinfonia* (1968–9) the finale recalls earlier material from the work before ending in a similar way to the first movement. A highly dramatic tension can result from the contrast between fundamentally simple elements and the vastly more complex details which may arise from their elaboration. Lutosławski and Ligeti both exploit this contrast with great skill, and

Sinfonia shows similar concerns. Its 'simple frames of reference',[24] principally chords built from thirds, come to act as clearly perceptible unifying factors.

The second and third movements of *Sinfonia* both share a kind of *cantus firmus* technique. In the second movement, a gentle invocation on the name of Martin Luther King, Berio employs a 21-note cantus which recurs four times and divides into three segments of four, seven and ten notes, each an elaboration of its predecessor. For the third movement, the 'cantus' is nothing less than the entire third movement of Mahler's Resurrection Symphony, on to which is grafted a spoken text from Beckett's novel *The Unnameable* and an immense amount of other verbal commentary and musical quotation. Berio has remarked that this is 'perhaps the most "experimental" music I have ever written,' and prefers to describe it as 'not so much composed as ... assembled.'[25] It may not solely be the relatively satisfying simplicity of the other movements of *Sinfonia* which makes one feel that the third movement is too congested: As in *Laborintus II*, the words and music seem to get in each other's way. Maybe the movement has exorcised once and for all Berio's obsession with attempting to translate the Joycean stream of consciousness into music. He has followed up the technique of assembling the music of different composers and periods, though without the superimpositions of *Sinfonia*, in his *Recital I (for Cathy)*, while at the other extreme a purely instrumental work like *Points on the curve to find* for piano and twenty-three instruments (1974) not merely avoids all literary and dramatic allusions and all indeterminate and electronic possibilities, but also involves a ten-note pitch-set in processes of transformation which show that Berio is still able to build on the earliest elements of his extraordinary adaptable and fluent style.

Pierre Boulez was born in 1925, the same year as Berio, and produced his first important compositions in his early twenties. *Psalmodies* for piano (1945) has been withdrawn, but the first two piano sonatas and the Sonatine for flute and piano, which all date from the years 1945 to 1948, mark one of the most assured debuts by any modern composer. The sheer speed with which Boulez digested and transformed existing techniques – it is characteristic that he should have been strongly impressed by one of the most elaborate, 'classical' twelve-note works, Schoenberg's Wind Quintet, and desired 'above all, to learn how it was written'[26] – brought him, in less than a decade, to a confrontation with two of the three major postwar innovations, 'total' serialism and electronics. Only after 1953 did he begin gradually to explore the possibilities of the third innovation, allowing performers a carefully controlled degree of choice in matters of rhythmic detail and structural sequence.

In his Darmstadt lectures, Boulez based his discussion of technique on the principle that 'the world of music today is . . . one where structural relationships are not defined once and for all according to absolute criteria, but are organised instead according to varying schemata'. He also affirmed that 'this world has arisen from the expansion of the idea of the series.' Schoenberg's concept of serialism is 'far wide of the mark, because it is applied to an idea as out of date as the harmonisation of a theme. . . . On the one hand, there is no truly *harmonic* function binding the theme to its accompaniment: it is a question of pure chromatic complementarity; on the other hand, instead of merging the two dimensions, this usage contrasts them artificially.'[27]

Boulez finds that 'the way ahead' can best be observed in Webern, notably the Second Cantata, Op. 31. Yet he is particularly hostile to what he terms the 'academicism' of most of Schoenberg's and Webern's serial works, arguing elsewhere that 'the peak of Webern is the Op. 9 *Bagatelles* for string quartet. That's really his most extraordinary work. Because he broke the form completely and had a free form, the language is *very* well organised both locally and generally (although on a small scale). From an aesthetic point of view that brought us something quite new.' By 'academicism' Boulez means the use of old forms – he instances what he calls Webern's obsession with them from the String Trio onwards – and the kind of 'conflict . . . between the series (and the principle of the series) and the theme' which he finds in Schoenberg's Orchestral Variations Op. 31. Even Berg fails to escape the charge: 'the form in *Wozzeck* is lively and non-academic but the form of *Lulu* is sometimes very academic.'[28]

There can be no doubt that these ideas must have crystallized at a remarkably early stage in Boulez's development, and even the very early works – notably the Piano Sonata No. 1 (1946) – show a flexible kind of total chromaticism presenting successions of cells, which gradually employ all the semitones within a specific area. In view of the later direction of Boulez's music it is useful to stress the 'mobility' of this evolutionary process, both with regard to the size of the individual cells and to the order of pitches within them. The assurance with which the young composer handles such a dangerously flexible technique makes it all the more surprising that he should have moved fairly rapidly towards what he himself has called the 'totalitarian' serialism of *Structure Ia* for two pianos (1952). Clearly, he felt that the possibilities of total serialism were worth investigation, and he acknowledged the particular stimulus of his former teacher Messiaen's *Mode de valeurs et d'intensités* by using one of the same pitch-sets for *Structure Ia*. Boulez, like Stockhausen, was also impressed by the pioneering Sonata for two pianos by the Belgian Karel Goeyvaerts (born 1923), which was completed in 1951. But such a strong degree of determinism was no more lasting in its appeal for Boulez than it was for Messiaen, and it was in the field of vocal music that the next significant step was taken.

Boulez had already used texts by the surrealist poet René Char in two works, *Le visage nuptial* (1946–51) and *Le Soleil des eaux* (1948–50, revised 1958 and 1965), and although these are by no means lacking in moments of expressionistic drama, the use of the French language itself seemed to ensure a degree of lyricism which in turn renders the employment of a relatively free and flexible technique appropriate.[29] Boulez's third composition to use poems by Char was *Le marteau sans Maître* (1953–5). This is in nine movements for mezzo-soprano and six instruments, and the relationships between the movements – settings of three poems with instrumental commentaries – are such as to suggest that an aleatory process is already at work, with the implied flexibility reaching deep into the (fully notated) musical fabric. The 'logical' scheme of the work could be as follows:

1a Avant *L'Artisanat furieux* (instrumental)
1b *L'Artisanat furieux* (vocal)
1c Après *L'Artisanat furieux* (instrumental)
2a *Bourreaux de solitude* (vocal)
2b Commentaire I de *Bourreaux de solitude* (instrumental)
2c Commentaire II de *Bourreaux de solitude* (instrumental)
2d Commentaire III de *Bourreaux de solitude* (instrumental)
3a *Bel édifice et les pressentiments* (vocal, first version)
3b *Bel édifice et les pressentiments* (vocal, second version)

but the actual scheme is 1a, 2b, 1b, 2c, 3a, 2a, 1c, 2d, 3b. Boulez comments that what might have been three separate cycles are 'interwoven, and by their layout form a kind of maze with turnings and returns'. It is in this sense that the structure foreshadows those later works whose schemes for alternative sectional succession observe certain requirements laid down by the composer. The purpose of the actual form of *Le marteau*, far from being to ensure an unpredictable discontinuity (the poems do not make conventional 'sense', still less tell a story), is to avoid the presentation of the three cycles 'in isolation', and this awareness of the validity of *integration* would certainly seem to be behind Boulez's preference for constantly evolving basic material. Nor does it exclude the use of repetition, or at least cross-reference: 'The last section of the work . . . integrates the three cycles one with another, either (literally) by quoting them in a new context, or by using their musical or instrumental characteristics.'[30]

Since *Le marteau sans Maître*, the basic principle of alternating, interwoven cycles has remained important to Boulez, and has been transformed into a concept of structure as something which itself can evolve, allowing a work to appear in different versions and to survive incomplete for long periods. The literary patron saint of this phase is the poet Stéphane Mallarmé, whose presence is most palpable in the largest of the completed works, *Pli selon pli* (1957–65). Subtitled 'portrait de Mallarmé,' this is in five movements, of which the first and last, 'Don' and 'Tombeau' are principally orchestral and related in structure. The three central movements, all called 'Improvisation' are anticipated in 'Don' (which was actually written after them) and the degree of freedom for the performers increases progressively until, in the third Improvisation – all employ Mallarmé poems – the conductor is allowed to choose between various alternative segments.

In 1956, Boulez began a Third Piano Sonata, but only two of the projected five movements have been completed. In both the order of events can vary within clearly defined limits. 'Trope' has four sections: Texte, Parenthèse, Glose and Commentaire, and the player may start with any, then follow the fixed order, with the additional proviso that Commentaire may be played before or after Glose. Parenthèse and Commentaire both contain segments in smaller type, marked 'libre', which may be omitted or not as the player decides (Ex. 73).

So too in 'Constellation-Miroir', which is intended to form the central movement of the completed work: 'the fragments are laid out on the page (as in Mallarmé's poem "a die cast will never abolish chance") like a constellation. The order among them is not fixed but controlled: each is to be followed by another chosen from among a limited number (from one to four): the direction chosen may imply a specific set of dynamic markings and tempo relationships. The real freedom of the performer – as in all music – lies in the imposition of continuity by the inflection of a phrase, and of dramatic clarity by articulation and spacing.'[31]

The flexibility of structure which results from degrees of inter-changeability has never encouraged Boulez to advance into such areas of indeterminacy as graphic notation or the 'text' piece: as he once tersely put it: 'I am not interested in giving the musicians cartoons to improvise.'[32] Of more value has been the association of performer-choice with the deployment of instrumental groups (and types of material). The first work to be completed since *Pli selon pli*, *Domaines* (1970), was first conceived for solo clarinet in 1968, but its final version also employs six instrumental groups: four trombones; string sextet; marimba and double bass; flute, trumpet, alto saxophone, bassoon and

Ex. 73

Parenthèse

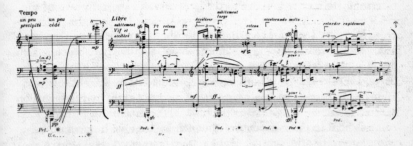

harp; oboe, horn and electric guitar; and bass clarinet. The clarinet soloist chooses the order in which he will play six passages of 'original' material, and he plays each in the 'domain' of one of the instrumental groups. The instrumental group whose domain the soloist is occupying then plays its own commentary on his 'original'. The soloist also has six 'mirrors' (modified retrogrades) of his 'originals', and in the second half of *Domaines* he plays these *after* the ensemble to which he has moved has played its own 'mirror' (the sequence of 'originals' and 'mirrors' need not be the same: in the recording made under the composer's supervision they follow the sequence: originals, ADCBEF: mirrors, DCEABF). The underlying symmetry of *Domaines* relates it both to *Pli selon pli* and to the intervening *Éclat* (1965; now grown to *Éclat/Multiples*), which has a fundamental 'arch' shape.[33] The musical material is shaped with that elegant rhetoric and purposeful coloratura which, while far removed from the regularly accented, 'on-going' manner which does so much to determine the character of Boulez's early compositions, is nevertheless instantly distinguishable from the static doodling of less talented imitators. Boulez's true skill is in ensuring that the parts never destroy the whole, and illuminate rather than undermine the basic form. This skill is perhaps even more immediately evident in ... *explosante/fixe* ... (1972), where the fundamental structure is less mobile than that of *Domaines* and 'the emphasis throughout is on obsessive return'.[34] Here there is only one 'original', a sustained E flat with decorations, and its recurrences contribute to the pervading 'sense of bleak austerity' which is also prominent in Boulez's more recent elegy, *Rituel: in memoriam Bruno Maderna* (1975). . . . *explosante/fixe* ... is Boulez's first work since *Poésie pour pouvoir* (1958) to use live electronics. While he was still not satisfied with the results, it may well be that his own activities as Director of the Music Research Centre in Paris will involve increasing exploration of the possibilities in the electronic field.

Hans Werner Henze and Karlheinz Stockhausen were born in the same region of Germany, Henze in Gütersloh on 1st July 1926, Stockhausen near Cologne on 22nd August 1928. Both therefore grew up during the Second World War, and both were deeply affected by their experiences. Henze's development has been determined not only by his revulsion against fascism – a revulsion which has its origins in his father's total commitment to the Nazi cause – but also by his love-hate relationship with late-romantic music. Mahler, the ostracized Jew, has had a profound influence on him, but Wagner, the anti-Semite and favourite composer of Hitler, was for long anathema, although a recent work, called *Tristan* (1974), may have begun the process of exorcism. Given the strength of his feelings, and the view that 'fascism had precise social and economic roots',[35] it is not surprising that Henze eventually found it impossible to live in Germany and adopted left-wing views. In 1953 he settled in Italy, but his involvement with the West German and Austrian cultural establishment continued, and it was only at the Salzburg première of *The Bassarids* in 1966 that complete disillusionment with the bourgeois glorification of expensive and exclusive theatrical display set in. Since then, Henze has not turned his back on the traditionally élitist forms of music-making, but has sought to change the content of his works, and to give them political relevance without radically simplifying his actual techniques of composition.

Stockhausen, though an inveterate traveller, has remained a West German citizen and resident. He was more deeply involved than Henze in the postwar avant-garde renaissance, when the serial music suppressed by the Nazis at last became available for study and emulation. Yet Stockhausen has developed, not in terms of sudden crises involving the desire to reject aspects of the existing situation, but in response to a constant urge to explore, while at the same time preserving a continuity of outlook and experience.

Henze's work falls into three periods, each linked with three main phases of his life: involvement in the postwar avant garde (1946–53); reaction and residence in Italy (1953–67); involvement with Marxism (1967 onwards). The potential for conflict in the personality of a young man who attended Leibowitz's revelations of Schoenbergian procedures at the Darmstadt summer schools in 1947 and 1948, and who was able to get his first opera (*Das Wundertheater*) produced in 1949, was considerable, since the intellectual interest and the instinctive flair were likely to pull in different directions. From the first Henze was prolific, but the type of operatic subject to which he felt drawn and the type of vocal writing which he determined to cultivate led him decisively away from a strict serial technique. 'The vocal implications was [*sic*] one reason why I left the twelve-tone camp – earlier than anybody else, I may say.'[36] To the more puritanical radicals of the early 1950s, Henze's second opera, *Boulevard Solitude* (1952), with its updating of the Manon story and its use of that essentially nineteenth-century feature, the ballet, must have seemed like cynical opportunism of the most blatant commercial kind, and *König Hirsch* (1952–5, revised 1962), his first 'Italian' opera (written for a German company to a German text, though later revised and translated), has an expansive spontaneity of style which suggests total rejection of avant-garde austerities.

Peter Heyworth has rightly stressed that 'the importance of *König Hirsch* in Henze's development lies far less in its much-discussed Italianate elements than in the fact that it marks the emergence of a style that drew sustenance from the music of both Schoenberg and Stravinsky.'[37] Such eclecticism has obvious dangers, yet the fundamental features of heightened lyricism – often achieving the full force of atonal expressionism – and sharply coloured rhythmic dynamism prove that Henze was quite capable of transforming Schoenbergian and Stravinskian elements into stylistic features of his own: what took time was getting the balance right, and for five years after the completion of *König Hirsch* his music stressed lyricism at the expense of dramatic tension – an especial fault of the opera based on Kleist's play, *Der Prinz von Homburg* (1958). In 1961, however, Henze completed *Elegy for Young Lovers*, and here, perhaps because of his particular personal involvement in this story of an anti-social artist, he achieved a new toughness and clarity without sacrificing lyric beauty: the right balance had been struck. Ex. 74 is from Act One Scene Ten.

Ex. 74

Henze's artistic success continued unabated into the early 1960s, when his works became disconcertingly uneven in quality. The lightweight Fifth Symphony (1962) was written for Bernstein and the New York Philharmonic, and seems all too obviously designed to produce a brilliant, not in the least disturbing, up-to-date effect with the minimum demands on the performers. Yet in the same year Henze completed the much more substantial and rewarding cantata, *Novae de Infinitio Laudes*, to texts by Giordano Bruno, the Italian philosopher martyred by the Inquisition. Henze's flair for exploiting the dramatic potentialities of any story involving the persecution of the visionary by the intolerant majority links him with Benjamin Britten, and he has been less successful when, instead of a single heroic or hypersensitive protagonist, his dramatic subjects have attempted to place more generalized social corruption and upheavals in the foreground. Of the two operas of the mid-1960s, *Der junge Lord* (1964) is an attempt to expose the social and moral defects of a small German town; but as an act of political criticism it lacks the bite of the later pieces of 'music theatre'. *The Bassarids* (1966) is an altogether more serious and complex examination of the forces making for social upheaval and disruption, but since the work is rooted in psychological rather than political or economic issues it is perhaps not surprising that it led directly to Henze's 'conversion', while displaying purely musical defects which that conversion has not so far been able wholly to cure.

The Bassarids has provoked widely differing reactions. Those who admire the works of Henze's second period more than those which have followed it often hail it as a masterpiece, pointing to the gigantic synthesis which *The Bassarids* presents: its 'symphonic' form, its references to earlier tonal music, its mythological subject, all seem to proclaim the imperishability, the *adaptability*, of fundamentally traditional aesthetic forms and concepts. Yet the extraordinary breadth of the harmonic resources – from simple triad to twelve-note cluster – can seem a substitute for a truly coherent harmonic language, and as a result the music often stagnates. Henze had achieved an explicit synthesis of the traditional and the modern only to find himself in an impasse where success had encouraged self-indulgence, and the absence of genuinely new forms is keenly felt.

If Henze's more recent music were as simple as his political philosophy, then it might be easier to make up one's mind both about their relevance to each other and their relationship to the earlier music. Many of the works written since 1966 display similar ambiguities, a similar eclectic elaboration courting featureless flux. His new openness to indeterminate notation certainly helped to sharpen the dramatic edge of *El Cimarrón* (1970) and the use of taped elements and amplification likewise benefits the Violin Concerto No. 2 (1971). More than the similarly motivated but disturbingly heterogeneous *Der langwierige Weg in der Wohnung der Natascha Ungeheuer* (also 1970), *El Cimarrón*, a seventy-six-minute 'recital' for an actor-singer and three instrumentalists which recounts the adventures of a runaway Cuban slave, brilliantly conveys the atmosphere of expressionistic intensity in which lyricism is present only as a ghost (a highly effective one) of its former self. Henze is at his best in vocal works in which, as he puts it, 'I fought my own conventions', and the dramatic impact involves a clear contrast between simple and elaborate textures: the 'oratorio volgare e militare' *Das Floss der Medusa* (1968), the *Essay on Pigs* (1969) and the huge twenty-two movement cycle *Voices* for mezzo-soprano, tenor and fifteen instrumentalists (1973) all impress simply because they do not veil their simple structures, or their eclecticism, in abstract processes which so easily dissolve into protracted note-spinning.

Writing in 1970, Peter Heyworth questioned whether socialism could ever provide a 'comparable intellectual and emotional challenge' to that posed by the two Auden-Kallman librettos,[38] *Elegy for Young Lovers* and *The Bassarids*. Had it led Henze to regard his function as the production of simple political tracts it would obviously not have done. But it seems that Henze would prefer the workers to write their own marching songs. He continues to act as a goad and a conscience to the intellectual élite which provides the audiences for all forms of serious music. So his collaboration with Edward Bond on *We Come To The River* (1976), for the Royal Opera House, Covent Garden, is no confession of political disillusionment, no compromise with decadent cultural forces, but a continuation of his attempt to effect positive change from the inside.

The end-product of Henze's war-time experiences seems therefore to be a conviction that fascist decadence must be combated by an alternative, opposed set of political principles. Stockhausen, by contrast, rejects 'ideology' altogether: 'I would never let myself become a horse for one group of people and serve their exclusive interests. I learnt during the war and after it that specific ideology would bring trouble and hatred and destruction.' Even more specifically, however, the differences between Stockhausen and Henze stem from the fact that Stockhausen succeeded at an early stage in coming to terms with the past: 'I was very much aware in 1951 that I was part of a new epoch; and that an epoch that had started hundreds of years ago, even 2,500 years ago with the way of thinking of the ancient Greeks, had finished during the last war.'[39] Nevertheless, Stockhausen the composer did not start from scratch, but with transformations of existing techniques. While Henze was achieving early success with operas and symphonies, Stockhausen was creating controversy even within the narrow world of summer schools and contemporary music festivals where he first came to be known. The rapidity with which he developed so many different aspects of music is a direct reflection of his interest in, and aptitude for, different disciplines: notably phonetics and communications theory. In Paris in the early 1950s he attended Messiaen's classes, and as a result of contact with the composers of *musique concrète*, 'I did the first, the very first composition with synthetic sound'.[40] Such an openness to new sound sources, coupled with the rigorous examination and exploitation of existing ones, led to a remarkable sequence of works spanning the years 1951 to 1956, in which the serial principle was extended beyond the mechanistic formulae which so repelled Boulez, electronic music was explored and degrees of indeterminacy were employed. In *Kreuzspiel* (1951), *Formel* (1951), *Kontrapunkte* (1952–3) and *Gruppen* (1955–7), a serial method, which has its origins in the symmetries and all-embracing potentialities of Webern's twelve-note music, flowers into an organizing principle of remarkable breadth and pervasiveness.[41] Yet in 1956, responding like Boulez and others to the ideas of Cage and the American experimentalists, Stockhausen completed Piano Piece XI, whose nineteen different segments can be played in any sequence the player chooses, according to certain simple guidelines as to tempo, dynamics and mode of attack. In that same year he also finished *Gesang der Jünglinge*, in which a recording of a boy's singing voice and electronic sounds are brought together.

Stockhausen's most important contribution to the progress of music has lain in his search for new forms: forms which, while they may have certain unavoidable points of contact with those of the past, are essentially different. The principal point of contact is, quite simply, the fact that, even if the same thing is never heard twice, 'one has the clear feeling that an immutable and extremely homogeneous continuity is never abandoned. There is a hidden power of cohesion, a relatedness among the proportions: a structure. Not similar shapes in a changing light. Rather this: different shapes in a constant, all-permeating light.' This point of contact also centres on a fundamental belief in 'the power of transformation' . . . 'Hence a refusal of repetition, of variation, of development, of contrast. Of all, in fact, that requires "shapes" – themes, motives, objects, to be repeated, varied, developed, contrasted; to be dismembered, rearranged, augmented, diminished, displayed in modulation, transposition, inversion or retrograde.'[42]

Undoubtedly the most important new form that Stockhausen has developed – itself a natural progression from his earlier Group-form – is Moment-form. In essence, Moment-form presents a number of musical entities, or Moments, each of which is 'individual and self-regulated, and able to sustain an independent existence. The musical events do not take a fixed course between a determined beginning and an inevitable ending, and the moments are not merely consequents of what precedes them and antecedents of what follows; rather the concentration on the NOW.' In place of the progress through conflict and contrast to resolution, 'a composer is no longer in the position of beginning from a fixed point in time and moving forwards from it; rather he is moving in all directions within a materially circumscribed world'.[43]

Momente for soprano, four choral groups and thirteen instrumentalists (1962–4, revised version 1972), retains its links with Stockhausen's personal concept of serialism and, while highly variable in form, is in no sense 'indeterminate'. 'The fact that any number and combination of Moments can change position means that there is a very large number of possible forms. On the other hand the polynuclear arrangement of the Moments means that a Moment can be replaced only by another Moment belonging to the same structural level, and that the number of different positions which each individual Moment can occupy is relatively limited so that all possible connections can be foreseen.'[44] Moment-form is certainly of central importance in establishing Stockhausen's pre-eminence in the field of avant-garde music today. But he has continued to explore many different kinds of composition involving many different types of sound source and many different notations. He has provided texts to stimulate improvisation (*Aus den Sieben Tagen, Für kommende Zeiten*) while still not rejecting the fully-notated, instrumental-plus-live-electronic composition (*Kontakte, Mixtur* and *Mantra*).

In terms of notational procedures, the 'plus-minus' technique has the particular virtue of simplicity. For example, a line from the piano part of *Prozession* (Ex. 75) contains only four symbols, though the score as a whole does employ a few other simple signs and, as usual with Stockhausen, there is a substantial preface of preliminary instructions.

Ex. 75

+ means higher or louder or longer or more segments
− means lower or softer or shorter or fewer segments
= means the same (similar) register, dynamics, duration, timbre and
   number of segments
PER means use regular periodicity

The actual material to which these symbols are applied is not printed in the score, but is taken from earlier works of Stockhausen – in the pianist's case the eleven *Klavierstücke* and *Kontakte*. Stockhausen refers to such material as 'a sequence of events', each successive sign or vertical combination of signs referring to one event. A full explanation of the notation and of the whole vital question of the interaction between the players is given in the composer's preface to the score.

Stockhausen has continued to employ all kinds of different spatial groupings, environments (including large-scale outdoor schemes) and theatrical techniques. If he is sincere in his belief that he is producing models of tomorrow's music, it is a hopeful sign that he already finds so many eager disciples as well as many more passive enthusiasts. He has not been able to escape all the pressures of commercial success, and he is quite capable of allowing trivial and tedious enterprises to bear his name. But the power of his music to disturb and excite is an indication of the urgency with which its principles and practice require further exploration.

It was argued in Part One of this book that the best modern traditionalists were those who proved positively adaptable, treating the symphonic form with a freedom and flexibility which is only possible when a structural principle has a long history behind it. Such adaptability may continue to be the most acceptable attitude in the very different world of Moment-form. It is certainly appropriate that Stockhausen, who now regards Cage as an anarchist, should be the true heir of Varèse. Varèse was a poet of the Waste Land, the pioneer who, of all modern masters, now seems most significantly to bridge the gap between Debussy and Stockhausen himself, and in his ultimate pessimism to reflect the turmoil and tragedy inherent in the 'civilized life' during the first half of the century. Stockhausen may at times seem like the self-appointed prophet of a New Heaven and a New Earth, but it is his concern to mediate between diversities rather than to synthesize them into a higher unity which is his most 'avant-garde', his most forward-looking attribute. It is no easier to predict the long-term future of music than of any other phenomenon: but it will surely continue to change, and to relate to the time of its creation.

All seven composers discussed in this chapter remain prominent, and highly regarded, a decade later. Signs of mellowing or tendencies to focus more consistently on pet obsessions or particularly ambitious projects can certainly be found, although it would be wrong to assume that such tendencies, in part the consequence of success, involve any loss of individuality or any selling-out to either commerce or conservatism. There has been progress, but no startling about-turns. Lutosławski has not rejected aleatory counterpoint, but the search for what he terms simpler techniques of chord construction has made possible an increasing sense of pitch-centredness, if not of tonality, notably in the Symphony No. 3 (1983). Like Messiaen and Tippett in their seventies, Lutosławski may to some degree be rediscovering his musical roots, and giving them a new lease of life without compromising his hard-won radical initiatives. Xenakis has certainly not compromised, either. His interest in computer calculations and various mathematical strategies remains, but the violent energy and vertical density so characteristic of his music have been offset to some degree by the use of scalic figures and melodies that invoke the idioms of folk music. Such a development is not as surprising as may at first appear: at an early stage of his musical career Xenakis declared that his strongest desire was for a closer association between Greek folk music and certain aspects of Western art music. And that development is given impetus by Xenakis's continued reliance on forms assembled from widely diverse components, as can be heard in such characteristically pugnacious compositions as *Dikhthas* for violin and piano (1979) and *Keqrops* for piano and orchestra (1986).

The recent music of Ligeti, notably the Trio for violin, horn and piano (1982) and the first version of the Piano Concerto (1987), has also revealed an openness to aspects of traditional harmonic procedure that by no means requires the abandonment of those techniques that made his earlier music so distinctive: indeed, in *Drei Phantasien* (1983) for 16-part mixed chorus, the intricate yet lucid counterpoint both recalls and refines the dense textural play of the earlier orchestral works. Ligeti has been occupied with a second opera — *The Tempest* — during these years, and opera has also been a prime concern of Luciano Berio, though there has been all too little opportunity to see stagings of his two full-length collaborations with Italo Calvino, *La vera storia* (1981) and *Un rè in ascolto* (1984). Two earlier, major concert works are also distinctly dramatic. *Coro* (1976) is an impassioned composition for chorus and orchestra that deals with the contrast between private, personal expressions of love and grief and the need for collective consciousness of political repression. *Ritorno degli snovidenia* (1977), in effect a cello concerto, and written for Rostropovich, is more consistently private. The title, meaning 'the return of dreams', adumbrates a complex, enigmatic meditation on Russian folk materials, all-pervading yet never heard untransformed. Berio's music remains a tantalizing, elusive blend of density and directness, the kind of contrast that he himself might describe in terms of Lévi-Strauss's celebrated metaphor of the raw and the cooked. No less determinedly than Xenakis, Berio has spoken of his desire to integrate folk and serious music, and his more recent works are arresting instances of the impact that grappling with these issues — as much political as aesthetic — can create.

Pierre Boulez's musical concerns have remained more abstract, despite the obvious political dimension of his relationship with the French establishment and the practical, technological realities of life at IRCAM. Since the completion of *Rituel*, Boulez's work as a composer has remained frustratingly fragmentary. Apart from continuing to rework pieces which date back to his earliest years (*Notations*) he has in his major and still unfinished work of the 1980s, *Répons*, allowed recurrent rhythmic patterns and even audibly focal pitches to create an absorbingly immediate argument that seems less restive than formerly at the prospect of association with tradition, and uses technology — a group of tuned percussion instruments (including piano and harp) have their sounds transformed by computer operations — to intensify the sense of drama and excitement that the music so vividly conveys.

Hans Werner Henze has remained faithful to his relatively conservative language during this period, and the fact that he can still provide convincing reinterpretations of traditional genres is well demonstrated by two large-scale works, *Le miracle de la rose* (1981), a concerto for clarinet and thirteen players, and the Symphony No. 7 (1984). Henze may at times deliberately court associations with specific traditions, as in the opera *The English Cat* (1983), but his own identity is not diminished by this propensity. It does, however, intensify the always intriguing contrast between him and Stockhausen. Stockhausen has pursued an ambitious aesthetic of mediation between the extremes of textural and technological complexity and an at times very simple, melodically-based music in his huge, seven-opera cycle *Licht* (to date, *Donnerstag*, 1981, and *Samstag*, 1984). In this project mystical obsessions, highly autobiographical in essence, and technological ambitions interact in the most powerful and provocative fashion.

By the late 1980s several younger composers have consolidated reputations that were already strong many years before: in Great Britain Harrison Birtwistle and Peter Maxwell Davies (both born 1934) are the obvious examples. Yet it is difficult to claim with any confidence that any composer currently under the age of fifty is the equal, or potentially the superior of his seniors. As the end of the century approaches, the future is opaque, the succession wide open.

Notes on the Text

INTRODUCTION

1. 'The War and the Future of Music', *Musical Times* lv, September 1914, pp. 571–2.
2. Cf. the introduction by Martin Cooper to *The Modern Age, New Oxford History of Music* Vol. X, London 1974, for an expression of this view.
3. A. Schoenberg (ed. L. Stein), *Style and Idea*, London 1975, pp. 180, 50.
4. Op. cit., p. 299.
5. In P. H. Lang (ed.), *Problems of Modern Music*, New York 1962, pp. 54–5.
6. Cf. the absorbing consideration of these issues in Part Three of L. B. Meyer, *Music, the Arts and Ideas*, Chicago 1967.
7. W. Mellers, *The Twilight of the Gods*, London 1973, pp. 189–90.
8. Ibid., p. 26.
9. Ibid., p. 86.
10. R. M. Pirsig, *Zen and the Art of Motorcycle Maintenance*, London 1974, p. 117.
11. Ibid., p. 169.

CHAPTER I: SYMPHONIC MUSIC I

1. Schoenberg, quoted in W. Reich, *Schoenberg, a critical biography* (transl. L. Black), London 1971, p. 241.
2. *Sibelius and Nielsen, a centenary essay*, London 1965, pp. 4, 6.
3. Cf. J. C. G. Waterhouse, 'Nielsen reconsidered', *Musical Times* cvi, June, July, August 1965.
4. Simpson, op, cit., pp. 24–6.
5. G. Abraham (ed.), *Sibelius*, London 1947, p. 35.
6. Simpson, op. cit., p. 34.
7. Cf. H. Ottaway, *Vaughan Williams Symphonies*, London 1972, p. 59.
8. D. Drew in H. Hartog (ed.), *European Music in the 20th Century*, Harmondsworth, Middlesex 1961, p. 258.
9. Ibid., p. 259.
10. Ibid., p. 257.
11. Ibid., p. 256.

CHAPTER 2: BÉLA BARTÓK

1. *The Life and Music of Béla Bartók*, revised ed., London 1964, p. 54.
2. Available in English in an unsatisfactorily compressed version as *Béla Bartók, an analysis of his music*, London 1971.
3. Golden Section is the division of a structure so that the relationship of one segment to the other is as the other to the whole. A Fibonacci sequence of numbers is one in which each term is the sum of its two predecessors: 1,2,3,5,8, etc.
4. Quoted in Stevens, op. cit., p. 280.

CHAPTER 3: IGOR STRAVINSKY

1. I. Stravinsky, *Autobiography*, New York 1962, p. 132.
2. I. Stravinsky and R. Craft, *Expositions and Developments*, London 1962, p. 113.
3. R. Craft, *Stravinsky: Chronicle of a Friendship, 1948–1971*, New York 1972, p. 185.
4. I. Stravinsky and R. Craft, *Conversations with Igor Stravinsky*, London 1959, p. 48.
5. Delivered at Harvard in 1939-40; the final version of the original French text was produced by Roland-Manuel.
6. R. Craft, *Stravinsky*, p. 63.
7. Ibid., p. 103.
8. Ibid., p. 215.
9. Cf. E. Salzman, *Twentieth-Century Music: an Introduction*, 2nd ed., Englewood Cliffs, N. J. 1974, pp. 208–14.
10. *Stravinsky: the Composer and his Works*, London 1966, p. 296.
11. Cf. 'Stravinsky's Oedipus as 20th-century Hero' in P. H. Lang (ed.), *Stravinsky: a new appraisal of his work*, New York 1963, pp. 34–46.
12. In M. Cooper (ed.), *The Modern Age*, p. 390.
13. Cf. E. T. Cone, 'The Uses of Convention: Stravinsky and his Models', in P. H. Lang (ed.), *Stravinsky*, pp. 21–33.
14. I. Stravinsky and R. Craft, *Dialogues and a Diary*, London 1968, pp. 50–2.

CHAPTER 4: SYMPHONIC MUSIC II

1. Cf. D. Drew, 'Musical Theatre in the Weimar Republic', *PRMA* 88, 1962, p. 97.
2. For a detailed comparison of the Fourth and Fifth Symphonies from this standpoint, cf. T. Souster, 'Shostakovich at the Crossroads', *Tempo* 78, 1966, pp. 2–9.
3. Souster, op. cit., p. 5.
4. R. Layton in R. Simpson (ed.), *The Symphony*, Vol. 2, Harmondsworth, Middlesex 1967, p. 228.

5. *I am a composer* (transl. W. O. Clough and A. A. Willman), London 1966, p. 79.

CHAPTER 5: OPERA

1. Cf. R. Holloway, 'Strauss' Last Opera', *Music and Musicians* xxi, August 1973, pp. 37–8.
2. E. Padmore, 'Kurt Weill', *Music and Musicians* xxi, October 1972, p. 34.
3. 'Weill's debt to Busoni', *Musical Times* cv, December 1964, pp. 897–9.
4. D. Drew, 'Brecht versus Opera', *Score*, July 1958, p. 8.
5. D. Drew, 'Topicality and the Universal: the strange case of Weill's *Die Burgschaft*', *Music and Letters* xxxix, July 1958, p. 243.
6. This can be found in H. Hollander, *Janáček, his life and works* (transl. P. Hamburger), London 1963, p. 152.
7. In H. Hartog (ed.), *European Music in the Twentieth Century*, p. 256.
8. I. Nestyev, *Prokofiev*, London 1960, p. 445.
9. Cf. R. McAllister, 'Natural and supernatural in Prokofiev's "Fiery Angel" ', *Musical Times* cxi, August 1970, p. 787.
10. A. Payne, 'Prokofiev's *The Fiery Angel*', *Tempo* 74, 1965, p. 22.
11. Nestyev, op. cit., p. 270.
12. Op. cit., pp. 313, 318.
13. Cf. G. Abraham in M. Cooper (ed.), *The Modern Age*, p. 669.
14. R. McAllister, 'Prokofiev's Tolstoy Epic', *Musical Times* cxiii, September 1972, p. 851.
15. Ibid., p. 854.
16. Nestyev, op. cit., p. 403.
17. Cf. P. Evans, 'Britten's "Death in Venice" ', *Opera* xxiv, June 1973, pp. 490–6.

CHAPTER 6: ARNOLD SCHOENBERG

1. W. Reich, *Schoenberg*, p. 131.
2. *Structural Functions of Harmony*, 2nd, rev. ed., London 1969, p. 194.
3. Reich, op. cit., p. 159.
4. Ibid., p. 168.
5. H. Keller, 'Schoenberg's Comic Opera', *Score*, July 1958, p. 33.
6. 'Moses and Aaron', *Musical Times* cvi, June 1965, p. 425.
7. M. Babbitt, 'Three Essays on Schoenberg' in B. Boretz and E. Cone (eds), *Perspectives on Schoenberg and Stravinsky*, Princeton 1968, p. 55.
8. Babbitt, op. cit., p. 59.
9. Reich, op. cit., p. 198.
10. Babbitt, op. cit., p. 49.
11. *Schoenberg*, London 1968, p. 55.
12. Op. cit., p. 56.

13. Schoenberg's notes on the Fourth String Quartet are published in U. Rauchhaupt (ed.), *Schoenberg, Berg and Webern. The String Quartets: a documentary study*, Hamburg 1971, pp. 58–64.

CHAPTER 7: ALBAN BERG

1. *Serial Composition and Atonality*, 2nd ed., London 1968, p. 34.
2. Cf. Berg's letter to Schoenberg of 9th February 1925, quoted in W. Reich, *The Life and Works of Alban Berg* (transl. C. Cardew), London 1965, p. 143.
3. Perle, op. cit., p. 78.
4. Perle, op. cit., pp. 101–2.
5. D. Jarman, 'Some Row Techniques in Alban Berg's *Der Wein*', *Soundings* 2, 1971–2, p. 55.

CHAPTER 8: ANTON WEBERN

1. A. Webern (ed. W. Reich), *The Path to the New Music* (transl. L. Black), Bryn Mawr, Pennsylvania 1963, p. 51.
2. Op. cit., p. 55.
3. Op. cit., p. 44.
4. Op. cit., p. 54.
5. 'Composition and Precomposition in the music of Webern', in D. Irvine (ed.), *Anton von Webern: Perspectives*, London 1967, pp. 95–6.
6. L. Smith, op. cit., p. 98.
7. A. Webern (ed. J. Polnauer), *Letters to Hildegard Jone and Josef Humplik* (transl. C. Cardew), Bryn Mawr, Pennsylvania 1967.
8. Cf. U. Rauchhaupt (ed.), *Schoenberg, Berg and Webern. The String Quartets*, pp. 132–6.
9. Rauchhaupt, op. cit., p. 127.
10. Quoted in W. Kolneder, *Anton Webern, an Introduction to his works* (transl. H. Searle), London 1968, pp. 154–6.

CHAPTER 9: THE SPREAD OF SERIALISM

1. Cf. *The Poetics of Music*, pp. 40–1, and *Conversations*, p. 24.
2. 'Remarks on the Recent Stravinsky', in B. Boretz and E. Cone (eds.), *Perspectives on Schoenberg and Stravinsky*, p. 184.
3. *Stravinsky*, 2nd ed., London 1967, p. 221.
4. I. Stravinsky and R. Craft, *Expositions and Developments*, London 1962, p. 107.
5. 'Schoenberg in the United States', *Tempo* 103, 1972, p. 16.
6. Issued with the recording, ZRG 702.
7. *Score*, September 1956, pp. 61–72.
8. *Score*, May 1952, pp. 23–5.
9. *The Listener*, 24 July 1969, p. 121.

10. Issued with the 1965 EMI recording, ALP 2063.
11. Gerhard, see above, p. 185.
12. 'Meeting with Webern: Pages from a Diary', *Tempo* 99, 1972, p. 2.
13. Op. cit., p. 3.
14. R. Smith Brindle in F. Sternfeld (ed.), *Music in the Modern Age, A History of Western Music* Vol. V, London 1973, p. 298.
15. Ibid., p. 299.
16. Ibid., p. 298.
17. P. Evans in M. Cooper (ed.), *The Modern Age*, p. 421.
18. Note issued with the recording, TV 34515S.
19. B. Boretz in J. Vinton (ed.), *Dictionary of Twentieth-Century Music*, London 1974, p. 48.
20. To be found in R.S. Hines (ed.), *The Orchestral Composer's Point of View*, Norman, Oklahoma 1970, pp. 12–38.

CHAPTER 10: THE RADICAL AESTHETIC

1. M. Nyman, *Experimental Music*, London 1974, Chapter One.
2. *Silence*, London 1966, p. 82.
3. P.D. Templier, *Satie* (Transl. E. L. and D. S. French), Cambridge, Mass. and London 1969, p. 45.
4. C. Tomkins, *Ahead of the Game*, Harmondsworth, Middlesex 1968, p. 98.
5. Cf. D. Drew in H. Hartog (ed.), *European Music in the Twentieth Century*, pp. 265–71.
6. Op. cit., pp. 83–4.
7. Cf. F. Ouellette, *Edgard Varèse* (transl. D. Coltman), London 1973, p. 72.
8. Cf. Ouellette, op. cit., pp. 178, 84.
9. Cf. Chou Wen-Chung, 'Varèse: a Sketch of the Man and his Music', *Musical Quarterly* lii, April 1966, p. 156.
10. K. Wörner, *Stockhausen. Life and Work* (transl. G. W. Hopkins), London 1973, p. 139.
11. Cf. Chou Wen-Chung, op cit., p. 161.
12 'The Liberation of Sound' in B. Boretz and E. Cone (eds), *Perspectives on American Composers*, New York 1971, p. 30.
13. Cf. Wörner, loc. cit.
14. *Genesis of a Music*, 2nd ed., New York 1974, p. xviii.
15. R. Kostalanetz (ed.), *John Cage*, London 1971, pp. 116–18.
16. *A Year from Monday*, London 1968, p. 42.
17. M. Nyman, op. cit., p. 3.
18. R. Smalley, 'Experimental Music', *Musical Times* cxvi, January 1975, pp. 23–5.
19. R. Smalley, reviewing the score in *Musical Times* cxiii, December 1972, p. 1222.
20. M. Nyman, op. cit., p. 119.

21. *Music and Musicians* xxiv, December 1974, p. 8.
22. *Musical Times* cxii, March 1971, p. 230.

CHAPTER 11: THREE INDIVIDUALISTS

1. Cf. C. Samuel, *Entretiens avec Olivier Messiaen*, Paris 1967, p. 181.
2. R. Sherlaw Johnson, *Messiaen*, London 1975, p. 32.
3. A. Edwards, *Flawed Words and Stubborn Sounds. A Conversation with Elliott Carter*, New York 1971, p. 61.
4. The quotations in this and the two following paragraphs are taken from the composer's sleeve-note on Nonesuch H–71234.
5. Cf. Tippett's notes issued with the Philips recording 6500 534.
6. Cf. Tippett's notes issued with the Philips recording 6500 662.
7. Cf. Tippett's notes issued with the Philips recording 6500 534.
8. Sherlaw Johnson, op. cit., p. 105.
9. Cf. Carter's notes issued with the Nonesuch recording H–71249.
10. Cf. Carter's note in the score.
11. Cf. the review by R. Moevs in *Musical Quarterly* lxi, January 1975, pp. 159–60.
12. Edwards, op. cit., pp. 87–8.

CHAPTER 12: SEVEN EUROPEANS

1. Cf. O. Nordwall (ed.), *Lutosławski*, Stockholm 1968, pp. 54, 88.
2. Ibid., pp. 109, 112.
3. Ibid., p. 57.
4. Ibid., p. 88.
5. Cf. R. S. Hines (ed.), *The Orchestral Composer's Point of View*, p. 145.
6. E. Cowie, 'Mobiles of Sound', *Music and Musicians* xx, October 1971, p. 35.
7. Cf. M. Bois, *Iannis Xenakis. The Man and his Music*, London 1967, pp. 9–16.
8. I. Xenakis, *Formalized Music*, Bloomington 1971, p. 23.
9. M. Bois, op. cit., p. 12.
10. P. Griffiths, 'Xenakis: Logic and Disorder', *Musical Times* cxvi, April 1975, pp. 329–30.
11. C. Butchers, 'The Random Arts: Xenakis, Mathematics and Music', *Tempo* 85, 1968, p. 5.
12. M. Bois, op. cit., p. 15.
13. C. Butchers, op. cit., p. 4.
14. M. Bois, op. cit., p. 12.
15. P. Griffiths, op. cit., p. 330.
16. 'Xenakis and the Performer', *Tempo* 112, 1975, pp. 17–22.
17. R. Steinitz, 'Connections with Alice', *Music and Musicians* xxii, December 1973, p. 42.

18. Cf. his essays in *Die Reihe* 4 and 7.

19. R. Steinitz, loc. cit.

20. Cf. Ligeti in *Music and Musicians* xxii, July 1974, p. 25.

21. Ibid., p. 30.

22. Cf. M. Donat in *Tempo* 101, 1972, pp. 57–9.

23. B. Rands, 'The Master of New Sounds', *Music and Musicians* xx, August 1971, p. 34.

24. D. Osmond Smith, 'Berio in London', *Music and Musicians* xxiii, March 1975, p. 19.

25. Cf. Berio's note with CBS recording no. 61079.

26. Cf. S. Bradshaw and R. R. Bennett, 'In search of Boulez,' *Music and Musicians* xi, January 1963, p. 11.

27. *Boulez on Music Today* (transl. S. Bradshaw and R. R. Bennett), London 1971, pp. 35, 132.

28. Cf. 'The Second Viennese School. Boulez talks to Tim Souster', *Musical Times* cx, May 1969, pp. 474–6.

29. Cf. G. W. Hopkins, 'Debussy and Boulez,' *Musical Times* cix, August 1968, pp. 710–14.

30. Cf. Boulez's note in BBC Promenade Concert Programme, 3rd September 1968.

31. Charles Rosen's note with his recording on CBS 72871.

32. *Music and Musicians* xxii, November 1973, p. 34.

33. P. Griffiths, 'Boulez reflects', *Musical Times* cxii, August 1971, pp. 753–4.

34. P. Griffiths, *Musical Times* cxiv, July 1973, p. 733.

35. *Observer* Magazine, 6th October 1974, pp. 59–61.

36. *Observer*, 23rd August 1970, p. 19.

37. 'Henze and the Revolution', *Music and Musicians* xix, September 1970, p. 38.

38. Op. cit., p. 40.

39. Cf. 'Spiritual dimensions: Peter Heyworth talks to Karlheinz Stockhausen', *Music and Musicians* xix, May 1971, pp. 36–8.

40. Loc. cit.

41. Cf. the recent analytical books on Stockhausen by J. Harvey and R. Maconie.

42. Cf. K. H. Wörner, *Stockhausen*, p. 30.

43. R Smalley, '*Momente*: material for the listener and composer', *Musical Times* cxv, January 1974, pp. 25–6.

44. Ibid., p. 28.

Bibliography

This is a selective list, comprising only the principal books with which any serious student of the period should be familiar. Reference to other sources, especially to articles, will be found in the Notes printed between pp. 267 and 273.

Babbitt, M., *Words about Music*, Madison, Wisconsin, 1987.

Berio, L., *Two Interviews* (transl. D. Osmond-Smith), New York and London 1985.

Boretz, B. and Cone, E. (eds), *Perspectives on Schoenberg and Stravinsky*, Princeton 1968.

Boretz, B. and Cone, E. (eds), *Perspectives on American Composers*, New York 1971.

Boulez on Music Today (transl. S. Bradshaw and R. R. Bennett), London 1971.

Boulez, P., *Orientations* (transl. M. Cooper), London 1986.

Cage, J., *Silence*, London 1966.

Carter, E. (ed. E. Stone and K. Stone), *The Writings of Elliott Carter*, Bloomington and London 1977.

Craft, R., *Stravinsky: Chronicle of a Friendship, 1948-1971*, New York 1972.

Del Mar, N., *Richard Strauss: a critical commentary on his life and work*, 3 volumes, 2nd ed., London 1978.

Edwards, A., *Flawed Words and Stubborn Sounds. A conversation with Elliott Carter*, New York 1971.

Evans, P., *The Music of Benjamin Britten*, London 1979.

Griffiths, P., *György Ligeti*, London 1983.

Griffiths, P., *Olivier Messiaen and the Music of Time*, London 1985.

Henze, H. W., *Music and Politics: collected writings 1953-81* (transl. P. Labanyi), London 1982.

Hines, R. S. (ed.), *The Orchestral Composer's Point of View*, Norman, Oklahoma 1970.

Hitchcock, H. W., *Music in the United States: a historical introduction*, New York 1969.

Hollander, H., *Janáček, his life and works* (transl. P. Hamburger), London 1963.

Jarman, D., *The Music of Alban Berg*, London 1979.

Keller, H. and Cosman, M., *Stravinsky seen and heard*, London 1982.

Kemp, I., *Hindemith*, London 1970.

Kemp. I., *Tippett: the composer and his music*, London 1984.

Kennedy, M., *The works of Ralph Vaughan Williams*, London 1964.

Kostalanetz, R. (ed.), *John Cage*, London 1971.

Lang, P. H. (ed.), *Problems of modern music*, New York 1962.

Lang, P. H. (ed.), *Stravinsky: a new appraisal of his work*, New York 1963.

Layton, R., *Sibelius*, London 1965.

Lendvai, E., *Béla Bartók, an analysis of his music*, London 1971.

Maconie, R., *The works of Karlheinz Stockhausen*, London 1976.

Matossian, N., *Xenakis*, New York 1986.

Messiaen, O., *La technique de mon langage musicale*, Paris 1944; English transl. J. Satterfield, London 1957.

Moldenhauer, H., *Anton von Webern: a chronicle of his life and work*, London 1978.

Nestyev, I., *Prokofiev*, London 1960.

Nyman, M., *Experimental Music*, London 1974.

Ouellette, F., *Edgard Varèse* (transl. D. Coltman), London 1973.

Payne, A., *Schoenberg*, London 1968.

Perle, G., *Serial composition and atonality*, 4th ed., London 1977.

Perle, G., *The Operas of Alban Berg: I Wozzeck, II Lulu*, Berkeley, Los Angeles and London 1980 and 1985.

Rauchhaupt, U. (ed.), *Schoenberg, Berg and Webern. The String Quartets: a documentary study*, Hamburg 1971.

Reich, W., *Schoenberg, a critical biography* (transl. L. Black), London 1971.

Rufer, J., *The works of Arnold Schoenberg* (transl. D. Newlin), London 1962.

Schiff, D., *The music of Elliott Carter*, London 1983.

Schoenberg, A. (ed. L. Stein), *Style and Idea*, London 1975.

Schoenberg, A., *Structural Functions of Harmony*, 2nd rev. ed., London 1969.

Schwarz, B., *Music and musical life in Soviet Russia, 1917-1970*, Bloomington, Ind. 1983.

Simpson, R., *Carl Nielsen, symphonist*, 2nd ed., London 1979.

Simpson, R., *Sibelius and Nielsen, a centenary essay*, London 1965.

Stevens, H., *The life and music of Béla Bartók*, rev. ed., London 1964.

Stravinsky, I., *The Poetics of Music* (transl. A. Knodel and I. Dahl), New York 1947.

Stravinsky, I., *Autobiography*, New York 1962.

Stravinsky, I. and Craft, R., *Conversations with Igor Stravinsky*, London 1959.

Stravinsky, I. and Craft, R., *Expositions and Developments*, London 1962.

Stravinsky, I. and Craft, R., *Dialogues and a diary*, London 1968.

Stucky, S., *Lutosławski and his music*, Cambridge 1981.

Templier, P.-D., *Erik Satie,* Paris 1932; English transl. E. L. and D. S. French, Cambridge, Mass., and London 1969.

van den Toorn, P., *The Music of Igor Stravinsky,* New Haven, Conn., and London 1983.

Vinton, J. (ed.), *Dictionary of Twentieth-Century Music,* London 1974.

Webern, A. (ed. W. Reich), *The Path to the New Music* (transl. L. Black), Bryn Mawr, Penn. 1967.

Webern, A. (ed. J. Polnauer), *Letters to Hildegard Jone and Josef Humplik* (transl. C. Cardew), Bryn Mawr, Penn. 1967.

White, E. W., *Stravinsky: the composer and his works,* London 1966.

Index of Names and Titles